Second Edition

MARKETING CULTURE AND THE ARTS

Second Edition

MARKETING CULTURE AND THE ARTS

FRANÇOIS COLBERT

with Jacques Nantel, Suzanne Bilodeau and J. Dennis Rich

Foreword by William D. Poole

Chair in Arts Management

PRESSES HEC

National Library of Canada Cataloguing in Publication Data

Colbert, François
   Marketing culture and the arts

2nd ed.
Translation of: Le marketing des arts et de la culture.
Includes bibliographical references and index.
ISBN 2-9803081-8-8

   1. Arts—Marketing. 2. Cultural industries—Management. 3. Marketing. I. Nantel, Jacques, 1956- II. Bilodeau, Suzanne III. Rich, J. Dennis IV. École des Hautes Études Commerciales (Montréal, Québec). Chair in Arts Management V. Title.

NX634.C6413 2001   380.1'457   C2001-901404-X

Translated from *Le marketing des arts et de la culture*, © 1993, 2000
Gaëtan Morin Éditeur ltée
All rights reserved.

First English Edition:
© Gaëtan Morin Éditeur ltée, 1994

Publishing assistant: Louise St-Pierre
Copy editing: Jane Broderick
Cover design: Stéphane Lortie, Atelier de graphisme de l'École des Hautes Études Commerciales
Layout: Rolande Trudeau, Atelier de graphisme de l'École des Hautes Études Commerciales

© 2001 Chair in Arts Management, École des Hautes Études Commerciales (HEC), Montréal.
All rights reserved for all countries.
Distributed by the Chair in Arts Management, École des HEC, 3000, chemin de la Côte-Sainte-Catherine, Montréal (Québec), Canada, H3T 2A7, tel.: (514) 340-5629, www.hec.ca/artsmanagement/mca

Legal Deposit – Bibliothèque nationale du Québec – National Library of Canada, 2001

To Maxime, Simon and Julien

Acknowledgments

The author would like to thank Jacques Nantel for his contribution to chapters 4 and 5, J. Dennis Rich for the sections on sponsorship in chapters 3 and 8, and Suzanne Bilodeau, who lent her practical expertise and critical acumen to the book and helped develop some of the concepts presented. The author is also grateful to William D. Poole, director of the Centre for Cultural Management (Canada), for his in-depth review of the manuscript of the first edition of this book.

Professor Colbert also expresses his thanks to Dan Martin of Carnegie Mellon University (United States) for his helpful comments, as well as to Jennifer Radbourne of Queensland University of Technology (Australia) for contributing the Australian examples, and to Herwig Poeschl of the International Centre for Culture and Management (Austria) and Ugo Bacchella of the Fondazione Fitzcarraldo (Italy), who were responsible, respectively, for the German and Italian versions of this book. Finally, the author would like to thank Elena Levshina of the St. Petersburg Theatre Arts Academy for her work on the Russian version of this publication.

Foreword

In the Foreword to the first edition (1994) of *Marketing Culture and the Arts,* I positioned this important new book squarely in the context of the ongoing discussion on the need to develop trained arts managers for Canada. More specifically, I noted that in March 1983 the Canada Council had funded an inquiry into the state of arts administration in Canada. A result of this inquiry, hosted by the Banff Centre, was the founding, in 1984, of the Canadian Association of Arts Administration Educators (CAAAE). The Association soon concluded that more in-depth work was needed and in 1986 began that work. The result was the *Final Report of the Study of Management Development Needs of Publicly Funded Not-for-Profit Arts and Heritage Organizations in Canada*, released in 1987.

By publishing *Le marketing des arts et de la culture* in 1993, and the English-language edition the following year, François Colbert took a significant step towards meeting the need – identified at Banff a decade earlier and reiterated in the *Final Report* – for Canadian course materials appropriate for cultural managers working in English or French.

While *Marketing Culture and the Arts* was acknowledged to be Canadian in context, it was clear even in 1994 that the need for a text of this calibre was by no means limited to Canada. A revised edition would, it was anticipated, find a ready market in the United States, Europe, Australia, and other jurisdictions facing the same challenges and responding to the same needs as those identified by the CAAAE. The global appetite for a high-quality arts marketing book was, if anything, seriously underestimated. With hindsight, it is now clear that *Marketing Culture and the Arts* was at the forefront of an explosion in academic and practical interest in the field of arts and cultural management worldwide. The fact that Professor Colbert's book is now available in German and Italian as well as French and English is a clear indication of that global interest.

Other indicators of that interest, and of the need for and timeliness of a revised edition, are the proliferation of arts management programs worldwide – with the concomitant evolution of the Association of Arts Administration Educators (AAAE) – and the blossoming of the International Association of Arts and Cultural Management/Association Internationale de Management des Arts et de la Culture (AIMAC), a research network whose main function is to hold biennial conferences as a forum for the exchange of insights in cultural management and consumption.

The final contributing factor in the emergence of arts and cultural management as an established discipline was the launch, in 1998, of the *International Journal of Arts Management,* with François Colbert as Editor. *IJAM* is published on a not-for-profit basis by the Chair in Arts Management of the École des Hautes Études Commerciales (HEC) de Montréal (Université de Montréal), in collaboration with AIMAC. The Journal publishes refereed research papers and case studies on the management of arts and cultural organizations.

While *Marketing Culture and the Arts* will continue to be an invaluable resource for arts administration students and instructors around the world, its use is not limited to the classroom. Managers of a wide range of arts and cultural organizations will also want to have this stand-alone marketing resource close at hand as they prepare to meet the challenges of the twenty-first century.

William D. Poole, Director
Centre for Cultural Management
University of Waterloo
Waterloo, Ontario, Canada

Contents

2 THE PRODUCT

3. THE MARKET

4. CONSUMER BEHAVIOURS *(by Jacques Nantel)*

5 SEGMENTATION AND POSITIONING *(by Jacques Nantel)*

6. THE PRICE VARIABLE

7 THE PLACE VARIABLE

8   THE PROMOTION VARIABLE

9 MARKETING INFORMATION SYSTEMS

10 PLANNING AND CONTROLLING THE MARKETING PROCESS

Plan

CHAPTER 1
Cultural Enterprises and Marketing

OBJECTIVES

- Understand the specificity of cultural enterprises
- Pinpoint the artist's role in a cultural enterprise
- Make the distinction between the arts sector and cultural industries
- Understand the evolution of marketing
- Distinguish between traditional marketing and the marketing of culture and the arts

INTRODUCTION

This chapter sets out the distinguishing characteristics of the marketing of culture and the arts. In the first section, we consider cultural enterprises as a whole by examining their place in our society, the artist's role within them, and their mission in terms of a product. We then determine what sets different cultural enterprises apart and, more specifically, what differentiates cultural industries from those attached, by definition, to the arts sector.

In the second section, we review the history of marketing, from its humble beginnings to the rise of specializations – in particular, the marketing of culture and the arts. We then define this specialization by comparing the traditional model of marketing with one adapted to the reality of an artistic product.

Lastly, we provide a broad overview describing each component of the marketing model used in upcoming chapters.

1.1 CULTURE AND THE ARTS

1.1.1 The Position Held by Cultural Enterprises within Society

Cultural enterprises or organizations have an important place in society. They reflect cultural identity through the content of the works offered (values, issues, taboos), the form used (technology), the intensity of their presence (number of venues in a city), and the type of consumption involved. Type of consumption may be illustrated by the following example: a dance could be either performed by all attending or, as a performance event, watched by an audience.

The notion of a cultural enterprise may be viewed narrowly or broadly. In the narrow view, it represents production and distribution companies specialized in the performing arts, such as theatre, music, opera, or dance, in the visual arts found in galleries and museums, and in libraries and heritage sites. In a broader point of view, the notion of a cultural enterprise expands to include the cultural industries (films, sound recording, musicals, publishing, crafts) and the media (radio, television, newspapers, periodicals).

1.1.2 The Artist's Role within the Cultural Enterprise

The artist plays a key role in any cultural undertaking. In fact, all cultural products rely upon this highly specialized labour force. Beyond traditional disciplines, artists may be categorized by the work they produce. There are creators – playwrights, choreographers, composers, writers, lyricists, painters, and sculptors. They are followed by performers – actors, dancers, instrumentalists, and singers. There are also designers who create set mock-ups, costumes, lighting effects, book jackets, and so on. Another group includes camera operators, set and props builders, wardrobe staff, stage managers, lighting technicians, and typesetters and book binders. As well, there are all those who direct or co-ordinate the entire production team – the directors, producers, and conductors. Lastly, there are the artistic directors, who recruit, mobilize, and support other artists in producing a work.

Obviously, without artists there could be no cultural enterprise. Moreover, the artist is indispensable to other industries that fall outside the traditional definition of cultural activities. In advertising, for example, the artist is the basic resource used in creating an advertising product. In fact, filming a commercial involves a producer, musicians, actors, set designers, and so on. Often, the actors are the same ones seen on stage, television, or the big screen.

1.1.3 The Mandate of Cultural Enterprises in Terms of Product

All cultural enterprises share two characteristics: they give the artist an important role and they deal with the product of a creative act. Often, this artistic act is independent of any organization or firm, especially in disciplines such as the visual arts or literature, where the artist usually works alone. As well, if products vary substantially from one discipline to the next, cultural enterprises

may play quite different roles vis-à-vis the product. Roles may range from designing, producing, and reproducing, to distributing or preserving the product (see figure 1.1). Depending on the mission of the cultural enterprise, it may perform one or several of these functions. Various combinations are possible, but the organization's mission determines the number of functions performed.

In the performing arts, some theatre companies create, produce, and distribute their works themselves, while others count on a specialist to distribute the product that they create and produce. Touring companies are an example of this distinction. Thus, an enterprise may have a mandate to handle only the distribution of a play without any participation in its creation or staging. The same pattern can be seen in the visual arts, where exhibition halls simply show works, while museums also conserve them.

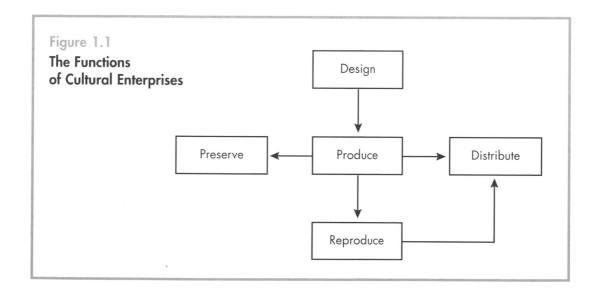

Figure 1.1

The Functions of Cultural Enterprises

1.1.4 Distinctions among Cultural Enterprises

Cultural enterprises vary considerably in size, structure, discipline, and function. It would therefore be difficult to speak of a national museum, a record company exporting abroad, and a small modern-dance troupe in the same breath, even though they are all cultural enterprises. Perhaps the best way to proceed is to differentiate and then recategorize cultural enterprises according to specific criteria.

The first criterion concerns the orientation of the enterprise's mission, which can be positioned on a continuum that has product focus and market focus as its extremes. An enterprise oriented toward (or centred on) the product would focus on the product as its *raison d'être*. Examples include a chamber-music ensemble, a children's-theatre festival, or a contemporary-art museum. At the other end of the continuum is the market-oriented or market-centred enterprise, which concentrates on the market that supports it. Between these two extremes lie a vast range of different possibilities.

The second criterion applies to the way works of art are produced. The production of an artistic work is analogous to building a model or prototype. There is no recipe or set of instructions to guarantee the outcome. Consequently, there is a healthy dose of mystery in the assembly of each product, be it a show, a painting, or a sculpture.

On the other hand, for some disciplines and product types, the prototype is specifically designed to be mass produced in order to have many copies simultaneously. This is the case for films, records, and books.

Obviously, for any product to be reproduced, there must be an original – a manuscript, master, prototype, or model. The task of producing or reproducing may be handled by one or several companies.

This second criterion clearly distinguishes between unique products not designed to be reproduced (a prototype industry) and products manufactured in runs or batches using a prototype so that many copies appear at the same time.

By combining these two criteria, as shown in figure 1.2, it is easier to distinguish between cultural industries and enterprises in the arts sector.

Quadrant 1 of figure 1.2 represents product-centred enterprises whose *raison d'être* is the unique product or prototype. As a group, these enterprises form what is commonly called the "arts sector." Usually, they are small non-profit groups; however, there may be significant exceptions.

In the diagonally opposite corner, quadrant 3, are the market-centred enterprises, which reproduce a product. Of course, these are the profit-generating firms, which include most cultural industries.

Quadrants 2 and 4 represent mixed cases. Quadrant 4 includes Broadway productions like *Les Misérables* or *Phantom of the Opera*. Although these companies do produce unique works similar to a prototype, they are first and foremost market-centred companies. These are the cultural industries. In quadrant 2 is the product-centred enterprise, which nevertheless produces many copies of a work. A non-profit publisher printing a volume of poetry would fit into quadrant 2. This type of firm, though con-

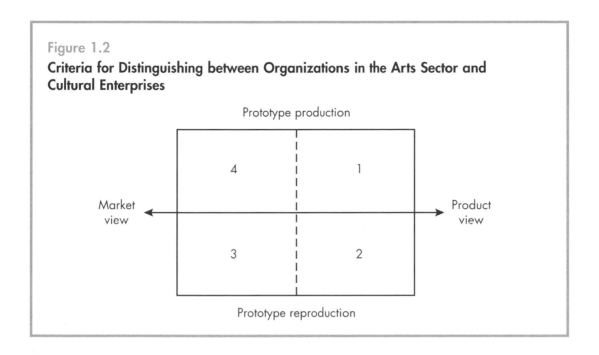

Figure 1.2

Criteria for Distinguishing between Organizations in the Arts Sector and Cultural Enterprises

sidered a cultural industry, often has more in common with the arts sector.

The other two criteria used here provide some interesting nuances; they are the size and the legal status of the enterprise.

The legal status of the enterprise quite often confirms whether it is market- or product-centred. Naturally, this is a general rule that does have its share of exceptions. Take as an example a cultural centre whose mission is to serve a linguistic minority through an entertainment program. This centre could very well be both a not-for-profit organization and market-centred. This criterion no longer distinguishes but certainly adds a nuance relevant to the description of the organization.

Size is the last criterion. Obviously, multinational firms are typical in the cultural industries. The legal status and, most of all, the mission of an enterprise in the arts sector are incompatible with the expansion of activities implied by the very concept of a multinational enterprise. The average size of firms in the arts sector is, therefore, much smaller than that of firms in the cultural industries.

This classification system will be useful in the chapters to follow, since the approach specific to marketing culture and the arts applies only to certain types of enterprises. Other types tend to use the traditional approach. Any detailed discussion of this distinction between traditional marketing and the marketing of culture and the arts should first put these approaches into perspective. What follows is a brief description of the evolution of marketing since the beginning of the twentieth century.

1.2 THE EVOLUTION OF MARKETING

1.2.1 A Definition of Marketing

The goal of marketing is optimization of the relationship between companies and customers and maximization of their mutual satisfaction.

The *Dictionary of Marketing Terms*[1] published by the American Marketing Association[2] defines marketing as "the process of planning and executing the conception, pricing, promotion, and distribution of ideas, goods, and services to create exchanges that satisfy individual and organizational goals." The definition given in *The Fundamentals and Practice of Marketing*[3] is "the management process responsible for identifying, anticipating, and satisfying customer requirements profitably."

The notion of marketing implies essentially four elements: a consumer need, satisfaction of this need, a link between the company and the consumer, and optimization of profits. The distinction between optimization and maximization is important. The maximization process attempts to generate the highest profits possible. Optimization seeks to obtain the highest possible profits while taking into account organizational or environmental elements, such as ensuring employee welfare, creating a solid corporate image, satisfying the customer, or getting the company involved in its community.

1.2.2 The Birth and Development of Marketing

Marketing as a science developed in parallel with improved material well-being in the industrialized world and as a result of the development of trade.

During the nineteenth century, supply clearly created the demand. At this time, the average consumer did not have much of an income and manufacturers could barely satisfy the basic needs of the population. The distribution system for goods was made up of small manufacturers on the one hand and small shopkeepers on the other. Wholesalers and various intermediaries served to link the two extremes. It was definitely a seller's market as opposed to a buyer's market.

Industrialization dramatically changed these conditions. At the beginning of the twentieth century, manufacturing costs were lowered through assembly-line procedures. As a result, the size of manufacturers and stores grew. Clusters of firms developed in certain industries. Competition intensified on both the local and international level. At the same time, firms broke with the custom of pricing a product based on its manufacturing costs. Manufacturers realized that consumers with increased spending capacity wanted goods that would satisfy not only their needs but also their tastes and desires. They were no longer necessarily ready to buy the lowest-priced product on the market.

Economists were the first to reflect upon the problems related to market and demand. In the early days, marketing actually borrowed a great deal from economics. Bartels, in *The History of Marketing Thought*,[4] traces the first marketing course to the University of Michigan in 1902, followed closely by Ohio State University. These courses focussed essentially on the various means of product distribution within the United States. The first studies were oriented toward a simple description of marketing activities.

Around 1910, the term "marketing" began to mean something more than distribution or trade. At that time, three approaches were used to study the reality of trade and industry. The first was the institutional approach, which described institutions and their operations while focussing on the various agents, such as wholesalers, retailers, and brokers. The second was the commodity approach, which studied the marketing of a product – for example, through a detailed analysis of how a car is launched and marketed. The third was the functional approach, which examined each marketing function, such as credit, sales, or advertising.

It was not until the 1920s that the first marketing studies and textbooks were published. At that time, other publications came out on retail, sales, and advertising techniques.

Meanwhile, the distributors continued to grow. This expansion led to the first internal conflicts. Basically, each one wanted to take control of distribution. Manufacturers used advertising to generate brand loyalty among their customers so that they would ask their retailers or wholesalers for these brands. In return, retail chains created their own house brands and undercut national-brand prices. This tactic effectively weakened the manufacturers' power. As illustrated in table 1.1, several marketing practices still popular today were born well before the word "marketing" itself.

The spread of supermarkets and shopping centres was brought about by various factors, including the postwar boom in both the birth rate and the size of the pay packet, the sudden popularity and affordability of refrigerators, and the increase in the number of car owners. The refrigerator enabled consumers to buy and store large amounts of food, and the car allowed them to transport these or other purchases more easily. Supermarkets caused the demise of small, independent grocers, while shopping centres dealt a harsh blow to downtown stores. In the end, shoppers went to the suburbs. Without a doubt, the refrigerator and the car were two innovations leading to today's commercial mosaic. Other such innovations include super-drugstores, home delivery, discount stores, vending machines, fast food, credit and debit cards, warehouse shopping, self-service, automatic tellers, and "teleshopping."

1.2.3 The Advent of Modern Marketing

Sometime during the 1950s, the focus shifted from product and sales – the view that a product sells if promoted well – toward a marketing view based on the consumer. This shift heralded the advent of modern marketing. Rather than applying a series of principles and rules, marketing now concentrated on managing the function itself. Marketing management was considered a three-part process that included analysis, planning, and action. In 1948, for the first time, James Culliton[5] used the expression "marketing mix" to describe the combination of key elements involved in any marketing decision. Culliton divided these elements into two groups:

Table 1.1
Dates of Introduction of Some Basic Marketing Practices

1670	The Hudson's Bay Company commences retailing in Canada
1704	Newspaper advertising begins in the United States
1744	Benjamin Franklin publishes the first mail-order catalogue
1841	Volnez B. Palmer opens the first advertising agency in Philadelphia
1850	Singer offers a payment-by-instalment plan
1865	John Wanamaker offers money-back guarantees
1880	Macy's starts setting prices that are not rounded off
1890	The Shuster department store in Milwaukee invents trading stamps
1898	C.W. Post launches discount coupons
1911	The Curtis Publishing Co. starts doing market research
1927	Procter and Gamble sets up the first product-manager system
1930	King Kullen opens the first supermarket in the New York area
1950	Allied Stores builds its first regional shopping centre in Seattle
1976	The Carrefour chain in France launches no-name (generic) products

Source: American Marketing Association. *Marketing News*. 1982.

---

1) Market forces:
- consumers' buying behaviour
- trade behaviour (wholesalers, retailers)
- competitors' position and behaviour
- government behaviour

2) Marketing elements:
- product planning (including packaging and branding)
- pricing
- place (managing distribution channels and physical plant)
- promotion (advertising, sales promotion, personal selling, public relations)
- servicing
- fact-finding and analysis

In 1960, McCarthy[6] reorganized the elements of the marketing mix into the four Ps we all know: product, price, place, and promotion. According to McCarthy, the notion of service was included as part of product management, market research was part of planning, and environmental forces were considered when creating a marketing strategy.

Between 1945 and 1960, the postwar baby boom and the swelling middle class encouraged marketing specialists to survey the needs and desires of potential consumers, who now had enormous purchasing power. With a view to knowing the clientele better, marketing experts delved into such social sciences as psychology and sociology in their quest to understand individual and collective consumer behaviour. This vast subject generated a great deal of data which, during the 1960s, started to be generated according to the latest quantitative and computerized methods. Thus, although marketing may have started with the application of economic theory, it was later enriched by knowledge gleaned from other sciences and then applied to create a separate discipline.

During the 1970s, marketing went from fairly general and standardized to specialized. This was also the time when a new dimension emerged – social or societal marketing. According to Kotler,[7] the concept of societal marketing "holds that the organization's task is to determine the needs, wants, and interests of target markets and to deliver the desired satisfactions more effectively and efficiently than competitors in a way that preserves or enhances the consumer's and society's well-being."

Marketing had thus reached the stage where specialists studied its application to particular economic sectors. Reference material now dealt with marketing in small and medium-sized businesses, hospital settings, service industries, and non-profit organizations, as well as industrial sectors. The concept of marketing expanded and found new applications in the marketing of people, political entities, social causes, and institutions. In 1977, Gaedeke[8] wrote,

References are made to the "broadening," "deepening," or "expanding" role of marketing. For instance, examples are used to illustrate how people (politicians, athletes, movie stars, etc.), places (cities, states, nations, etc.), causes (family planning, equal rights, anti-smoking, etc.), and institutions (hospitals, universities, Red Cross, etc.) apply marketing techniques.

In the second half of the 1970s and in the 1980s, marketing expanded into the service and "grey matter" industries. This period also marked the beginning of philanthropic marketing and the first attempts at integrating these concepts into the arts sector.

1.3 MARKETING CULTURE AND THE ARTS

In 1967, for the first time, the question of marketing cultural enterprises was raised by an academic. Kotler,[9] in his introductory textbook, pointed out that cultural organizations, be they museums, concert halls, libraries, or universities, produce cultural goods. All of these organizations are now realizing that they had to compete for both the consumer's attention and their own share of national resources. In other words, they were facing a marketing problem.

The first books specializing in marketing culture soon followed, including works by Mokwa et al.,[10] Melillo,[11] Diggles,[12] and Reiss.[13] These texts, which focus on managing culture and the arts, offer a few definitions of marketing that diverge from the traditional ones. Diggles,[14] for example, states that "the primary aim of arts marketing is to bring an appropriate number of people into an appropriate form of contact with the artist, and in so doing to arrive at the best financial outcome that is compatible with the achievement of that aim."

CAPSULE 1.1   **THE TEACHING OF MARKETING
IN ARTS MANAGEMENT PROGRAMS**

Within the university setting, marketing has developed and spawned a number of specialized courses. Students are offered courses on specific aspects of this discipline as varied as advertising, sales-force management, retailing, international marketing, and consumer behaviour.

The teaching of marketing adapted to the context of cultural enterprises began on university campuses when arts-management programs were introduced. Two phases can be identified in terms of the development of training programs in arts management; the first period, one of slow growth, lasted from 1966 to 1980, while a second, more rapid, period of growth stretches from 1980 to present. Yale University in the United States is generally credited with having created the first university program in this field, by offering, in 1966, a major in arts management as part of its Master's Degree in Fine Arts (M.F.A.). Similar offerings were subsequently made by other universities, including City University in England in 1967, St. Petersburg Theatre Arts Academy (Russia) in 1968 and York University in Canada in 1969. Close to thirty such programs had been created by 1980, and this number had climbed to over 100 by 1990; our most recent count reveals that nearly 400 programs were being offered in 2000.

In looking at the different types of programs offered, two aspects of the question should be taken into account: the academic level for which each program is intended, and the paternity of the program within the institution.

We can identify three levels of training in arts management: seminars for managers, undergraduate programs, and graduate programs. Some institutions offer development seminars intended for managers of cultural enterprises. These short-term seminars allow managers to acquire specific skills and do not usually lead to a diploma. Most of the existing programs, however, do lead to some form of formal recognition: many are programs at the graduate level, but a number of programs are also offered leading to an undergraduate degree. It is interesting to note that arts management is taught not only in traditional management schools or faculties; a number of programs have been created within arts faculties, particularly in theatre and art history programs (museology). Students graduating from this type of

(continued)

Diggles's definition unequivocally places the artist, and hence the artistic product, in the foreground of any marketing strategy. The accent is on the contact between the artist's work and the consumer, and the idea is to bring as many people as possible to the point of making this contact. The initial goal is not to satisfy any consumer need, but to invite consumers to get to know and appreciate a work. This goal bears no secondary financial gain. According to Diggles, marketing culture and the arts essentially seeks to distribute or disseminate a work and generate the best possible financial results. The ultimate goal is artistic rather than financial. Unlike the commercial sector, which creates a product according to consumer needs, artistic concerns create a product first and then try to find the appropriate clientele.

Mokwa's[15] definition stresses that "marketing does not tell an artist how to create a work of art; rather, the role of marketing is to match the artist's creations and interpretations with an appropriate audience."

On the topic of the performing arts, Melillo[16] states:

"The performing arts, by their essentially artistic nature, require marketing principles (and the resulting processes and techniques) to be transformed before they are integrated into the creative process. Only then are they ready to find an audience for a performing-arts event. You will find that the marketing principles have a constancy, while the process is always an organic element of the situation."

Mokwa and Melillo agree with Diggles that marketing must adapt to artistic organizations and that in this highly specific context the product leads to the public, not the inverse.

Hirschman[17] concurs that the traditional concept of marketing, which considers the satisfaction of a market need as the *raison d'être* of a product, cannot be applied to artistic products, given the very nature of art. In fact, Hirschman feels that artistic products contain their own reason for existing, since they do not necessarily fulfil any needs other than that of the artist for self-expression.

Based on the notion of satisfaction in the exchange between product and market, Hirschman outlines three market segments, as illustrated in figure 1.3. The three segments are defined according to the artist's creative orientation and goals. The first market segment is the artist or creator. In this case, creativity is said to be self-ori-ented and the artist's goal is simply to satisfy an individual's need to express oneself. The second segment comprises peers – other artists, critics, or other professionals in a particular discipline – and creativity is said to be peer-oriented – the artist seeks recognition in a particular milieu. The third segment, the public at large, can be divided into several sub-segments; hence, the artist's creativity is said to be commercial or market-oriented. The primary objective in this case is most often financial gain. Artists may create in the hope of reaching one or another of these segments, or even all three at once. Even if artists are trying to reach all three segments, they should still

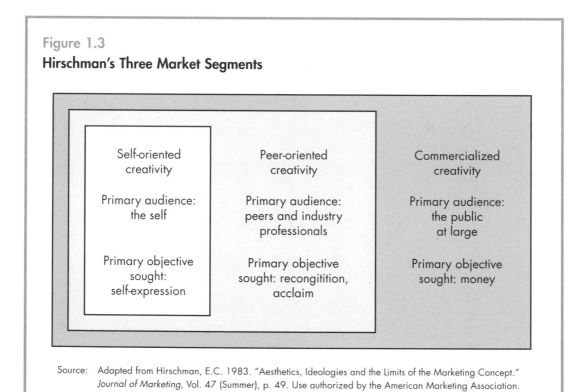

Figure 1.3
Hirschman's Three Market Segments

Self-oriented creativity

Primary audience:
the self

Primary objective sought:
self-expression

Peer-oriented creativity

Primary audience:
peers and industry professionals

Primary objective sought: recongitition, acclaim

Commercialized creativity

Primary audience:
the public at large

Primary objective sought: money

Source:　Adapted from Hirschman, E.C. 1983. "Aesthetics, Ideologies and the Limits of the Marketing Concept." *Journal of Marketing*, Vol. 47 (Summer), p. 49. Use authorized by the American Marketing Association.

find satisfaction in their work. In fact, one artist may choose to create different products for each segment.

Whenever the work produced stems from self-oriented creativity, the marketing process is product-centred and distinct from the traditional, market-centred, process. In this case, the artistic organization must find consumers who are likely to appreciate the product. Evrard[18] describes this reality as "marketing the supply."

We could combine the above definitions by saying that cultural marketing is

"the art of reaching those market segments likely to be interested in the product while adjusting to the product the commercial variables – price, place and promotion – to put the product in contact with a sufficient number of consumers and to reach the objectives consistent with the mission of the cultural enterprise."

1.4   THE MARKETING MODEL

Marketing theoreticians use a model to describe in simplified fashion how a company markets a product. Since the reality of the cultural or artistic milieu is different from that of commerce or industry, the marketing model must be adjusted to account for this difference.

1.4.1 The Traditional Marketing Model

In the traditional model, which describes the reality of commercial and industrial firms, the components must be considered a sequence that starts in the "market" square (see figure 1.4). This theory maintains that a company seeks to fulfil an existing need among consumers. Using data provided by the company's marketing-information system, the company evaluates the existing need and its capacity to meet that need, given current resources and the corporate

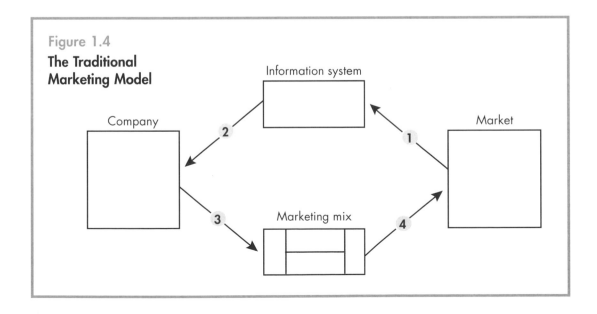

Figure 1.4
The Traditional Marketing Model

mission. The company then takes the four elements of the marketing mix and adjusts them to produce the desired effect on the potential consumer. The sequence here is as follows: market – information system – company – marketing mix – market. The market is thus both the starting and the finishing point for this process.

1.4.2 The Marketing Model for Culture and the Arts

Although this model contains the same components as the traditional marketing model, the marketing process for product-centred cultural enterprises is different. As a result, the traditional marketing model cannot adequately reflect the reality of the artistic milieu. As figure 1.5 shows, the process starts within the enterprise, in the product itself, as stated in the definition adopted above. The enterprise tries to decide which part of the market is likely to be interested in its product. Once potential customers are identified, the company will decide on the other three elements – price, place, and promotion – for this clientele. In this type of company, the process order would be company (product) – information system – market – information system – company – marketing mix – market. The starting point is the product and the destination is the market. This "product-to-client" approach, while applicable to other types of companies, is truly typical of the arts sector.

This model could also describe the reality for other types of companies. For example, in industry and commerce, the discovery of a new product or application leads to a search for a market where the product can be introduced. In this particular case, therefore, the point of departure lies in the company and its product, just as in a cultural venture. There is still, however, a consider-

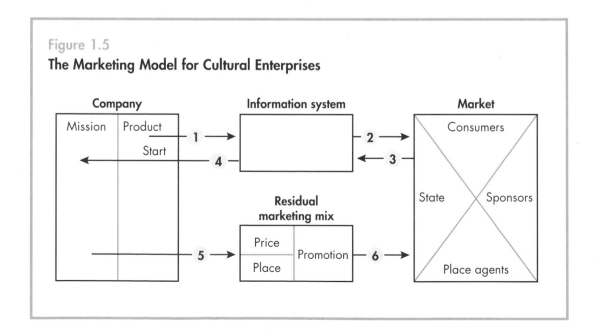

Figure 1.5
The Marketing Model for Cultural Enterprises

able difference between the two situations. Essentially, the objectives are different: the commercial firm seeks a market where profit may be optimized, or it will abandon the market due to lack of consumer interest; the product-centred cultural enterprise has art rather than profit as its ultimate objective. Reaching the artistic goal is a truer measure of success for the company executing an artistic rather than a financial project.[19]

As we have seen, some cultural enterprises are basically market-centred, with a financial rather than an artistic goal. In their case, the traditional marketing model would best describe the marketing process.

1.4.3 Marketing and Cultural Enterprises

Looking again at the model presented in section 1.1.4, we can not only distinguish between enterprises in the arts sector and those defined as cultural industries, but also clearly see in which instances tradi-tional marketing or marketing of culture and the arts is appropriate (see figure 1.6).

Quadrant 3 contains market-centred companies, whose marketing approach would be essentially traditional. On the other hand, in quadrant 1, where the companies are basically product-centred, the marketing approach would correspond to the marketing model for culture and the arts.

Beyond these two opposing situations, enterprises may shift, to various degrees, toward one approach or the other. For example, firm A would have a clear market orientation even if its product were unique, such as a Broadway type of show. Firm B would consider market conditions, but less rigidly than firm A. This difference would distinguish firm B from the companies in quadrant 1. Similarly, if we look at firms C and D, two companies reproducing artistic works, firm C has a clear-cut product orientation, while firm D has a less definite product orientation. This is also the

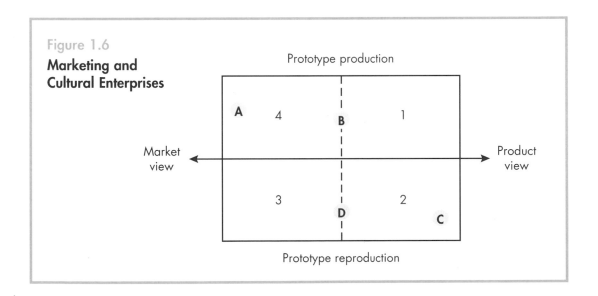

Figure 1.6

Marketing and Cultural Enterprises

Prototype production

A   4   B   1

Market view ←——————→ Product view

3   2   C

D

Prototype reproduction

difference between firm D and the companies in quadrant 3.

These examples reveal three different marketing situations: firms using a "pure" traditional marketing approach (quadrants 3 and 4), those with a "pure" approach to cultural marketing (quadrants 1 and 2), and a third category whose mixed approach allows for some compromises on product or adjustments to the product according to consumer preferences (situations B and D).

1.5 COMPONENTS OF THE MARKETING MODEL

1.5.1 The Market

A market is a group of consumers expressing desires and needs for products, services, or ideas. The notions of need and desire are the cornerstone of marketing and the key to any marketing strategy.

Thus, a consumer expresses needs, which a company seeks to meet through a range of products and services. A commercial organization would study these needs before designing a product. A cultural enterprise, on the other hand, would seek out consumers with needs likely to be met by the works produced. These consumers could be either individuals or other organizations. The term "consumer" itself is used here in the broadest sense to cover all economic agents. Needs and desires, given their rather subjective nature, are not always as easily defined. Even at the movies, a consumer may distinguish the broad categories (comedy, horror, and action) yet remain unaware of the countless nuances of potential benefit or interest.

By buying products or services, consumers create what economists call "the demand," or the amount of a good or service that economic agents acquire in a given market.

A market may be divided into subgroups or segments according to the consumer's tastes and needs. A commercial enterprise or organization designs a product with a clientele in mind. The product is shaped to meet the needs of those potential customers. The company thus sets itself apart from the competition, whose product offering is not marketed the same way. The company with a clear-cut advantage over its competitors thus consolidates its market position. By creating market segments, a cultural enterprise identifies a clientele made up of individuals likely to appreciate the features of its product.

1.5.2 The Environment

A marketing strategy cannot be drawn up in a vacuum; there are many external restrictions affecting the market and the firm. The environment, including both the company and the market, is composed of two elements which constantly influence all organizations: competition, over which the company has some control, and macro-environmental variables, also known as "uncontrollable variables."

Competition is often defined as a semi-controllable variable. That is, even if a competitor's strategy cannot be directly affected, there are various ways to react – for example, following the opponent's lead by lowering prices or matching a lively advertising campaign with an equally lively promotional campaign. A firm is not as powerless when confronted with semi-controllable variables as it is when facing macro-environmental variables.

Macro-environmental, or uncontrollable, variables constantly affect the life of any corporation, which may have to adapt to radical changes yet never have the chance to act upon the causes of these changes.

There are five main variables in the macro-environment: demographic, cultural, economic, political legal, and technological. They will be described in detail in chapter 3.

1.5.3 The Marketing Information System (MIS)

Marketing information systems rely on three key components: internal data, secondary data published by private firms or government agencies, and the data collected by the company itself.

"Internal data" means all information available from within the firm itself. The firm's accounting system actually provides more than financial analysis; it is a rich source of internal data for the marketing specialist.

If managers want to compare their company's results with those of the competition or of the market in general, they must gather data from external sources. These data fall into two categories: those published by public- and private-sector organizations, and those gathered by the company directly.

The term "secondary data" is used to describe data published by public-sector agencies, such as statistics bureau, arts councils, or ministries of culture, and private-sector firms that specialize in producing research reports. These publications are usually available in the business library of colleges and universities or through the public-library system. Before a market study is initiated, the main sources of secondary data must be consulted – if only to ensure that the proposed study does not already exist!

If all the internal and secondary data do not provide the information required in the decision-making process, it may be useful to gather primary data. In other words, the consumer must be questioned directly. This is commonly called a market study. The goal may be to determine consumer purchasing habits, tastes, and preferences or to test public reaction to an advertising poster or different endings for a film.

1.5.4 The Marketing Mix

Every marketing strategy is composed of the same four components: price, product, place, and promotion. Together, the "four Ps" make up what is known as the marketing mix. Successful marketing depends on a skilful balance of these components. A great distribution network and a powerful promotion campaign will not sell a product that consumers do not want, no matter how cheap it may be! The same applies to a fine product badly priced or inadequately distributed because of an error in promotion strategy. These are the fundamentals of any marketing strategy, and all firms aim at creating synergy through the combined strengths of all four. Synergy exists when the overall effect of several elements is greater than the sum of the effect of the elements taken separately.

Although the four Ps form a whole, there is a logical order in defining them. Even in the commercial sector, marketers must first know the product being sold before pricing it or deciding on its distribution. Similarly, a promotional campaign would be impossible without knowledge of the product offering, the price, and points of sale. Initially, decisions are made following this pre-established sequence. Later on, a firm or organization may learn by experience how to blend the components.

The components of the marketing mix are called "controllable variables," in contrast with competition, which is a semi-controllable variable, or the macro-environment, which is considered uncontrollable.

Product

The product is the centrepiece of any enterprise. This statement becomes particularly meaningful in the cultural sector, in which the product constitutes the starting point of any marketing activity.

In this book, the term "product" is used in its broadest sense to mean a tangible good, a service, a cause, or an idea. "Product" is associated with any result of the creative act – for example, a performance, an exhibition, a record, a book, or a television program.

Price

Every product has a price, which is normally expressed as the monetary value attributed to that product. Price also includes the effort a consumer must expend in the act of buying the product. Thus, there is always a price to pay for a product, even when it is free.

The amount paid for a product is not necessarily proportionate to its manufacturing cost. The same thing may be said of the value attributed to it. The admission fee for a movie has nothing to do with a film's production costs. On the contrary, the uniqueness, fame, and symbolic value of an object may increase the price consumers are willing to pay. A work of art could, for instance, fetch a very high price that has nothing to do with the cost of creating it.

The fairest price is, therefore, the one that the consumer is prepared to pay. It is this price that a company should use to develop its strategies.

Place

Place is composed of several elements. The main ones are physical distribution, distribution channels, and commercial venue. First, the logistics of distributing the product, be it a theatrical tour or a book delivered from the publisher to the reading public, are considered. Then, the focus shifts to the relationships and the various agents within a channel – in an artistic example, the network from artist to producer to broadcaster. Lastly, location is an important factor in the success or failure of companies selling directly to the consumer. The location of a bookshop, movie theatre, hall, museum, or even a traditional business must be carefully selected.

Promotion

Promotion comes last in the first sequence of this definition of the marketing mix. In the pre-preparation stage of a promotional campaign, a company must know which product is offered at which price and where. It must know beforehand the main characteristics of the targetted consumers and, in particular, the most convincing selling arguments for those consumers.

Since the same consumers are targetted by advertising, promotion, and marketing campaigns, these three areas are often confused. They are inclusive, since promotion is made up of four distinct components: advertising, personal selling, sales promotions, and public relations, and since marketing includes promotion.

1.5.5 Two Influential Elements

Two other elements must be considered in any marketing analysis: time, and the specificity of the firm (see figure 1.7).

Time

All companies must work within a changing environment. Market conditions evolve over time, as do consumer needs and tastes.

The variables of the macro-environment may be modified and the competition may adjust its strategies. An excellent marketing strategy may seem outdated after a few years, or even a few months. The marketing professional must constantly review the current strategy. Time is also important to the company's own growth, since corporate objectives – and hence marketing policies – may be altered. Marketing should be considered an evolving process, and any strategy must be periodically reviewed and adjusted according to the environment and corporate priorities.

Specificity of the Firm

Every organization has its own personality and acts as an individual entity. What may

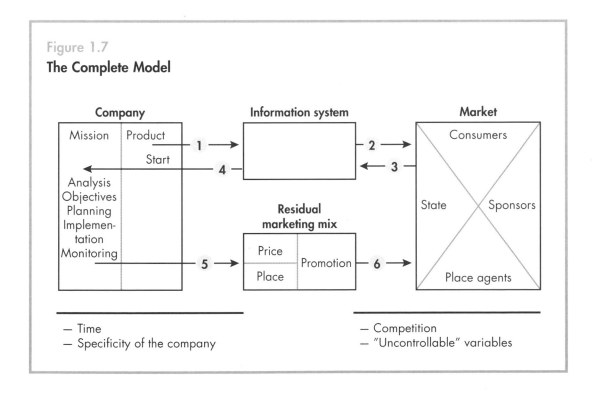

Figure 1.7
The Complete Model

be an excellent marketing strategy for firm A may prove hopelessly inadequate for firm B. Neither their products nor their market shares are necessarily the same. Their corporate images may also vary. It would therefore be risky to try to transplant a strategy from one firm to another. In some instances, however, a successful competitor's strategy may serve as inspiration. Many small companies successfully imitate the products and marketing policies of their competitors and manage to save enormous sums on marketing studies. Rarely, however, can all the elements of a strategy be borrowed from a competitor.

1.5.6 The Company and Its Marketing Management

Decisions on marketing strategies must always conform to the company's mission and objectives. These decisions must also take into account the organization's human, financial, and technical resources.

The marketing management process may be broken down into five key steps: analysis, setting of objectives, planning, implementation, and monitoring. First, marketers analyze the situation by looking at the relevant market and at the company's objectives and resources. This analysis enables them to set marketing goals that are compatible with the current situation. At the planning stage, marketers focus on both the strategic aspects (product positioning, competitor's predicted reaction, most suitable distribution channel) and the more operational aspects (sales-force meetings, distribution of advertising material at the right time and place, etc.).

Implementation of a marketing plan requires the skilful co-ordination of all parties involved and the participation of all corporate sectors. For example, production must be included to ensure that resources are available. Finance must be on board to make funding available. Personnel must be advised in case additional staff is needed. As soon as a strategy is set up, corporate executives must be kept up to date on the operation. Monitoring allows the company to compare results with objectives and, if need be, address any discrepancies through corrective measures.

1.5.7 The Interdependence of the Elements

Although the various elements of the marketing model have been presented individually, they are interdependent. In fact, they form a whole in which one or all may influence the others.

Marketing managers must be well acquainted with the market and the variables likely to influence it. They must correctly determine consumers' needs, measure the level and development of the demand for a particular good, and divide the larger market into sub-markets or segments in order to take advantage of opportunities and gain a distinct advantage over the competition. They must also study the different variables within the macro-environment. Competition in any form may affect product sales. Demographics, culture, economics, laws and regulations, and technology constantly change the rules of the game. As a result, marketing professionals must use their information system wisely and know how to juggle the variables of the marketing mix.

SUMMARY

Cultural enterprises play an important role in society. Their products or activities revolve around or stem from an act of artistic creation. The artist thus holds a pivotal position in such an enterprise and can be found at the many different stages of production, creation, and diffusion.

There are many differences among cultural enterprises, which are usually divided into two sectors: the arts and the cultural industries.

Cultural companies can be further divided by their mission, which may be market- or product-oriented, and the nature of their product, which may be unique (a prototype) or mass produced. Their orientation obviously affects their size and legal status.

The approach specific to marketing culture and the arts does not consider all cultural enterprises, only those that are market-oriented. For others, the traditional approach is quite adequate.

The traditional marketing model must be adjusted to reflect the reality of companies in the arts sector. Although the components are the same, their sequence may be different. The product is more than a simple variable in the marketing mix, since it is the company's *raison d'être*, regardless of market needs.

Marketing, as a discipline within the management curriculum, emerged at the beginning of the twentieth century. It now comprises a mixed body of knowledge separate from any other science. Marketing knowledge expands constantly and has an increasing number of applications in specific sectors, as is the case in marketing culture and the arts.

Over all, marketing must be seen as a set of activities designed to draw company and consumer together. The four components of marketing are the market, the marketing information system, the company, and the marketing mix.

QUESTIONS

1. Why is the artist the cornerstone of the marketing strategy of any cultural enterprise?
2. What are the four criteria that enable us to distinguish between the arts sector and cultural industries?
3. What is the difference between traditional marketing and marketing in the arts? Between traditional marketing and marketing in the cultural industries?
4. In most definitions of the term "marketing," we find the idea of exchange. Why?
5. Give some highlights from the history of marketing.
6. What does "supply marketing" mean?
7. Why do people who are not in the field often confuse marketing and advertising?
8. Why do we call each of the four elements of the marketing mix "controllable"?
9. Why do we put the product and the company in the same box in the marketing model for the cultural sector?
10. Why do we call competition a "semi-controllable" variable?
11. According to Hirschman, how can artists themselves form a market segment?
12. Can you find examples of companies in the arts sector that are obviously market-oriented? Companies in the cultural industries that are clearly product-oriented?

Notes

1. Bennett, P.D. 1988. *Dictionary of Marketing Terms.* American Marketing Association.

2. In North America, researchers, academics, and marketers form the American Marketing Association.

3. Wilmshurst, J. 1978. *The Fundamentals and Practice of Marketing.* London: Institute of Marketing and CAM Foundation.

4. Bartels, R. 1976. *The History of Marketing Thought, 2nd ed.* Columbus, Ohio: Grid.

5. Quoted in N.H. Borden. 1964. "The Concept of the Marketing Mix." *Journal of Advertising Research*, Vol. 4, n° 2 (June), p. 2–7.

6. McCarthy, E.J. 1971. *Basic Marketing: A Managerial Approach, 4th ed.* Homewood, Illinois: R.D. Irwin (1st ed. 1960).

7. Kotler, P., and B. Dubois. 1977. *Marketing Management, Analyse, planification et contrôle, 3rd ed.* Paris: Publi-Union.

8. Gaedeke, R.M. 1977. *Marketing in Private and Public Nonprofit Organizations: Perspectives and Illustrations.* Santa Monica, California: Goodyear.

9. Kotler, P. 1967. *Marketing Management: Analysis, Planning and Control.* Englewood Cliffs, New Jersey: Prentice-Hall.

10. Mokwa, M.P., W.M. Dawson and E.A. Prieve. 1980. *Marketing the Arts.* New York: Praeger.

11. Melillo, J.V. 1983. *Market the Arts.* New York: Foundation for the Extension and Development of the American Professional Theater.

12. Diggles, K. 1986. *Guide to Arts Marketing: The Principles and Practice of Marketing as They Apply to the Arts.* London: Rhinegold.

13. Reiss, A.H. 1974. *The Arts Management Handbook, 2nd ed.* New York: Law-Arts Publishers (1st ed. 1979).

14. Diggles, K. 1986. *Guide to Arts Marketing: The Principles and Practice of Marketing as They Apply to Arts.* London: Rhinegold.

15. Mokwa, M.P., W.M. Dawson and E.A. Prieve. 1980. *Marketing the Arts.* New York: Praeger.

16. Melillo, J.V. 1983. *Market the Arts*. New York: Foundation for the Extension and Development of the American Professional Theater.

17. Hirschman, E.C. 1983. "Aesthetics, Ideologies and the Limits of the Marketing Concept." *Journal of Marketing*, Vol. 47 (Summer), p. 40–55.

18. Evrard, Y. 1991. "Culture et marketing: incompatibilité ou réconciliation?"in *Proceedings of the First International Conference on Arts Management*, F. Colbert and C. Mitchell, eds. Montreal: Chaire de gestion des arts, École des HEC (August), p. 37–50.

19. Colbert, F. 1989. *La recherche et l'enseignement en gestion des arts à l'aube des années 1990*. Cahier de recherche GA89-01, Montreal: Chaire de gestion des arts, École des HEC (December).

For Further Reference

Bendixen, P. 2000. "Skills and Roles: An Essay on Concepts of Modern Arts Management." *International Journal of Arts Management*, Vol. 2, n° 3 (Spring), p. 4–13.

Botti, S. 2000. "What Role for Marketing the Arts? An Analysis of Art Consumption and Artistic Value." *International Journal of Arts Management*, Vol. 2, n° 3 (Spring), p. 14–27.

Evrard, Y. 1993. *Le management des entreprises artistiques et culturelles*. Paris: Economica.

Killacky, J.R. 1998. "Corporate Research and Venture Capital Models for the Arts." *International Journal of Arts Management*, Vol. 1, n° 1 (Fall), p. 4–8.

Kotler P., and J. Scheff. 1997. *Standing Room Only*. Boston: Harvard Business Press.

Plan

CHAPTER 2
The Product

OBJECTIVES

- Define "cultural product"
- Set out the main characteristics of a cultural product
- Explore the idea of a product life cycle
- Apply the life-cycle concept to cultural products
- Understand the risks cultural organizations face

INTRODUCTION

The product is the cornerstone of every cultural enterprise, and hence of every marketing strategy. In the first section of this chapter, we look at the product from various vantage points.

In the second section, we introduce an important concept in managing products: the product life cycle. This model, which describes the different stages in the life cycle according to how the market and corporate environment develop, enables marketing professionals to create various corporate survival strategies.

In the third and last section, we look at the specific type of risk cultural companies face, by examining the way in which new products are designed – in particular, cultural products vis-à-vis mass consumer products.

2.1 PRODUCT

The term "product" is used here in its generic meaning – that is, as a service, an object, or an experience.

2.1.1 The Concept of Product

The concept of "product" may be defined in several ways. This chapter presents a classification system based on the amount of effort the consumer expends to acquire the product. The product is then broken into its components. Lastly, an attempt is made to define the characteristics of a cultural product.

The Classification of Products Based on the Effort Expended by the Consumer

In marketing literature, there are several ways of classifying products. Here, we describe the best-known method, which involves classifying products, according to the amount of effort expended by the consumer, into convenience goods, shopping goods, and specialty goods.

Convenience goods are those that the consumer buys often, though with very little brand loyalty. The normal brand of milk, bread, or butter, for example, is easily replaced by whichever brand the corner store sells when a consumer does not want to travel all the way to the supermarket.

If a purchase is well thought out, however, the consumer will buy only after comparison shopping among substitute products. When clothes shopping, for example, most consumers compare the style, colour, and fabric of several similar garments before finding the one that meets their current criteria best.

A specialized purchase involves a product, often a particular brand, for which the consumer is prepared to make a significant effort. The consumer will refuse all other brands if the product desired is unavailable, and will even make a special trip to wherever that product is sold.

Cultural products usually fall under the category of specialty goods. The consumer wants to see a particular show or film and/or buy a specific recording by a favourite performer. This consumer will not compromise and will put considerable effort into buying tickets in advance, lining up for hours or even travelling great distances to the venue where the event is being held.

In some situations, a cultural product can be categorized as a thought-out purchase (shopping goods). For example, in buying a book, a consumer might browse through a bookshop for something that suits his or her mood. This consumer may opt for a novel and then leaf through the best-sellers or read jacket blurbs before choosing one title out of a group of interesting novels.

The Three Components of a Product

Most products have the following main components:

1) the central product or object itself;

2) related services;

3) the value, be it symbolic, affective, or other, that consumers attach to the product.

In buying a car, the consumer acquires a means of transportation (central product), but also certain services, such as a warranty and a service contract. There is also, of course, a symbolic value, which may be prestige, power, or the fulfilment of a dream.

The reasons behind choosing a particular brand or product may vary from one consumer to the next. The car example comes to mind once again. Some people make their decision based on purely technical criteria, such as fuel consumption – in

other words, based on the central product. Some may choose one brand over another because of the manufacturer's warranty or the dealer's post-purchase maintenance service plan – that is, according to services associated with the product. Still others may base their decision on the social standing linked to product use. Sometimes this symbolic value becomes the main reason for buying a product.

The Three Dimensions of a Cultural Product

Another way of approaching the notion of a product, which applies in the case of a cultural product, is to define the artistic work using three dimensions (see table 2.1): referential, technical, and circumstantial.[1]

The referential dimension enables consumers to situate a product according to various points of reference (field, genre, history, etc.). These reference points increase or decrease according to the individual consumer's experience or knowledge of the product. This dimension defines the product through comparison with both whatever else exists and what once existed. A

Table 2.1

The Three Dimensions of an Artistic Work

Referential dimension	Technical dimension	Circumstantial dimension
Discipline Genre History Competitors' products Substitute products	of the product consumed of the production process	Ephemeral components The consumer The artist

contemporary-dance work, for example, could be situated as a product in comparison with other pieces in the same show, with the artist's other works, or with other styles in dance (modern, jazz, etc.). This product could also be situated in relation to dramatic works, which also compete for audiences, or to other leisure activities. When the product is evaluated, it is also situated within a certain context of distribution or diffusion and within a particular market where other products exist or existed. This inherent complexity explains why the critic's task is exceedingly difficult, since he or she must be aware of these several reference points.

Similarly, certain consumers are better able to judge the quality of a glass-maker's craftsmanship, and thus to distinguish the work of a less experienced or less talented artisan from that of a master craftsman. This complexity also explains why some artistic products are more popular than others. For example, the average consumer is surrounded by popular music from childhood on, thus acquiring, over the years, references that shape his or her choices and preferences; on the other hand, the language of dance is not nearly as pervasive in everyday life, making this art form less penetrable to the average consumer.

The technical dimension includes the technical and material components of the product as received by the consumer. It could be the product itself (a sculpture), the vehicle (a record or book), or a component of the performance of the work (a show). The consumer buying a compact disk is acquiring the technical dimension of an artistic work. As a spectator, however, the same consumer may see the technical dimension integrated into the work but be unable to possess it. In any event, the technical dimension influences the quality of the work produced.

The circumstantial dimension is related to the ephemeral circumstances surrounding product perception. An artistic work cannot be seen twice in exactly the same way – even by the same person! Consumer perceptions are a basic, indispensable component in the appreciation of a product. The same may be said of the perception of the context in which the product is presented. For example, a sculpture will look different with a sunset as a backdrop rather than a cloudy sky. Moreover, the individual perceiving the product has different moods, physical states, comfort levels, and so on. All of these fleeting factors play a role in the overall perception of a product and influence the consumer's opinion. Indeed, as soon as human perception is part of the equation, it becomes a key variable.

Although the consumer's perception is an influential factor for all products, it must be noted that perception plays a special role in the performing arts, where an artist's mood, physical condition, and perception of the audience's reaction are also circumstantial factors influencing product quality and proving once again that a product cannot be the same twice.

2.1.2 The Cultural Product: A Complex Product

The complexity of a product may vary greatly according to the specific features of the product, the consumer's characteristics, or the consumer's perception of the product.

Some products are considered more complex because their technical specifications require substantial personal effort on the part of the consumer just to be familiar with product features. The first-time, inexperienced buyer of a personal computer, for example, confronts technical complexity. This shopper may find the emotional burden associated with buying a computer rather unsettling. Before buying a new car, a consumer may seek advice from several friends, since their opinions are important in combatting emotional complexity. This consumer will buy other products automatically, however, as is the case for many common convenience goods, which could be called "simple products."

Most cultural products may be defined as complex, especially when the works produced require specific knowledge or rely on abstract notions that require the consumer's ability to appreciate such concepts. Complexity becomes even greater when the consumer is unfamiliar with a particular type of product.

The cultural or artistic sector does, nonetheless, include less complex products, such as work drawing on stereotypes known to most people or using very concrete concepts. These products are often labelled popular. "Pop" music and summer-stock theatre may be considered simple products in comparison with a classical repertoire or an avant-garde production.

2.1.3 Defining the Term "Product"

A market specialist might define a product as:

The set of benefits as they are perceived by the consumer.

A product may be described by its technical dimension or symbolic value, yet, in the end, what the consumer buys is a set of benefits, real or imaginary. Consumers agree to invest money and effort in obtaining the product according to the importance of their needs and the resources available to them.

For any company, a product is defined as a set of technical characteristics, which are perceived differently according to the specialization or department of the employee working at the company. From one employee's point of view, the product is a set of material components. For another employee, the same product constitutes a series of selling features. For a third, the product is a collection of financial aspects. In developing effective marketing strategies, however, a company would be wise to consider and use the consumer's point of view.

2.1.4 Product Lines and Ranges

Darmon et al.[2] define a firm's product line as "a group of products that are fairly closely related"; the term "depth of product line" is used to describe the number of different items offered in a product line. Novels bought at a bookshop are a line of products, while periodicals, dictionaries, and children's books are three other product lines.

A product mix is made up of all the lines offered by one company. The bookseller's product mix is made up of all the lines found on the store's shelves.

Many theatre companies, especially touring ones, perform only one production per season. These are "one-product" companies for whom the idea of a line or mix does not exist. The theatre company that has its own venue and offers five productions per season would be offering its clientele a line of products. Each work performed, though part of the theatre category, constitutes a separate product. Unlike a firm that produces books, records, or videos, all of which may be a line offered simultaneously, a theatre group presents a line of products offered sequentially.

The notion of a product mix is easily applied to companies whose mission is to promote and distribute entertainment. A presenter or promoter offering a variety of artistic products – theatre, classical music, dance, variety shows – each operating as a line, is in effect offering audiences a mix of products. A major arts centre can offer a theatre line, a dance line, and so on, whereas a small presenter can offer only a limited mix with only a few product lines, possibly comprising one product each.

Cultural enterprises do tend, however, to create spin-off products that are related to the main artistic product yet constitute other product lines. A symphony orchestra may offer a concert series, record part of their repertoire, and sell promotional items such as T-shirts. Museums, for example, not only present permanent and temporary exhibits but also offer a series of educational and cultural activities including workshops, guided tours, and conferences. Most also have a restaurant and a gift shop.

On the topic of the extended product mix offered by museums and its impact on the organization and the main product(s), Benghozi and Bayart[3] observe that:

"the possibility of major gains on related products encourages producers to rethink their strategies. Cultural objects such as films, exhibitions, books, concerts, etc. are seen as part of a co-ordinated product mix whose markets must be mutually reinforcing... Two-thirds of the museums surveyed do offer their public at least a library, a projection or conference room, a gift shop, and a restaurant or cafeteria."

These observations result from a study based on a sampling of American and French museums. The results of the study reveal the potential revenue spin-off products can generate.

2.1.5 Brand

For most businesses, the use of a brand is an important component of their marketing strategy. Consumers differentiate among products based on their recognition of a product's attributes as conveyed by the brand. The brand can be either a name or a symbol (design).

All cultural enterprises have a brand or trademark. The name of a well-known company conjures up images in the mind of the consumer, who associates a particular product with that name. Even people who have never set foot in Milan's La Scala or New York's Museum of Modern Art have some idea of what these institutions represent.

A strong brand not only attracts consumers, but enables the creation of franchises. The Guggenheim Museum, for example, has capitalized on the strength of its brand name to expand its market and establish franchises throughout the world: there is now a Peggy Guggenheim Collection in Venice, the Deutsche Guggenheim Berlin, and the Guggenheim Museum Bilbao.[4]

2.2 THE PRODUCT LIFE CYCLE

2.2.1 The Concept of a Life Cycle

The concept of a life cycle for a product stems from the notion that everything, from people to products, is born, grows, and dies. Some products know moments of glory, only to fall later into disuse or oblivion. This is the case for papyrus, the quill and inkwell, and the gramophone and record player. All of these products were replaced by easier-to-use, more efficient products that fulfilled certain needs better than their predecessors did.

In short, the idea of a product life cycle exists because consumer needs and preferences change as technology continues to evolve. Taste and technology are two interdependent phenomena that influence each other and often speed up a product's life cycle.

The following four stages make up the life cycle of a product: introduction, growth, maturity, and decline. Although it is diffi-cult to pinpoint the exact stage a product may be in at any given moment, each phase does have specific characteristics. Figure 2.1 shows the theoretical curve of the life cycle.

This curve is actually the demand curve for a product over a period of time. Unfortunately, the elegant line shown in figure 2.1 is rarely reproduced in reality, where each phase may not be equal in length. Demand for a product may be a mere flash in the pan or may blossom slowly to reach maturity only years after the introduction stage. The number of possibilities is infinite. Figure 2.2 shows a few examples.

The expression "product life cycle" should be considered in its broadest sense. The concept may apply to a group of products offered on the market (market life cycle) or to a specific brand or product. Generally, the life cycle of a market is composed of a series of superimposed product life cycles, which, in turn, are made up of superimposed brand life cycles.

The notion of a life cycle in the arts can be seen more clearly with the concrete

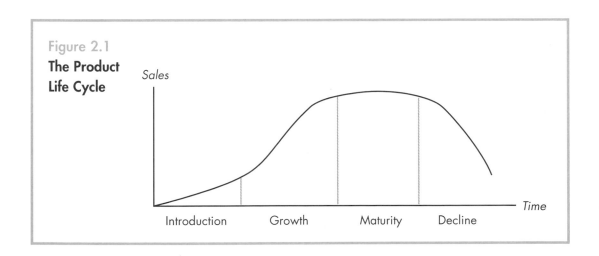

Figure 2.1
The Product Life Cycle

Sales

Time

Introduction   Growth   Maturity   Decline

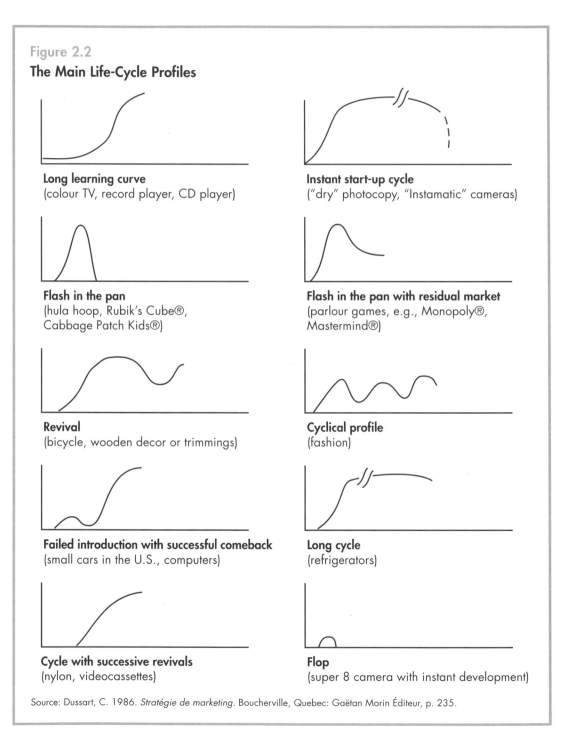

Figure 2.2

The Main Life-Cycle Profiles

Long learning curve
(colour TV, record player, CD player)

Instant start-up cycle
("dry" photocopy, "Instamatic" cameras)

Flash in the pan
(hula hoop, Rubik's Cube®,
Cabbage Patch Kids®)

Flash in the pan with residual market
(parlour games, e.g., Monopoly®,
Mastermind®)

Revival
(bicycle, wooden decor or trimmings)

Cyclical profile
(fashion)

Failed introduction with successful comeback
(small cars in the U.S., computers)

Long cycle
(refrigerators)

Cycle with successive revivals
(nylon, videocassettes)

Flop
(super 8 camera with instant development)

Source: Dussart, C. 1986. *Stratégie de marketing*. Boucherville, Quebec: Gaëtan Morin Éditeur, p. 235.

example of summer-stock theatre and summer theatre festivals in the province of Quebec, Canada. Figure 2.3 follows the life cycle of summer-stock theatre from its inception to the late 1990s.

The product was introduced gradually. As a result, the number of summer-stock theatres rose slowly from 1957 to 1974, a period corresponding to the introduction phase. The year 1974 marked the start of tremendous growth, which stopped in the early 1980s, when the market hit the ceiling (100 productions), corresponding to the start of the maturity phase. The number of troupes and products remained stable until 1990. After this period, the proliferation of festivals and other popular events caused the number of productions to fall to twenty-nine.

The museum product, as a whole, has long been considered elitist. During the 1970s, the client base was broadened and the number of visits rose. Some people have called this the democratization of museumgoing. Marketing specialists, however, might consider it an example of a market life cycle that has experienced a new growth stage after years spent at one level. This market, however, has not developed evenly. Art museums, for example, were slow to draw a large clientele. Indeed, only in the past decade have they managed to increase their popularity. On the other hand, museums of civilization, a newer product, were an instant success and remain quite popular. Science museums also attract ever-increasing numbers of visitors.

2.2.2 The Product-Adoption Process

Although some consumers are hesitant to stop using a product, others are constantly looking for novelty and are always ready to try something new. As we have seen, the

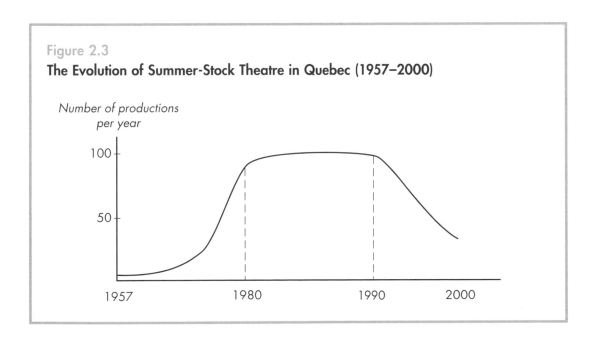

Figure 2.3

The Evolution of Summer-Stock Theatre in Quebec (1957–2000)

Number of productions per year

demand for a product corresponds to the number of units purchased by consumers. The greater the number of units, the stronger the demand. However, not all potential consumers will become customers at the same time. Some take more risks and agree to consume a product just introduced; others are more conservative and wait until the product has passed the test of public approval. Rogers[5] created a model that describes how innovations are diffused. He based his research on how quickly American farmers adopted new products. Figure 2.4 illustrates the results of Rogers's study.

So-called innovators are prepared to consume a new product as soon as it goes on the market. After a certain period, the initial consumers, a group characterized by strong personal leadership, play a key role in spreading the innovation. These initial consumers gather in their wake the early and late majorities. The laggards are the last to both start and stop using the product.

When the cycle occurs as illustrated in figure 2.4, consumer purchases create, over time, a curve representing the demand. This curve can be seen as the life cycle of the product. In fact, when only the so-called innovators buy a new product, its life cycle does not go beyond the introduction stage. If, however, adoption of the product progresses quickly, the maturity stage will soon be reached. Of course, if the adoption process is swift because of the characteristics of consumers within the target market, other factors may play a major role. One factor is certainly the lower selling price of the product, if it is a durable good. The video-cassette recorder/player provides an excellent example of this factor. The VCR spread like wildfire throughout the industrialized

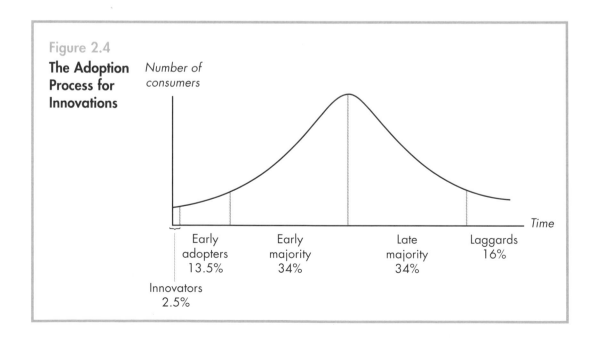

Figure 2.4

The Adoption Process for Innovations

Number of consumers

Early adopters 13.5%   Early majority 34%   Late majority 34%   Laggards 16%

Time

Innovators 2.5%

countries: the percentage of households owning a videocassette player hovered at 0% in 1980 and shot up to 70% within one decade; today, ownership rates surpass 80% in many countries. Although this piece of equipment cost several thousand dollars in the early eighties, it can now be found for less than five hundred dollars. The onslaught of the VCR led to a boom in the number of video clubs, creating a whole new industry. In turn, this phenomenon helped develop the market potential for the VCR itself.

In short, the curve representing the diffusion of an innovation is the graphic image of the number of consumers purchasing a product. The curve representing the product life cycle illustrates the demand for that product.

2.2.3 The Four Stages of a Life Cycle

Introduction

In a life cycle, the introduction of a new product is characterized by slow starting sales, financial losses, and the absence of competitors. This stage can covers a fairly long period of time, depending on consumer response. The sooner the bulk of consumers change their habits and adopt an innovation, the sooner the growth stage is reached. Market penetration may be slowed by a variety of factors, such as the consumer's resistance to change, a distribution network that limits accessibility to the new product, a robust offensive by companies selling substitute products, an overly high price, and so on.

Normally the selling price is highest during the introduction stage, when the manufacturer has enormous expenses to cover. Not only are manufacturing costs per unit high, but promotion costs have to be included in the selling price to ensure that the innovation is accepted. The manufacturer must also include a certain percentage to amortize the design and development of the product.

Table 2.2 shows four product-introduction strategies based on a combination of two

Table 2.2
Product-Introduction Strategies

		Promotion	
		Heavy	Light
Price	High	Top-of-the-line strategy	Selective penetration strategy
	Low	Massive penetration strategy	Bottom-of-the-line strategy

hypotheses of price and promotion: low or high price and light or heavy promotion.

The "top-of-the-line" strategy involves launching a product at a high price through a powerful promotional campaign. This strategy is applicable when the potential market does not yet know the product – for example, a real novelty item – but a sufficient number of consumers are likely to buy it even at a high price. The company, in this case, foresees competition in the near future and seeks to forge a strong brand image.

The massive penetration strategy consists of launching a product at a relatively low price with a very strong promotional campaign. The company is then likely to obtain a high level of market penetration and capture a large share of the market. This second strategy is useful if the product is little known but likely to interest a vast market of potential price-conscious consumers. The number of units produced must allow for economies of scale[6] in order to ensure profitability.

The third strategy, called the "bottom-of-the-line" strategy, enables a company to increase profits by economizing on promotional costs. In this case, the market must be extremely large, the average consumer must be price-conscious, and the type of product must already be known, even if the brand is new.

Last is the selective penetration strategy, which involves launching a new product at a high cost with little promotional input. This approach may be used if competition is weak, if the generic product is known, and if the consumer is prepared to pay the price. Marketing this product allows for a high profit margin with little money spent on promotion.

Growth

As more consumers join the innovators, the product enters the growth stage. The ranks of the "early adopters" are swelled by the "early majority." At this point, the demand becomes strong enough to allow a drop in the price, to encourage other groups of consumers to buy the product.

This stage is characterized by a rapid jump in sales figures and a noticeable increase in competition, since the market can now absorb new competitors. The arrival of additional consumers enables new manufacturers to earn enough without jeopardizing the sales of existing companies. In the consumer-goods sector, this is a period when both the number of consumers and the rate of consumption per person rise.

During this period, companies face a major dilemma: should they take immediate advantage of the short-term profits generated, or invest those profits in the hope of developing a better competitive stance during the next stage of the product life cycle? In taking the second option, an executive could choose to allot a percentage of corporate profits to improving the product, expanding distribution routes, seeking new categories of consumers, intensifying promotional campaigns, and so on. In all of these cases, immediate profits are sacrificed for the betterment of the company's future position.

Maturity

Sooner or later, once all potential customers have been reached and the rate of consumption per person has stabilized, overall demand will plateau. This is the maturity stage, which generally lasts longer than the previous stages.

The maturity stage may be subdivided into three periods. The first is increasing maturity, at which point the rate of sales growth starts to slow down. Although laggards start adopting the product and join the crowd of current buyers, they are relatively few in number. Product sales then reach a plateau. This is the saturation period, during which the demand comes essentially from replacement sales. The third period is that of declining maturity, characterized by a drop in sales volume, since some consumers are already looking at substitute or new products.

When demand levels off, there are serious consequences in terms of competition. Although the market is saturated, new companies or product brands are constantly springing up and trying to find a niche. The increasingly intense competition forces the most vulnerable companies to close their doors.

Strategically, a company may now choose among three different approaches: modify the market, modify the product, or modify other variables in the marketing mix.

The market may be modified by seeking out new, as yet untapped segments. The company must then either persuade consumers to buy more of the product or reposition the brand by modifying the average consumer's perceptions of the product.

Product modification consists of reviving sales by improving quality, changing style, or developing features specific to that product. This tactic is effective as long as the consumer perceives these changes as both real and relevant.

Lastly, a company may choose to adjust other variables in the marketing mix. It may lower prices, attack the market through a powerful promotional campaign, hold a contest, offer coupons, or turn to higher-volume distribution channels, such as discount stores.

It is not always easy to recognize where a product is in its life cycle. Although the introduction and growth stages are usually the easiest to pinpoint, the other stages may prove difficult to analyze in detail. For example, how can a temporary plateau in sales be distinguished from the saturation phase? A diagnostic approach would likely include the following three elements: the product's rate of penetration, the possibility of finding new market segments, and the amount of consumption per person. If a company cannot increase the number of consumers in a given segment or hunt down other segments likely to buy the product, and it is impossible to increase consumption per person, the market saturation point has been reached.

Decline

The decline stage is undoubtedly the most difficult for any company to handle. In fact, the company may not even be able to tell whether its product has really started to decline or its sales have simply slumped temporarily. Only a detailed analysis of the situation can provide any answers to this question, and even then no one can be sure. The problem of distinguishing between a temporary decrease and a definitive drop in sales should not be underestimated. This kind of uncertainty leads to difficult decisions, especially if the product was marketed over a very lengthy period. The human factors involved in this type of decision should not be underestimated either. A sentimental attachment or a resistance to the idea of defeat may make a promoter insist on pursuing a project.

A company may prefer to pull its product off the shelves, maintain the status quo, or adopt the concentration strategy. This strategy involves concentrating efforts on the most profitable market segments and distribution channels. A company may also decide to use a pressure strategy, which lowers promotion costs and allows the product to "float" while generating short-term profits.

The main indicator used in diagnosing the decline stage is the presence of superior substitute products. This stage is usually reached as soon as superior substitute products that cannot be outdone hit the market. The compact disk, which almost completely eliminated the vinyl record, is an excellent example of this indicator. Yet even with this indicator nothing is certain. Some thought that television would sound the death knell for radio, but this was not the case. TV and radio seemed like the same product, using two different technical supports, destined for one and the same market. Some products were transferred – for example, radio soap operas to TV "daytime dramas"; however, each mode of communication developed its own specialties, so as to co-exist with the other yet still serve the same clientele for different needs and in different circumstances.

2.2.4 The Limitations of the Life-Cycle Concept

Some authors have seriously questioned the value of the concept of a product life cycle.[7] Their main argument is that the concept is modelled after the human life cycle, which has strict time definitions (childhood, adolescence, adulthood, and old age). Products, on the other hand, may experience a revival, extend their growth stage, or even become eternal! Products that follow the elegant curve shown in figure 2.1 are actually rare. Jagged, less symmetrical curves are the norm.

Unfortunately, the model is not very useful during the course of business. In fact, a product's current stage is never known for sure, especially with respect to the decline and maturity stages. Although some indicators do help marketing professionals to determine approximately where the product is in its life cycle, much remains uncertain. As a result, a drop in sales may not necessarily mean that the product is in decline, and hasty corporate decisions made at that point may later be regretted.

For some cultural products, especially those whose technical dimension cannot be bought, the model is not very useful at all. In fact, the life cycle of a product is often predestined at its launching. Many cultural products, particularly in the arts sector, are created to be performed or exhibited for a limited time only. They have a set number of performances or a pre-scheduled exhibition length, then they disappear. Even if the production is a success, it closes by a certain date. This style of product management is imposed by the restrictions inherent in the cultural sector. For example, a theatre company may offer a seasonal subscription and therefore be obliged to set dates and reserve seats. Meanwhile, performers accept or decline contract offers according to the date of their last performance. In most cases, the company cannot "hold over" the life cycle indefinitely, since contracts have been signed with the theatre and cast. Few theatres want to remount a play for either artistic or financial reasons (more rehearsals, another promotional campaign, different performers and hence a different product). A tour offers an interesting way of extending the life cycle of a product, but it may not always correspond to the company's mission.

The typical life cycle of the cultural product described above therefore follows a curve similar to that shown in figure 2.5.

As for productions that, once mounted, are allowed to run as long as there is still demand for them, they generally follow the standard product life cycle curve. This is the case of many of the commercial productions that play on New York (Broadway) and London stages, but also of repertory theatres that perform productions once or twice a week in rotation with the other productions in the company's repertory, until demand for them has run out. This type of concept is found at La Comédie-Française in Paris and in several Eastern European countries.[8] These companies typically have a permanent troupe of actors who appear in some capacity in nearly all of its productions. Often, actors will rehearse a new production in the morning and dedicate the afternoon to rehearsing the production they are to perform that very evening.

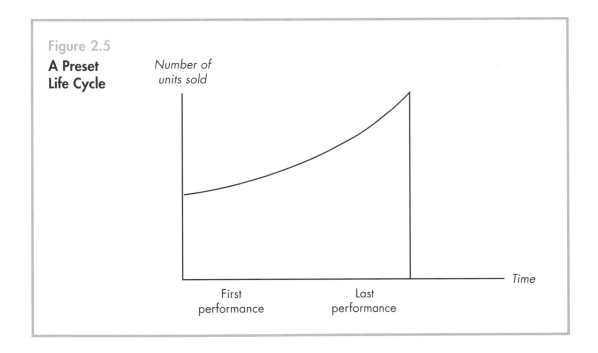

Figure 2.5
A Preset Life Cycle

Number of units sold

First performance

Last performance

Time

2.3 DESIGNING NEW PRODUCTS

2.3.1 Research and Development

Large manufacturing firms have a special department working on new products. The research and development (R and D) department has the exclusive task of developing product ideas. All expenses are financed through the profits generated by products sold by the firm. Large firms accept the fact that they must invest sizable sums of money in R and D to ensure the future success of both new products and the organization itself.

The idea of special units devoted to research and development is foreign to the cultural milieu. As a matter of fact, the role of R and D is played somewhat by specialized companies, which must obtain a significant percentage of their revenue through government grants. These groups are not mandated to both do research and market successful products. Normally found in cultural industries and the arts, they bear names beginning with adjectives like "contemporary," "alternative," or "parallel."

In a manufacturing firm, new products designed by the R and D department are evaluated by a series of specialists in engineering, marketing, or finance. Their expert opinions are given throughout the product-development process using product prototypes that are not yet marketed or ready to be field-tested by a sampling of the population. In the cultural sector, a product usually undergoes this critical process after it has been marketed, unveiled, or premiered. The specialists, in this instance, are the critics or members of the artistic community and the "connoisseurs" in the general public.

The development and marketing of new products is an extremely risky undertaking for any organization, regardless of its sector. Administrators seek to minimize the inherent risk by using a very rigorous development process.[9] This process (see figure 2.6) actually involves a series of precise steps, each one requiring a decision before continuing to the next step, in which the manager must once again decide whether or not to continue developing the product. Since the high cost of product development actually increases with each step, this process helps companies pinpoint losing projects early, and thus saves them a considerable amount of money.

The creative act characteristic of the development of any artistic product does not fit well with this process. In fact, in most cases, only on opening night can a company know how the product will be received by the audience. Even experts can be mistaken in their predictions of the commercial success of a script. There is, of course, an enormous difference between the text and the finished product. Casting, group dynamics at rehearsal, and direction are all intangible factors with a tremendous influence on this product. Obviously, certain elements surrounding the "manufacture" of an artistic product may be tested – for instance, elements in an advertising campaign. The product may also be adapted according to cultural differences when exported – for instance, a new ending to a film. These adjustments, however, are minor.

In the performing arts, the concept of a "work in progress" provides a noteworthy

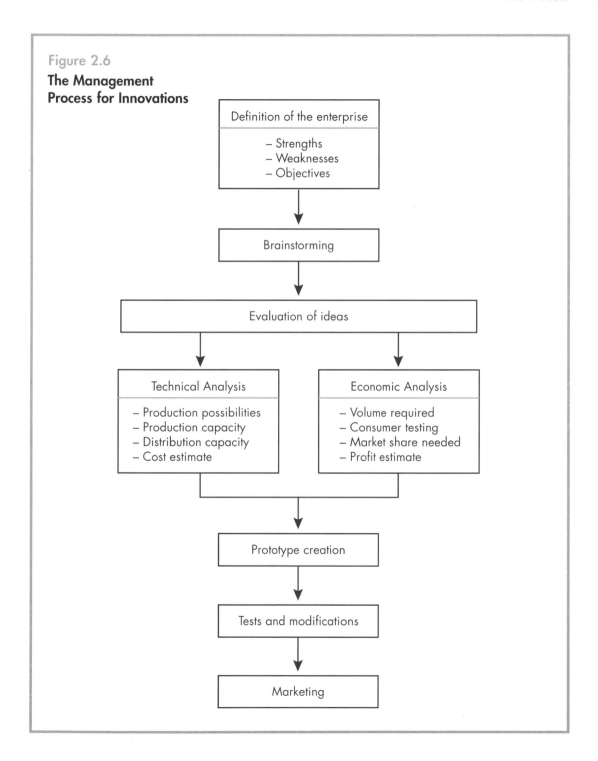

Figure 2.6
The Management Process for Innovations

exception. Several creative artists present the fruit of their labours to a limited audience prior to the final shaping of their work, after a certain stage has been reached in rehearsal but without all the production elements (sets, props, costumes, and lighting) in order to test certain ideas or effects on a select clientele.

2.3.2 Risk

The development and launching of a new product always involves a certain amount of risk for the producer – "risk" in the sense that the possibility of not satisfying the consumer or not meeting marketing objectives or corporate financial goals is ever-present. In manufacturing, for example, the product-mortality rate is extremely high: papers on marketing confirm that only one out of every sixty ideas ever blossoms into a product launched on the market. Of those few products launched, many flop. *Business Week* reported that has of "11,000 new products launched by 77 manufacturing, service, and consumer-products companies . . . only a little more than half – 56% – of all products that actually get launched are still on the market five years later."[10] The moral of the story is that commercial products are not as easily or successfully marketed as one might think.

Commercial success alone does not satisfy the corporate mission of many cultural enterprises, especially if they are product oriented. In their case, the risk is both financial and artistic. The following three factors determine the high level of risk experienced by cultural enterprises, in particular those devoted to the live performing arts:

- the impossibility of pretesting a newly launched product;
- a planned limited life cycle;
- the inability to stock the product.

To be consistent with their missions, most cultural companies must constantly launch new products without being able to pretest them. Obviously, probing audience reaction to a film or show would still mean that the company has to assume the inherent production and promotion costs before reaching the preview stage. Moreover, once launched, the cultural product can no longer be changed. A museum, for instance, launching a new exhibit, whether of Picasso's or a lesser-known artist's work, must sell the product as is to the potential "consumer." No artist or theme can be guaranteed success in advance.

Consumers, on the other hand, feel limited if they cannot taste or touch a sample of the product. Producers or distributors in the performing arts who own their own venues try to reduce this anxiety or pressure by offering potential consumers a season's subscription that includes several different productions. The perceived risk is thus lessened since the product, hence the company, is "tried and true." The viewer essentially "buys" the Royal Alexandra, the Comédie-Française, the Chicago Symphony Orchestra, or the Canadian Opera Company rather than *The Mikado*, Molière's *The Imaginary Invalid*, Beethoven's *Symphony No. 2 in D Major,* or *Madama Butterfly*.

Of course, the newer the product, as is the case for modern art, the greater the risk, in terms both of appreciation and of financial loss for the producer. For a classic product that is well known by the public, the risk is still present, but lower.

The second characteristic of the risk inherent in cultural products is the fateful date when the product is withdrawn from the marketplace. For most companies active in the performing arts, this date must be set with the possibility of additional performances tacked on, after which the work will be withdrawn from the market regardless of its success. Similarly for museums, the length of an exhibit is predetermined, since borrowed works are expected elsewhere after the show closes.

The third aspect of risk experienced frequently in the cultural sector is related to the fact that the product cannot be stored. Seats that remain empty during a performance represent lost revenues. This aspect also heightens the pressure for consumers to see the show while it is playing, and not whenever they have the time and money to do so. Often, a consumer must choose between two shows which, unlike books, cannot be consumed later on. This particularity of many cultural products has tremendous impact on the nature of the competition.

All of the elements noted above prove that cultural enterprises are high-risk ventures that have no equivalent in other sectors of the economy. The manager of an artistic product must invest massively in the creation of a product that cannot be pretested, knowing full well that the product must be deliberately withdrawn from the marketplace, regardless of its success. Moreover, even if the product is successful, the company cannot store that product at that moment for future use (even if sets and costumes can be stored). Knowing all this, the manager must also constantly start the whole process over, again and again, with other products.

SUMMARY

There are several recognized ways of defining products. One way is to classify them according to the effort consumers expend to purchase them. This is how popular consumer products are categorized. The notion of a product is, however, much broader than a simple physical entity. We can therefore distinguish among the central product, related services, and the symbolic dimension. The consumer may, in fact, want to buy any one or more of these components. A cultural product may be defined according to three dimensions: referential, technical, and circumstantial.

Cultural products are often perceived as complex, because the notion of aesthetics, a subjective, non-quantifiable element related to taste and upbringing, is involved. The degree of complexity of a cultural product may vary according to corporate mission. For the marketer, the product may be defined as the set of benefits the customer perceives.

A product line combines all models of one type of product offered by a company. A product range comprises all the lines offered by a company. The life cycle of a product is a key concept in marketing. It is usually defined in terms of four stages: introduction, growth, maturity, and decline. The life cycle is represented by a curve that actually represents the demand. The time line for the life-cycle curve varies according to the consumption level of the target market. The notion of a life cycle is useful but far from definitive. For cultural enterprises whose products have predetermined life spans, its practical application is extremely limited.

The launching of a new product represents a major risk for any firm. Production in the arts and cultural sectors must be considered a particularly high-risk venture, since each product is actually a new one. The normal risk is exacerbated by three characteristics of cultural products. First, in the performing arts, for example, the product cannot be tested before its opening night; hence, production and promotion costs must be assumed ahead of time. Second, these products often have a predetermined life span regardless of their commercial success. Third, this type of product cannot be stored by either the producer or the consumer. As a result, the level of risk rises and the nature of the competition is affected.

QUESTIONS

1. Why is the main or central product not always the most important aspect for the consumer making a purchase?

2. Why does the circumstantial dimension of an artistic product have a double impact in the performing arts?

3. How does a consumer's definition of what a product is differ from a company's definition?

4. Can you give some examples of product ranges in the cultural sector?

5. How is the notion of a product life cycle useful?

6. Can you describe how innovations spread?

7. What do "top-of-the-line" and "massive penetration" entail as strategies?

8. What are the characteristics of the growth phase in a product life cycle?

9. Which strategies are available to a company in the maturity stage?

10. What are the three elements that help us decide that a product is in the decline stage?

11. What risks are normally associated with the launching of a new product?

12. How is risk different for cultural products?

Notes

1. Colbert, F., N. Turgeon and S. Bilodeau. 1991. "Le développement de la connaissance du produit artistique." *Nouveau programme de formation des diffuseurs*. Ottawa: Touring Office, Canada Council.

2. Darmon, R.Y., M. Laroche and J.V. Petrov. 1990. *Le marketing, fondements et applications*, 4th ed. Montreal: McGraw-Hill.

3. Benghozi, P.-J., and D. Bayart. 1991. "La diversification des productions culturelles, l'exemple des musées," in *Proceedings of the First International Conference on Arts Management*, F. Colbert and C. Mitchell eds. Montreal: Chaire de gestion des arts, École des HEC (August), p. 275–300.

4. Caldwell, N.G. 2000. "The Emergence of Museum Brands." *International Journal of Arts Management*, Vol. 2, no 3 (Spring), p. 28–34.

5. Rogers, E. 1962. *The Diffusion of Innovations*. New York: Free Press.

6. "Economies of scale" refers to how a company can reduce unit costs by manufacturing in large quantities.

7. Dhalla, N.K., and S. Yuspeh. 1976. "Forget the Product Life Cycle Concept." *Harvard Business Review* (January–February), p. 102–112.

8. Levshina, E., and Y. Orlov. 2000. "General and Specific Issues in Russian Theatre." *International Journal of Arts Management*, Vol. 2, no 2 (Winter), p. 74–83.

9. Cooper, R.G. 1976. *Winning the New Product Game*. Montreal: Publication Services, McGill University.

10. *Business Week*. August 16, 1993, p. 77.

For Further Reference

Bennett, R. 2001. "Lead User Influence on New Product Development Decisions of UK Theatre Companies: An Empirical Study." *International Journal of Arts Management*, Vol. 3, no 2 (Winter), p. 28–40.

Leemans, H. 1997. "A PMC-Model for Cultural Organisations: The Case of a Public Library Private," in *Proceedings of the 4th International Conference on Arts and Culture Management*. San Francisco: Golden Gate University, p. 381–394.

Scott, C. 2000. "Branding: Positioning Museums in the 21st Century." *International Journal of Arts Management*, Vol. 2, no 3 (Spring), p. 35–39.

Plan

CHAPTER 3
The Market

OBJECTIVES

- Understand the specificity of the four markets open to cultural enterprises
- Give a profile of the culture consumer
- Point out the different levels of demand experienced by a company
- Explain the pressures exerted on the market by macro-environmental variables
- Understand the dangers of an obtuse view of the competition

3

INTRODUCTION

The market served by a firm is not homogeneous. Here, we have divided the market served by cultural enterprises into the following four groups: the consumer market, distribution agents, the state, and sponsors. By defining each of these markets, we can see why a company must formulate specific strategies for each one.

The demand generated by consumer purchases is constantly evolving, so this chapter will pay special attention to one market, the leisure market. One of the marketing manager's tasks is to measure the level of product demand, which may be real or potential, either for the market as a whole or specifically for his or her own company.

The marketing manager who wants to understand the forces influencing the market must adopt a broader view of the competition while taking into account globalization of the competition. Competition and globalization, combined with industry fragmentation in some cultural sectors, oblige companies to rely on a competitive advantage to ensure their own survival.

Lastly, in this chapter, we examine how environmental forces exert tremendous pressure on the market, the company, and even the competition.

3.1   THE MARKET

As a rule, one company targets several markets. A cultural company may serve four different markets: the ultimate consumer, the distribution agents, the state, and the sponsor. These are, in effect, distinct markets responding to different motivations. Decision makers in each market should be carefully studied so that a company can develop appropriate marketing strategies for each one.

3.1.1 The Consumer Market

The consumer market is composed of individuals who buy a specific good or service.

Rarely does one product interest the entire population. This statement applies even to staples, such as sugar, flour, and salt. A small percentage of households do not eat these products, so even if a company did target the entire population, not everyone would be a potential consumer.

The same statistical truth applies to cultural products. However, because of the extremely fragmented nature of the cultural sector, some distinctions are in order. For example, looking at this sector as a whole, it can be said that nearly 100% of the population consumes one type of cultural product or another. Indeed, in its broadest sense, the cultural sector encompasses everything from the arts (high and popular), to heritage, compact disks, movies, book and magazine publishing, and radio and television, with each of these disciplines appropriating a more or less important share of global demand.

In Canada for example, statistics[1] show that 36.4% of Canadian families go at least once a year to an event in the performing arts: 56.3% to the movies, 25.9% to museums and art galleries. In the United States, the figures are 15.6% for classical music, 4.7% for opera, 24.5% for musicals, 15.8% for plays,

5.8% for ballet, 34.5% for art museums, and 46.9% for historical parks.[2] In Australia,[3] the corresponding figures are: musical theatre 19.3%, classical music 7.7%, festivals 21.9%, concerts 23%, museums 27.8%. Of course, within each of these sectors, consumers cluster according to specific poles of interest. This leads to sharper market segmentation. The consumer makes a discriminating choice among various cultural products to obtain the type of product desired.

The distribution of consumers according to various market segments differs in both time and space. Markets undergo and reflect the influence of opinion leaders, trends, tastes, and societal characteristics. Markets also vary from country to country according to different social structures.[4]

Surveys[5] focusing on the sociodemographic profile of consumers of cultural products have been carried out in nearly every European country (both East and West), as well as in Canada, the United States, Australia, and Japan.[6] It is fascinating to note that, regardless of whether the surveys were conducted in the 1970s, 1980s, or 1990s, they all obtain the same attendance rates and the same sociodemographic profiles. Differences in the measuring tools used can sometimes make it difficult to compare countries (different nomenclature for sectors, questions formulated differently, etc.); nonetheless, these surveys have systematically, unequivocally, and consistently over the last forty years revealed a strong polarization among audiences and consumers from one country to another. They show, for example, that cultural products catering to high art attract educated consumers, while, conversely, those catering to popular culture draw upon a less-educated population segment. The proportion of university graduates making up Canadian audiences, for example, ranges between 50% and 70% in the first case (symphony orchestras, arts festivals, fine arts museums, etc.), compared with 10% to 25% in the second (popular music, historical parks, etc.). By way of comparison, the overall percentage of university graduates in Canada is 15%. Similar results have been found in other countries (appendix 3.2), including Russia, where university graduates make up 50% of performing arts audiences, while the proportion of university graduates in the general population is only 7%.[7]

Other sociodemographic variables are also linked to attendance; these include personal income (high in the first case and low in the second) and the type of occupation (white-collar in the first case and blue-collar in the second). Moreover, attendance rates at high-art performances is nearly identical across all industrialized countries, with some variations attributable to the specific cultural heritage of given countries (for example, attendance is higher for opera in Italy and for classical music in Germany). In addition, regular patrons account for only a small portion of the total population, as attested to by the findings for theatre compiled by the Council of Europe (1993) and presented in table 3.1.

Of course, this generalization is based on averages. Less-educated individuals with lower income may be great consumers of culture, as is the case for students and those specialized or working in the cultural milieu. Indeed, it is well known that, as a rule many people active in the arts are highly educated

Table 3.1
Regular Theatre Attendance

Country	Date	Attendance rate (%)	Frequency
France	1988	2.0	5 times or more per year
United Kingdom	1989	4.4[*]	4 times or more per year
The Netherlands	1987	4.0	1 time or more per month
Finland	1981	4.0	5 times or more per year

[*] This rate applies for "plays" only. The rate is 6.3% if Britain's statistical definition of theatre, which includes opera and ballet, is used.

Source: Conseil de l'Europe. 1993. *Participation à la vie culturelle en Europe, Tendances, stratégies et défis, Table ronde de Moscou –1991*, Paris, La Documentation française, 1993, p.75.

yet so ill paid that they struggle to stay above the poverty line. On the other hand, there are people with both very high salaries and very high educational levels who are not interested in the arts and gladly keep their distance. Four factors are known to influence an individual's penchant for complex cultural products: family values that encourage or discourage high art; the educational milieu and the value it places on high art; the fact of having attended performances or visited museums as a child; and amateur art practice.

A more detailed analysis of the typical cultural consumer's traits reveals other nuances; for example, dance audiences are relatively younger and even more female in composition than those of the other performing arts; similarly, more women than men read novels, although a larger proportion of men read daily newspapers. In the film sector, there are two very different segments of avid cinema-goers; one of these segments is dominated by a young clientele (15-25 years), while the other is made up of educated people. The majority of consumers in the film sector belong to one or the other of these two segments.

Companies that have a high proportion of university graduates in their audience are targetting a rather limited market, even if these people usually are great consumers of cultural products. On the other hand, popular art caters to a much larger market segment.

Figure 3.1 illustrates the relationship between the popular and high or fine arts, the number of units consumed, and the complexity of the product.

3.1.2 The Distribution Market

Although some companies sell their product directly to the ultimate consumer, many must use the services of an agent or intermediary. The decision to use an agent may be strategic, dictated by limited resources

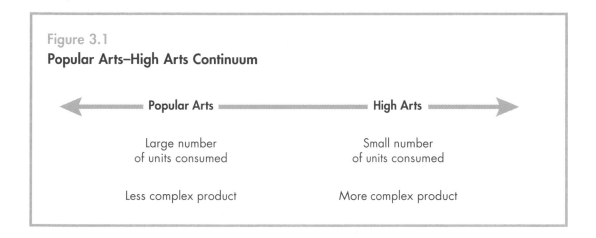

Figure 3.1
Popular Arts–High Arts Continuum

◄———————— Popular Arts ============ High Arts ———————►

| Large number of units consumed | Small number of units consumed |
| Less complex product | More complex product |

or the way a particular product is consumed. The distribution market comprises these agents or intermediaries.

In the performing arts, the presenter is a distribution agent. A touring company uses a presenter to reach consumers in a specific city or region. The marketing of a cultural product in this instance involves the following two steps: the touring company must convince the agent or presenter to include the show in the next season's line-up, and then the presenter must target potential consumers in the region. Usually, the producer develops a specific strategy to attract presenters and also foresees the promotional tools that will help the presenter or promoter market the show to the ultimate consumer.

There is a distribution market in almost all cultural sectors.

3.1.3 The State as a Market

"State" is used here to denote the different levels of government – federal, provincial (regional), and municipal (local) – that support cultural enterprises in various ways.

The state plays a dominant role in the cultural sector in most Western countries. Sometimes it acts as a consumer, or it may intervene to varying degrees, from simple partner to patron controlling the entire cultural sector of a nation.

The notion of the state as grant giver and as market implies that a cultural enterprise must define its own strategy to convince decision makers to become partners in its activities. This type of cultural enterprise faces competition from others in the same field, and the efforts of each company to obtain more state support are essentially efforts to capture a larger share of a specific market. Since the arts budget is not sufficient to meet the needs of the entire cultural sector, the arrival of a new company or the success of an existing one may mean that the money allotted to one company will be reallocated to the benefit or detriment of another company.

There are several government agencies prepared to assist cultural organizations and companies through various forms of financial support. Some programs allow for the funding of infrastructures; others allow for the completion of specific projects; and still others contribute to the operational budget of the company itself.

The level of public investment in the arts and culture varies according to each country's traditions. Countries in Continental Europe have a long history of state participation in this sector; major theatres and museums can expect to receive as much as 80 to 100% of their budget in the form of government funding. In the United States, on the other hand, public investment in the arts is much less pronounced, but the private sector and individual donors play a major role in the life of cultural enterprises. For example, on average, the performing arts receive only 6% of their budget from public sources in the United States.[8] The approach adopted by Canada and Australia is modelled after that of England, where the state has a hand in the cultural sector, but to a lesser degree than in Continental Europe.

With regard to the structures created to distribute these public funds, again the models vary from one country to the next. Some countries, such as France, have a centralized model in which a Minister of Culture fixes the priorities and objectives that define cultural policy. On the other hand, the United States has adopted a highly decentralized model based on the creation of nearly 3,000 Local Arts Councils that play a major role in the cultural life of communities; even the National Endowment for the Arts, whose budget is very low considering the country's size (less than US$100 million), is obliged to distribute a portion of its budget to the State Arts Councils and Local Arts Councils. In Canada, Australia, and England (whose model the first two countries have borrowed), a national arts council plays a major role in awarding funding for the arts; however, this strong presence does not preclude other ministries and regional authorities from establishing their own financial aid programs.

3.1.4 Sponsorship, Cause-Related Marketing, and the Donor Market (by J. Dennis Rich)

Overview of Philanthropic Activity

Fundraising is not a new concept to managers of culture and the arts. From the beginning of recorded history, philanthropy has had a place in human society. It arrived in America with the Pilgrims. A basic tenet of their society was that each member of the community should willingly assume responsibilities for the common good. An outcome of this historical circumstance was the association of volunteerism with philanthropy.

Communities preceded government in the New World, and one result of this was that community needs were met through co-operative volunteer effort. Leaders of such efforts were unpaid, but achieved elevated social status and, over the years, wealthy individuals made such institutions as universities, schools, and libraries possible. In addition, they often bequeathed a part of their fortunes to charitable organizations. As early as 1638, John Harvard bequeathed a portion of his estate and his library to found Harvard College. Benjamin Franklin's will not only provided for his children, but also included instructions concerning charitable donations.

As their circumstances improved, members of the U.S. middle class followed suit and began to make charitable gifts as well.[9]

By the nineteenth century, fundraising activity began to resemble modern philanthropic practice, as personal solicitation, fundraising events, letters soliciting contributions, and fundraising campaigns all came into being. In 1835, Alexis de Tocqueville (1805-1859) commented on the unique nature of American philanthropy, characterized by individual, private efforts and volunteerism. He was impressed by the willingness of people to give their own funds to support social improvements and observed that when Americans saw the need for a school, hospital, church, or cultural service, local citizens would form a committee to discuss the need, provide leadership, and seek out sources of support.

The Americans make associations to give entertainments, to found seminaries, to build inns, to construct churches, to diffuse books, to send missionaries to the antipodes; in this manner, they found hospitals, prisons, and schools. If it is proposed to inculcate some truth or to foster some feeling by the encouragement of a great example, they form a society. Wherever at the head of some new undertaking you see the government in France, or a man of rank in England, in the United States you will be sure to find an association.[10]

By the early part of the next century, wealthy individuals such as John D. Rockefeller and Andrew Carnegie set the stage for major support with the establishment of private foundations and with the assertion that the wealthy have a moral obligation to distribute their fortunes for the good of society.

World War I was the first time that U.S. citizens contributed to a cause on a substantial scale. Many communities established war chests and, in 1917, the American Red Cross raised $115 million in a single month.[11]

During the Great Depression of the 1930s, the U.S. government began both to help meet people's needs with such programs as the Works Progress Administration and the Civilian Conservation Core, and to encourage corporate giving with passage of the 1935 Revenue Act, which allowed corporations to reduce their taxes as a consequence of charitable contributions.

Beginning in the 1950s, personal incomes in the U.S. rose dramatically, as did taxes. One result was an upsurge in charitable giving and in the creation of family-sponsored and corporate foundations in an effort to gain some tax advantage. By the 1960s, during the "Great Society" era, U.S. citizens were supporting numerous causes, including the arts and culture. By 1965, when the National Endowment for the Arts and the National Endowment for the Humanities were established, Americans were giving to culture and the arts in record numbers.[12]

The Donor Market Today

In recent years, the competition for donated money has brought concepts traditionally associated with marketing into the cultural fundraising arena. Few arts organizations seek support solely on the basis of quality programs or even of the services they provide the community. It is common for cultural institutions today to refer to economic impact, the creation of jobs, or the role they play in attracting tourists. In essence, they are seeking to effect an exchange of value.

The sponsor and fundraising market comprises individuals, foundations, and private companies likely to provide support to cultural institutions. This is a special market in that, once again, cultural enterprises must often compete among themselves to capture the market share representing high potential earnings. Sponsors and donors, on the other hand, make support decisions using different criteria from the state and the consumer. Each sponsor has its own criteria for selecting a company to support.

Support may take two forms: contributions, or sponsorship of events or products. While contributions may be made by individuals, foundations, or companies, sponsorships come mainly from companies. A contribution is normally a philanthropic act, whereas sponsorship is a promotional initiative in exchange for publicity or advertising. Sponsorships are undertaken according to promotional benefits calculated in advance. The corporate sponsor then judges the performance of the investment in terms of visibility, top-of-the-mind awareness, and the vehicle's reach – that is, the number of consumers receiving the message.

Companies that sponsor artistic and cultural events are looking for prestige advertising vehicles. Their hope is that the popularity of the group sponsored and the public's affection for that group will be transferred to the sponsor. Usually, funds are drawn from the company's advertising or PR (public relations) budget. The public targeted by cultural companies is an extremely lucrative source for commercial enterprises seeking a market segment with strong purchasing power. In fact, several companies in the cultural industries serve a broad-based market and are therefore perceived by the private sector as excellent advertising vehicles. Faced with media fragmentation, companies are looking for new ways to get their message across in a cost-effective and competitively successful manner.[13] Sponsorship can meet this need.

The gamut of companies looking for a sponsorship role proves this point. Today, companies such as the Toronto Film Festival, the Chicago Symphony Orchestra, and the Salzburg Festival are so successful that major private-sector corporations do not hesitate to associate themselves with these events, which not only reach a large number of spectators, but also enjoy tremendous public approval and appeal.

Individual donors, on the other hand, provide assistance based on personal taste and commitment. In the case of a foundation, its mission and goals determine the choice of a cause. Donors usually are rewarded with some form of recognition, but this is not usually what motivates a philanthropic gesture.

In Canada, the private sector provides 15.6% of the revenue of companies in the performing arts.[14] In the United States, the figure can exceed 40%. In the U.S., government support from all sources for the performing arts averages 5.5% or less, while in Canada, support for all the performing arts from the different levels of governments amounts to as much as 40%.[15]

Certain fields are more highly subsidized than others by the private sector. In this sense, orchestras, opera companies, and musical societies are more successful than dance or theatre groups. The size of the artistic enterprise or event also influences donors or sponsors in their choices, the latter tending to prefer larger venues and groups.

The United States is an interesting case among the top industrialized nations in terms of private sector participation in supporting the arts. This may be partially explained by the lower rate of corporate taxation and the number of tax incentives available in the United States, where the state plays a lesser role in financing the arts. Indeed, the ratio of foundations supporting the arts in the U.S. in comparison with those in Canada is 35:1, whereas the population ratio is 10:1.[16] In Europe, the state historically has done little to encourage cultural enterprises to find partners in the private sector, though this is changing rapidly.

Cultural sponsorship in Western Europe started at the end of the 1970s. At the beginning, corporations in Germany, Spain, the Netherlands, and France limited their support to the collection of works of art. They gradually extended and broadened their assistance, subsidizing sectors like the visual arts (collections and exhibitions), heritage (restoration of monuments and buildings), and theatre and classical music (sponsorship of touring for well-known companies). Corporate support and sponsorship of the arts, and the implications of it, in Europe is still low, but is growing.

Donor support in the U.S. represents significant sums of money. In total, charitable giving in the U.S. for 1998 represented 2.1% of the gross domestic product,[17] or $174.52 billion. Of this total, *individuals* gave 85.1% (including bequests), *corporations* gave 5.1% (excluding sponsorship and cause-related marketing), and *foundations* gave the remaining 9.8%. Of the total amount, 6%, or $10.62 billion, was given to culture and the arts.[18]

In addition to giving financial support, about 50% of all American adults volunteer, giving their time to a charitable organization. Moreover, Americans who volunteer also tend to make larger financial gifts. Typically, in households in which adults volunteer their time and services, total charitable giving came to 2.5% of personal income in 1998. Among non-volunteering households in which adults made gifts, the average was 1.2% of income.[19]

3.2   MARKET DEMAND

3.2.1 Defining Demand

Market demand for a particular product is the expression, in volume or dollars, of purchases made. The demand may be expressed either quantitatively in units (volume) or monetarily (in dollars), according to need and availability of data.

Demand expressed in terms of volume often gives a more realistic picture of the market, since the results are not swollen through price increases. It is therefore easier to compare data from one year to the next since the basis of comparison is similar. Sometimes, an increase in demand in dollars is merely the result of higher prices, while the real market level remains the same. If the demand is given in dollars with no adjustment for price, the measurement is considered to be in current dollars. If a marketing analyst eliminates the inflation factor by using the same year of reference, the measurement is said to be in constant dollars. If data on volume are unavailable, demand must be calculated in constant dollars to neutralize variations in price and provide a true picture of the situation.

Although expressing demand in terms of volume may be useful, especially to see how demand evolves, it may at times be difficult to do. The data, as such, may not exist, or the product may comprise a range of diverse elements. In the leisure market, for instance, the demand cannot be evaluated in terms of volume because the category of products combines proverbial apples and oranges that do not add up – for instance, theatre seats, trips, and book purchases.

Market demand (MD) and corporate demand (CD) are normally considered separately. Corporate demand is the expression in volume or in dollars of purchases made of one product manufactured by a specific company. Market demand embraces all the corporate demands.

CD = Number of units sold by a company
$$MD = \sum CD_i$$

Since the market demand (MD) for a product consists of all the individual corporate demands (CD), the over-all demand may reveal one trend while the CD indicates the opposite. For example, the over-all demand for theatre tickets may have risen one year, while the demand for tickets for a particular theatre company may have plummeted during the same period. The same possibility exists in the over-all demand for a specific industry, such as leisure activities, with regard to the demand for its parts, such as shows or sporting events.

It is possible to measure demand at different points along the chain from creation to production to distribution to consumption. In this case, demand for a specific link is equal to the volume in units or dollars of purchases made by all those active in the following link.

Sometimes several firms or "players" join forces to stimulate over-all market demand. These firms presume that an increase in over-all demand is possible and beneficial to each firm in proportion to its respective importance in the marketplace. The Canadian Museums Association is an example of this type of group. The objectives of this association go beyond the exchange of ideas to joint strategies to stimulate collective interest in museums and thus stimulate more people to visit more museums more often. The annual national museums day organized by this association lets the public come and sample different museums' wares. Similar initiatives may take place at the local or regional level. In the United States, for example, some museums have formed associations with a view to joint promotional campaigns designed to increase the overall demand within a particular region.

3.2.2 Market Share

The market, as defined here, comprises all the individuals or companies consuming a product. Each firm encourages its part of the market segment to consume its product in order to acquire a percentage of the demand. In current marketing terms, this is called the "market share," and it describes not the consumers buying the products, but the proportion of the demand belonging to one company. It would be more accurate to speak of "demand share" rather than market share, but the accepted expression is market share. The term also means share of the demand and is used in that sense here.

The market share of a company is calculated as follows:

$$\text{Market share} = \frac{CD}{MD}$$

A company with sales of $400,000 in a very specific $1 million market that it shares with other companies is said to have a market share of 40% ($400,000 ÷ $1,000,000). This information is extremely useful, since it enables a firm to compare itself to other firms and thus determine its own position relative to the competition.

3.2.3 The State of the Demand

Demand for a product may be considered from two vantage points: real and potential. For each aspect, there are three periods: past demand, current demand, and forecast demand.

The Real Demand

The real demand of a company corresponds to its sales volume at a specific time. The same applies to the market demand, which is a measure of the demand at a specific moment, be it now or in the past. It is possible to obtain the historical background chronicling the dynamics of a sector, industry, or company by measuring the evolution of the demand from past years. At the same time, the future level of demand can be forecast for a company or market in general terms.

The Potential Demand

The potential demand is the maximum level that may be reached by a product in a given context. Not all consumers buy all the products offered on the market, although for commonly bought consumer goods consumption is often believed to be generalized. The entire consumer population is almost never reached. People who do not consume a particular product but may do so are called potential consumers. Manufacturers work to persuade these potential purchasers to try their products in order to increase sales. If the percentage of sales per capita can be increased, manufacturers will try to convince their clientele to consume more.

There is, however, a threshold for any demand. This level depends on the consumers' means, tastes, and preferences, as well as on their receptivity to a marketing strategy and their environment. The marketing manager's task is to estimate the maximum level of market demand at any given time – in other words, the potential market demand. Similarly, the manager can estimate the potential demand for the company.

Just as in the case of the real demand, the potential demand may be calculated at a point in the past or the present, or forecast for the future.

Market Demand in Different Situations

Real demand is often lower than potential demand. In this case, a company may hope to increase its sales or its market share. If the real and potential demand are equal, then the market is said to have reached the saturation point, after which the product enters the maturity stage of its life cycle.

Any sales projections must therefore take into account the foreseeable actions of the competition and the predicted evolution of the potential demand. The marketing manager may expect an increase in potential demand and an increase in company sales figures. On the other hand, when potential demand in a market dips, companies must expect to have greater difficulty in maintaining their current level of demand and market share (see figure 3.2).

These concepts apply not only to the demand but also to the market. A market may also be considered real or potential and be measured in the past, present, or future.

Here is a concrete example of these concepts. A touring theatre troupe offers its show to a presenter in a specific region. The current potential market for the troupe in that area corresponds to the total number of venues or presenters likely to buy the show. The real market is known, since the troupe knows which halls or theatres it has already played that year. The predicted market is composed of the number of buyers forecast for the following year. This forecast may be made by considering two different

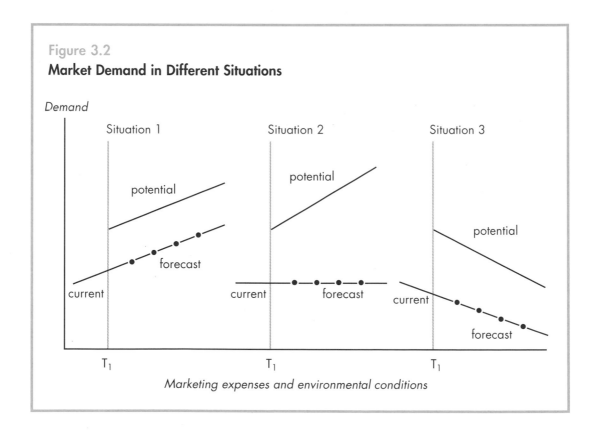

Figure 3.2
Market Demand in Different Situations

areas: the number of presenters in the market (potential market) and the number of presenters that will buy the show (real forecast market).

3.2.4 The Evolution of Demand in the Leisure Market

The world leisure market experienced tremendous growth between the 1960s and the 1980s; in Canada for example, the demand rose in constant dollars from $920 million (1964) to $3.93 billion (1982). This startling increase stems from the following four factors: a larger population, more leisure time, higher incomes, and higher levels of education.[20]

The increase in demand has benefitted almost all cultural sectors. It is worth noting that, in a country such as Canada, stage productions have surpassed sports events in terms of consumer popularity. Table 3.2 shows that in terms of the percentage of families responding, the percentage of dollars spent on these two leisure products reversed between 1964 and 1984, with stage productions surpassing sports events by far in popularity. This spectacular growth in demand for cultural leisure products can be partly explained by the fact that the clientele for these products is made up largely of women; indeed, the women's liberation movement of the 1960s, coupled with the mass integration of women in the labour market, created a new group of educated consumers with time and money on their hands and tastes differing from those of men.

The increase in demand that was seen between 1960 and 1980 is largely attributable to the coming of age of the baby boomers starting around 1960. This consumer group has dominated and set the tone for cultural behaviour for the past few decades. Moreover, it is a generation that chose to have children later in life and to have fewer of them. This caused a gradual decline in the number of children per

Table 3.2
Evolution of Average Family Expenditures on Cultural Outings

| | Sports events | | Stage performances | | Museums | | Cinema | |
	%	$ constant	%	$ constant	%	$ constant	%	$ constant
1964	35,5	10,6	26,0	5,1	n/a	n/a	61,0	16,1
1974	31,6	15,2	32,2	8,7	n/a	n/a	62,5	20,0
1984	28,4	8,3	43,1	11,8	39,5	5,4	59,9	13,4
1992	25,7	7,0	35,1	9,9	32,9	4,3	48,9	9,3
1996	22,3	7,0	36,4	11,8	25,9	3,5	56,3	11,2

Source : Statistics Canada, 2000. Family Expenditure in Canada. Catalogue 62.555

woman of child-bearing age, which was followed, starting in 1980, by an increase in the birth rate. This rise in the birth rate translates into an increase in the segment of the population that is presently under the age of 18. This new generation, often referred to as the echo generation, is larger than the generations preceding it but smaller than the baby boomer cohort, and it is expected to comprise an important segment of the market within the next ten to fifteen years.

In fact, by around 2015, the two largest segments of the market for cultural enterprises will be situated at opposite extremes of the age pyramid: the baby boomers, who will be over 50, and their offspring, who will be between the ages of 15 and 35. Each of these two segments will be larger than the third segment, made up of the 35-50 age group.[21] The main question raised by this phenomenon is whether these two consumer groups will have similar preferences, or whether they will be attracted to different cultural products. In the latter case, firms will be faced with a major dilemma: they will have to either choose between these two segments or adjust their products in order to reach both of these potentially incompatible segments at the same time. For companies that offer only one product, the dilemma will be absolute, while for those offering a program consisting of several performances or exhibitions, there will be greater room for adjustment, although this will not necessarily be easy to achieve.

Indeed, studies based on age cohorts in Canada, the United States, and Europe suggest that the behaviour adopted by younger generations differs from that of their elders,[22] all the more so when it comes to music. For example, the cohort born between 1966 and 1976 (thus ranging in age from 17 to 26 at the time of the American study) displayed a clear preference for jazz music and a marked lack of interest in classical music and opera. If this trend is carried over to the following generation (that born after 1976), barring a reversal, the audience for symphony orchestras and opera houses could go into a free fall within the next few years, especially in light of the drop in patronage observed among the very elderly.

This problem is compounded by the fact that senior citizens have very specific needs, described by Motta and Schewe[23] as being of both a physical and a psychological order. Their physical needs involve diminished hearing, vision, physical endurance, and mobility due to age, while their psychological needs have to do with a diminished capacity for abstraction and memory. For example, many elderly people are unable to perceive certain sounds, or they may like to sit down more frequently. Generally speaking, this age group prefers events which offer the opportunity to socialize with other people, as opposed to events involving more solitary contemplation.

Thus, beyond the preferences for particular works or a specific repertoire, it is the whole context of consumption that is affected by these trends.

3.3 MARKET AND COMPETITION

3.3.1 A Broad View of Competition

In any discussion of competition in culture and the arts, the cultural product must first be situated within a far broader context – the leisure market. Even if many people do not consider cultural products simply as pastimes, consumers can only consume these products during non-working and non-sleeping hours. The cultural product is therefore in competition not only with other cultural products, but also with various other products designed to occupy the consumer's free time, such as sports, other physical activities, travel, and continuing education.

There are essentially three types of competition. First, there is competition within one category of products. This is the case in a regional market, for instance, for an exhibit offered by different museums. There is also competition between different genres of cultural products – for example, a concert of classical music and a dance performance. Lastly, there may be competition between cultural products and other leisure products – for example, going to the movies or going skiing.

Competition is quite strong for leisure organizations trying to capture their share of the precious moments and dollars consumers allot to free time. Competition is fiercer in large cities, where the number of cultural products and leisure activities reaches dizzying heights. One look at the newspapers in a major city like New York, Sydney, Rome, or Toronto reveals a tremendous variety in the supply.

The competition is all the keener since the life span of these products is rather short and ephemeral. Exhibitions are offered for a limited time only, so these products cannot be stored for future presentation and the consumer cannot postpone consumption of the production beyond a certain date. The consumer's choice must therefore be made immediately. This time pressure exacerbates the competition among products.

As already seen, the demand for cultural products soared between 1964 and 1984. This increase was accompanied by an equally rapid rise in the supply. Starting in the mid-1960s, a profusion of artists and cultural products in all cultural domains – theatre, dance, and arts magazines, to name but a few – experienced tremendous growth. The same trend was seen in popular music, films, art galleries, and museums. The number of cable TV channels available also shot up. In the 1980s alone, the VCR and video market escalated dramatically.

Not only did the supply increase, but so also did the competition, which has now globalized.

3.3.2 The Effect of Globalization on Competition

Globalization of competition has opened up new vistas to consumers and made it possible to export certain cultural products. In exchange, other products can be imported from foreign countries. These imports mean additional competition for local products.

In the cultural industries, companies are clustered or concentrated, so that a small number of multinationals control creation of a large number of cultural products.[24] These multinationals diversify their activities so that each one controls businesses in each cultural sector: record production, entertainment equipment (CD players, VCRs, etc.), film production and distribution, publishing houses, radio and TV networks, stage productions, and so on. The cultural enterprises in a country with a small population must work together, using synergy to combat foreign competition. This united front, so to speak, must include not only products, but also the many other partners or links that form the production channel, including suppliers and the distribution network. This idea of the industrial cluster was part of Porter's[25] strategy for a country seeking to position itself advantageously at an international level. Porter also pointed out that, just like corporations, countries are competing among themselves.

3.3.3 Industry Fragmentation

Another trend that can intensify competition is fragmentation of the industry. Porter[26] gives five sources of pressure that might cause an industry to fragment (see figure 3.3). These are (1) intra-industry rivals; (2) new entrants – for example, companies just starting in the industry; (3) suppliers; (4) purchasers; (5) substitute products.

An industry is said to be fragmented if competitors are small yet numerous, if barriers blocking their entry into the industry are weak, and if buyers or suppliers have control over companies within the industry.

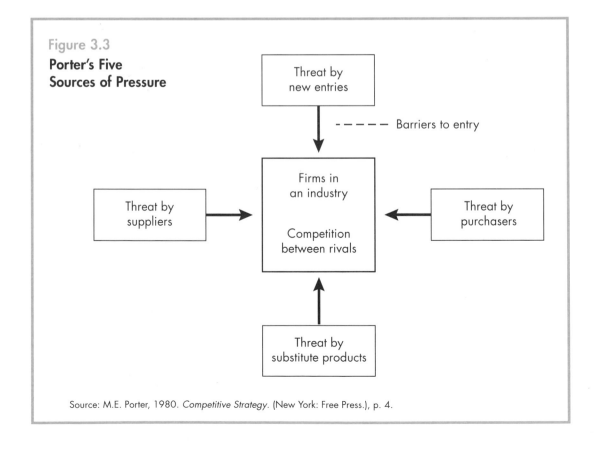

Figure 3.3

Porter's Five Sources of Pressure

Threat by new entries

- - - - - Barriers to entry

Threat by suppliers

Firms in an industry

Competition between rivals

Threat by purchasers

Threat by substitute products

Source: M.E. Porter, 1980. *Competitive Strategy*. (New York: Free Press.), p. 4.

This last point is particularly important when there are few suppliers or buyers and they are both large and powerful enough to lay down the law within that industry, and keep competitors small so as to enjoy their position of power. If, on top of that, the sector grows slowly and there is little possibility of differentiation among firms, competition becomes cut-throat among small firms that are unable to expand. The usual result is a perpetual price war. The competing firms may jeopardize their own profitability and end up bankrupt.

An industry may change from an extremely fragmented to a less fragmented one if that industry becomes highly concentrated. By concentrating, an industry can have a balanced number of large and small companies. The former regulate the market. Some industries, however, will never experience this type of concentration. Porter lists sixteen traits that may prevent concentration (see table 3.3), one of which is enough to sustain the fragmentation.

The high arts sector is just such a fragmented industry, with many small companies. The industry does not, however, offer any possibility for concentration, since it possesses at least four of the sixteen traits likely to block concentration. First,

Table 3.3
The Sixteen Causes of Industry Fragmentation

1. Low overall entry barriers
2. Absence of economies of scale
3. High transport costs
4. High inventory costs or erratic sales fluctuations
5. No advantages of size in dealing with buyers or suppliers
6. Diseconomies of scale in some important aspect
7. Low overhead crucial to success of operation
8. Made-to-measure products for diverse market needs
9. Heavy creative content in product
10. Close local control and supervision of operations required
11. A lot of personalized service
12. Local contacts required simply to do business
13. Exit barriers
14. Local regulation
15. Government prohibition of concentration
16. Newness of industry

Source: Porter, M.E. 1980. *Competitive Strategy*. New York: Free Press, p. 196.

fragmentation in the arts may be explained by the lack of barriers to entry. It is, in fact, easy to found a string quartet or a theatre troupe since little initial outlay is required, in comparison with the financing needed to open a traditional commercial enterprise like an auto manufacturing plant. Second, economies of scale are not possible due to the very nature of the product. A symphony orchestra, for example, always needs the same number of musicians and the same amount of rehearsal or performance time. Third, artistic content is very important for the cultural enterprise. In fact, this is the main distinguishing feature of companies active in the arts. Lastly, the "exit barrier" helps to explain why many artists prefer to toil away rather than renounce their art. Their devotion enables their employer (cultural enterprises) to survive.

A company in a fragmented industry must find its positioning in order to stand out from the crowd – in other words, the competition. The principle of a competitive advantage is, therefore, vitally important.

3.3.4 The Principle of a Competitive Advantage

Pressure from the competition in its broadest sense, including that from global competition, obliges any cultural enterprise to define and use its competitive advantage to appear unique in the consumer's eyes.

Any company must try to adopt a strong position that enables it to stand out. This position of strength is achieved only by highlighting some distinctive aspect or competitive advantage of the company or product. Naturally, this aspect must be positively perceived by consumers. The advantage may be a product feature, a promotional tool, a different way of using the distribution networks, or an interesting pricing policy. It is up to the company to find its own unique niche that will enable it to outdistance the competition.

3.4 THE MARKET AND MACRO-ENVIRONMENTAL VARIABLES

Macro-environmental variables, also known as uncontrollable variables, exert an ongoing influence on both the market and the life of an organization. Firms must sometimes adapt to radical changes over which they have no power to act. There are five main variables in the macro-environment: demographic environment, cultural environment, economic environment, political-legal environment, and technological environment.

3.4.1 The Demographic Environment

Demographics play a key role in the market, since a shift in the population may mean a rise or fall in the demand. How the population is spread out within an area, which age groups dominate, and which ethnic groups live there are only a few of the important dimensions of the environment that influence marketing. For example, teenagers 15–17 years old buy the most pop-music records, cassettes, and CDs. Naturally, a variation in the number of teens aged 15–17 will have a definite impact on the music sector. This is also the case for products designed for children, a product category that depends on the number of children in each age group.

3.4.2 The Cultural Environment

The values of a society, also called the cultural environment, play a leading role in the marketing of a product. As values change, so do consumer habits. Thus, what was unthinkable for our grandparents now seems normal. The traditional role of women, for example, was once that of homemaker, and a large family was the treasured ideal. This is no longer the case; most women over 18 are now in the job market. At the same time, modern couples are having fewer children and having them later in life – in their thirties rather than in their twenties. This example helps to explain why today's young couples have more leisure time in which to consume cultural goods. Naturally, these changes influence cultural organizations.

3.4.3 The Economic Environment

Firms, like individuals, must deal with their economic environment. Inflation, unemployment, and recession are all now household words. During a recession, for instance, there are fewer potential consumers and fewer dollars available per consumer. This situation affects not just cultural enterprises, but sponsors too: the corporate budget for sponsorships or donations shrinks immediately. Any corporation trying to cut costs will slash peripheral activities, and donations and sponsorships are the first to go. Entire towns may disappear when the international economic situation triggers a drop in the price of certain raw materials. At that point, shock waves travel throughout the cultural sector, since the cultural demand often absorbs the consumer's discretionary income.[27]

3.4.4 The Political-Legal Environment

Laws and regulations are another key variable, since government action can radically change the face of an industry. A direct tax on the price of cultural products may lower demand. The effect of government intervention or action may also be positive – for instance, tax measures designed to stimulate the film-making industry.

3.4.5 The Technological Environment

Every company is subject to influences from the technological environment. Science has made tremendous advances and discoveries that leave few areas untouched. Technology has also had an impact on the arts . In some areas, such as audiovisual equipment, there is ongoing competition spurred by innovations that constantly flood the market and may radically change the way a work is produced or distributed. At the other end of the spectrum, certain sectors may be less affected by technical developments. Traditional artisans whose craft often consists of using quite old methods would produce an entirely different product if they used modern technology. The development of holography and computer graphics, for example, have changed or enhanced traditional techniques in painting. Artists can now create new, more durable, and more soluble synthetic pigments. Recent chemical discoveries have led to new binding substances and varnishes that provide more malleable, reliable tools for the conservation of works of art.

Cinema provides a very dramatic example of technological impact on one market. Figure 3.4 illustrates the evolution of various film-viewing possibilities.[28] At first, a movie

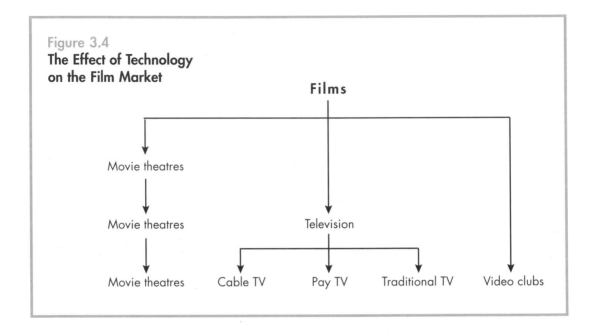

Figure 3.4
The Effect of Technology on the Film Market

Films

Movie theatres

Movie theatres   Television

Movie theatres   Cable TV   Pay TV   Traditional TV   Video clubs

was designed to be seen, or "consumed," in a room with a large screen. The rapid-fire succession of television, cable and pay TV, videocassettes, and satellite transmission has showered the consumer with an ever-increasing range of choices. For a night out, the choice is a movie theatre. For inexpensive entertainment, there's TV at home. In addition, there are pay-TV channels and video clubs that let subscribers or members view recent releases in the comfort of their homes. In 1950, there was only one choice; today, there are five different options!

If the 1950s were the television decade, the 1960s were the cable-TV decade, and the 1970s were the pay-TV years, followed by the 1980s, the video decade. The film industry has had to adapt to all of these changes; the proof of this can be seen on the small screen in made-for-TV movies. The next big challenge facing the industry in this age of the Internet and multimedia will most likely be that of convergence.

SUMMARY

The cultural market as an entity can be subdivided into four main groups: the consumer market, the distribution market, the state market, and the sponsorship market. Each one responds to different motivations and covers specific aspects of the product. It is, therefore, worthwhile to find different marketing strategies for each of these markets.

According to research carried out in several industrialized countries, the high-arts consumer has a higher than average income and level of education. However, fans of the popular arts have a lower level of income and education.

State subsidies represent a substantial chunk of the budget for cultural enterprises in most countries but not in the United States. However, the absence of government from the arts in the United States is offset by the fact that private enterprise and individual donors invest massively in the arts.

Demand is the expression in volume or dollars of purchases made by members of the market. The notion of demand is useful in accurately judging a company's competitive position in a given market in the past, the present, or the future.

Demand in the leisure market rose substantially from 1960 to 1980. The main factors were an increase in the population, an increase in leisure time available to consumers, and a rise in the levels of both income and education. The fact that the arts garnered a larger share of the leisure market than sports can be attributed to the emergence *en masse* of a female clientele in the 1960s.

Competition in the leisure and cultural-products markets may take many different forms, yet it remains fierce. If a company wants to survive, it must acquire some competitive advantage enabling it to resist competitive pressures, which are intensified by technological progress and the globalization of the marketplace. Moreover, the arts sector is fragmented, with many small companies, and is destined to remain that way.

QUESTIONS

1. What is the difference between the notion of demand and the notion of market?

2. What differences do you see in comparing current demand, forecast demand, and potential demand?

3. Why does stating that the consumer of cultural products is educated and well off not give a full picture of the situation?

4. The percentage of revenue from government sources is different for artistic enterprises and cultural industries. Why?

5. How important is the private sector in the budgets of cultural companies?

6. Can you describe how demand has changed since the 1960s in the leisure market?

7. What does the expression "gain a competitive advantage" mean?

8. What has been the impact of technological developments and the globalization of competition on cultural enterprises?

9. Why does the problem of fragmentation in the arts sector seem impossible to solve?

Notes

1. Statistics Canada. 2000. *Family Expenditure in Canada*. Ottawa: Author. Catalogue n° 62-555.

2. National Endowment for the Arts. 1997. *Survey of Public Participation in the Arts: Summary Report*. Washington: Author, p. 17.

3. Australian Bureau of Statistics. *Australia Now - A Statistical Profile*. http://www.abs.gov.au.

4. See Throsby and Whithers, as well as Myerscough, for a more in-depth discussion of cultural market differences by country: Myerscough, J. 1986. *Facts About the Arts 2: 1986 Edition*. London: PSI Policy Studies Institute; Throsby, C.D., and G.A. Withers. 1979. *The Economics of the Performing Arts*. New York: St. Martin's Press.

5. Without a central department gathering data on sales in each sector, it is difficult to judge levels of cultural consumption. It is, however, possible to use results from studies of consumer habits. Such studies enable a marketing manager to estimate the size of markets. Many studies are carried out over the telephone using the interview technique, as was the case for the figures quoted here. Unfortunately, the techniques used often lead researchers to grossly overestimate the situation. Here are some examples of how calculations are made.

First, researchers find out how large the population studied actually is. From that figure, they adjust for the children to obtain the net number of adults likely to consume cultural products. This number is then multiplied by the percentage (based on survey statistics) of respondents who say they buy cultural products, which gives researchers the number of adults who claim to consume specific cultural products. In order to estimate the overall consumption for a cultural product, the number of individuals partaking of a particular activity is multiplied by the average rate of consumption as set by the purchasers themselves through the survey.

Let us look at an example from Quebec cinema. The number of people aged 15 or older in Quebec in 1991 was 5.02 million. Approximately 60% of these people went to a movie theatre at least once, i.e., 3.01 million. Calculations based on the average frequency of film-going given by respondents to a survey suggested that 26 million movie tickets had been sold in Quebec. If we compare this estimate to Quebec Statistics Bureau figures showing that the actual number of cinema tickets sold was 13 million, we see that the survey overestimated reality by 100%.

It would seem that the consumption of cultural products is overestimated because of inflated research findings that, if multiplied among themselves, would lead to almost exponentially overestimated figures. Overestimating does not stem only from research findings. It may also stem from methodological problems caused by such things as a poor definition of what is actually being studied. It is therefore possible that theatre-goers include their attendance at performances by amateur groups in such a survey. Obviously, these should not be counted. Perhaps theatre-goers confuse their last evening at the movies with their last evening at the theatre. It may be that one person defines a musical comedy as a variety show rather than as a theatrical production. The possibility of distortion abounds in compiling statistics.

These exercises are not useless, however, since they do enable marketing managers to estimate consumption, albeit roughly, in certain sectors in which there are no reliable gauges. They also allow for studies of consistent groups over time. In this sense, they are useful and informative, since they can be interpreted with some distance and certain reservations.

6. See, for example: Conseil de l'Europe. 1993. *Participation à la vie culturelle en Europe, Tendances, stratégies et défis, Table ronde de Moscou-1991*. Paris: La documentation française; Donat, O. 1996. *Les amateurs : enquête sur les activités artistiques des Français*. Département des études et de la prospective, Ministère de la Culture, France; Fernandez-Blanco, V., and J. Prieto-Rodriguez. 1997. "Individual Choice and Cultural Consumption in Spain," in *Proceedings of the 4th International Conference on Arts and Cultural Management*. San Francisco: Golden Gate University, p. 193–205; Ford Foundation. 1974. *The Finances of the Performing Arts*, Vol. 2; Japan Council of Performer's Organisations. 1995. "Professional Orchestras in Japan." *Geidankyo News*, Vol. 1, (Spring), p. 6–7; McCaughey, C. 1984. *A Survey of Arts Audience Studies: A Canadian Perspective 1967-1984*, Ottawa: Canada Council for the Arts; Myerscough, J. 1986. *Facts About the Arts 2: 1986 Edition*, London. PSI Policy Studies Institute; Rubinstein, A. 1995. "Marketing Research into Theatre Audiences in Russia," in *Proceedings of the 3rd International Conference on Arts Management*. London: City University, p. 51–67; Throsby, C.D., and G.A. Withers. 1979. *The Economics of the Performing Arts*. New York: St. Martin's Press.

7. Rubinstein, A. 1995. "Marketing Research into Theatre Audience in Russia," in *Proceedings of the 3rd International Conference on Arts Management*. London: City University, (July), p. 51–67; Levshina, E., and Y. Orlov. 2000. "General and Specific Issues in Russian Theatre." *International Journal of Arts Management*, Vol. 2, n° 2 (Winter), p. 74–84.

8. Mulcahy, K.V. 1999. "Cultural Patronage in the United States." *International Journal of Arts Management*, Vol. 2, n° 1 (Fall), p. 53–59.

9. "Prologue." http://www.fundwell.com.

10. de Tocqueville, A. *Democracy in America*, Volume II, "Relation of Civil to Political Associations." http://www.xroads.virginia.edu/~hyper/detoc/home.html

11. Hopkins, K.B., and C.S. Friedman. 1997. *Successful Fundraising for Arts and Cultural Organizations*, 2nd ed. Phoenix, Arizona: Oryx Press, p. 14.

12. *Ibid*. p. 14.

13. Sponsorship Strategies. 1998. p. 3. http://www.amarach.com/.

14. Statistics Canada. 1997. *Canada's Culture, Heritage and Identity: A Statistical Perspective*. Catalogue n° 87-211.

15. National Endowment for the Arts. 1998. *Dance Organizations Report 43% Growth in Economic Census: 1987-1993*. Washington: Research Division Note #67 May. See also Kaplan, A.E. ed. 1999. *Giving USA: The Annual Report on Philanthropy for the Year 1998*. New York: AAFRC Trust for Philanthropy, p. 90. See also Opera America, http://www.operaam.org/ and tcg.org.

16. Davidson Shuster, J.M. 1985. *Supporting the Arts: An International Comparative Study*. Cambridge: Department of Urban Studies and Planning, Massachusetts Institute of Technology (March).

17. Kaplan, A.E. ed. 1999. *Giving USA: The Annual Report on Philanthropy for the Year 1998*. New York: AAFRC Trust for Philanthropy, p. 16–17.

18. *Ibid*. p. 16.

19. "The Relationship Between Giving and Volunteering." http://www.indepsec.org/GandV/s_rela.htm.

20. Colbert, F. 1997. "Changes in Marketing Environment and Their Impact on Cultural Policy." *Journal of Arts Management, Law and Society*, Vol. 27, n° 3 (Fall), p. 177–187.

21. Colbert, F. ed. 1998. "Changes in Demand and the Future Marketing Challenges Facing Cultural Organisations," in *Cultural Organisations of the Future*. Montreal: Chaire de gestion des arts, École des HEC, p. 69–87.

22. See Conseil de l'Europe. 1993. *Participation à la vie culturelle en Europe, Tendances, stratégies et défis, Table ronde de Moscou - 1991*. Paris: La documentation française; Pronovost, G. 1998. "Shifting Cultural Practices: An Intergenerational Perspective," in *Cultural Organisations of the Future*, F. Colbert, ed. Montreal: Chaire de gestion des arts, École des HEC, p. 89–110.

23. Schewe, C.D., and P.C. Motta. 1993. "Targeting Mature Adult Patrons: Some Marketing Directives," in *Proceedings of the 2nd International Conference on Arts and Cultural Management*. Jouy-en-Josas, France: Groupe HEC School of Management.

24. Pilon, R. 1991. "L'industrie mondiale des médias et du divertissement: des groupes et des chiffres," in *L'État*

des médias, groupes et stratégies, J.-M. Charron, ed. Paris: Éditions Boréal.

25. Porter, M.E. 1990. *The Competitive Advantage of Nations*. New York: Free Press.

26. Porter, M.E. 1980. *Competitive Strategy*. New York: Free Press.

27. Discretionary or disposable income is the portion of the consumer's income that remains after basic and essential needs have been met.

28. Colbert, F. 1984. "Le prochain défi de la commercialisation des produits culturels." *Questions de culture* (IQRC), n° 7, p. 127–138.

For Further Reference

Bourgeon-Renault, D. 2000. "Evaluating Consumer Behavior in the Field of Arts and Culture Marketing." *International Journal of Arts Management*, Vol. 3, n° 1 (Fall), p. 4–19.

Brokenshaw, P., and A. Tonks. 1986. *Culture and Community: Economics and Expectations of the Arts in South Australia*. Wentworth Falls, Australia: Social Science Press.

Cuadrado, M., and A. Molla. 2000. "Grouping Performing Arts Consumers According to Goals Atten-dance." *International Journal of Arts Management*, Vol. 2, n° 3 (Spring), p. 54–60.

Donat, O. 1994. *Les Français face à la culture. De l'exclusion à l'éclectisme*. Paris: La Découverte.

Donat, O., and D. Cogneau. 1990. *Les pratiques culturelles des Français 1973-1989*. Paris: La documentaion française.

Gainer, B. 1993. "The Importance of Gender to Arts Marketing." *Journal of Arts Management, Law and Society*, Vol. 23, n° 3, p. 253–260.

Gainer, B. 1997. "Marketing Arts Education: Parental Attitudes Towards Arts Education for Children." *Journal of Arts Management, Law and Society*, Vol. 26, n° 4, p. 253–268.

Kolb, B.M. 2001. "The decline of the Subscriber Base: A Study of the Philarmonia Orchestra Audience." *International Journal of Arts Management*, Vol. 3, n° 2 (Winter), p. 51–60.

National Endowment for the Arts. 1993. *Arts Participation in America: 1982-1992*, Washington: Author, Research Division, n° 27 (October).

Robinson, J., and G. Godbey. 1997. *Time for Life: The Surprising Ways Americans Use Their Time*. University Park: Pennsylvania State University Press.

Appendix 3.1
Attendance Rates for Arts Events, by Demographic Group, United States, 1997

	Jazz	Classical Music	Opera	Musical	Play	Ballet	Other Dance	Art Museum	Historic Park
All Adults	11.9%	15.6%	4.7%	24.5%	15.8%	5.8%	12.4%	34.9%	46.9%
Sex									
Male	13.2	14.2	4.0	22.3	14.6	4.1	11.7	34.3	48.2
Female	10.6	16.8	5.2	26.7	16.8	7.5	12.9	35.5	45.8
Race									
Hispanic	6.8	8.4	3.1	15.7	9.7	4.5	14.6	29.4	32.7
White	12.1	17.5	5.2	26.5	16.6	6.5	11.9	36.1	50.8
African American	15.6	9.6	2.1	22.4	16.4	3.9	13.4	31.1	36.5
American Indian	11.0	8.9	5.1	15.4	5.0	1.2	10.6	21.8	41.9
Asian	10.3	16.2	6.9	20.4	18.1	4.3	14.5	41.7	43.6
Age									
18 to 24	15.1	16.4	5.4	26.0	20.2	6.9	14.7	38.3	46.3
25 to 34	12.7	11.4	4.0	22.5	13.3	4.7	11.1	36.5	49.4
35 to 44	14.3	14.3	4.4	25.8	14.7	6.6	13.6	37.3	52.3
Education									
Grade school	1.8	2.1	.02	6.0	3.1	1.5	7.3	6.0	12.7
Some high school	3.4	3.9	1.5	12.6	7.2	1.8	6.6	14.4	26.6
High school graduate	6.8	8.3	1.7	15.7	9.1	3.6	9.2	24.6	40.5
Some college	15.4	18.1	5.2	28.4	18.9	6.5	13.7	43.2	56.3
College graduate	21.3	28.0	10.2	43.6	27.7	10.8	17.8	57.7	66.6
Graduate school	27.7	44.5	14.3	50.3	37.2	14.4	24.7	69.8	72.7

Source: National Endowment for the Arts.1977 Survey of Public Participation in the Arts: Summary Report.

Appendix 3.2
Arts Attendance According to Education Level and Socioprofessional Category

Annual Theatre Attendance Rates According to Level of Education (%)

Country	University	Secondary	Primary	None
United Kingdom	47	22	9	–
Italy	41	15	4	2
Austria	75	67	24	–
Czechoslovakia	83	73	33	–
France	39	24	16	7

Annual Theatre Attendance Rates According to Socioprofessional Category (%)

Country	Executives	Employees	Workers	Farmers
Finland	74	48	22	16
Norway	50	40	20	14
Czechoslovakia	71*		39	35
France	47	11	9	5

* Figure corresponding to the population of the service sector.

Opera Attendance According to Level of Education (%)

	University	Secondary	Primary	None
Austria	59	49	11	–
United Kingdom*	20	19	3	–
France	13	6	3	2
Germany	31	16	8	3

* At least once a year.

Annual Opera Attendance According to Socioprofessional Category (%)

	Executives	Employees	Workers	Farmers
France (1989)	15	3	1	1.0
Finland (1981)	16	8	6	0.5
United Kingdom (1990)*	16	8	3	–

* At least once a year.

(continued)

Appendix 3.2 (continued)

Dance Performance Attendance According to Level of Education (%)

	University	Secondary	Primary	None
France (1989)	17.0	13.0	5.0	3.0
Great Britain (1989)*				
classical ballet	19.0	9.0	3.0	2.0
modern dance	10.0	5.0	2.0	1.0
Spain	5.4	2.4	1.2	0.4

* At least once a year.

Professional Dance Performance Attendance in France in 1989 (%)

	Executives	Employees	Workers	Farmers
Annual attendance rate	20	7	5	3
Life-time attendance rate	52	25	15	10

Concert Attendance According to Level of Education (%)

	University	Secondary	Primary	None
Italy (1984)	25	6	3	2
France (1989)	31	15	6	5
Czechoslovakia (1989)	51	30	6	–
Austria (1989)	71	60	24	–
Germany (1989)				
Church music	30	23	14	11
Symphonic music with an orchestra or a solist	28	12	7	4
Chamber music, piano recital, or singing recital	24	11	9	4

Annual Classical Music Concert Attendance According to Socioprofessional Category (%)

	Executives	Employees	Workers	Farmers
Italy (1984)	13	6	4	–
France (1989)	42	6	5	4
Norway (1987)	28	18	8	13
	Service	Secondary	Primary	
Czechoslovakia (1989)	29	6	3	
USSR (1989)	10	6	2	

Source: Conseil de l'Europe. 1993. *Participation à la vie culturelle en Europe – Tendances, stratégies et défis – Table ronde de Mosour-1991*. Paris : La documentation française.

Appendix 3.2 (continued)

Performing Arts Attendance According to Education Level and Socioprofessional Category, Quebec, Canada, 1994

According to Level of Education

Diploma	Regular season theatre	Opera	Classical dance	Modern dance	Classical concert	Sports match
University	36.7	10.5	9.1	7.2	24.0	41.9
College	25.7	5.7	4.8	4.9	9.5	40.0
Secondary	17.4	2.3	3.0	2.1	4.4	35.5
Primary	11.2	0.7	3.8	1.9	2.5	21.1

According to Socioprofessional Category

	Regular season theatre	Opera	Classical dance	Modern dance	Classical concert	Sports match
Professionals, executives of large companies	40.3	10.1	9.2	6.8	20.4	47.6
Semi-professionals	36.3	5.3	6.3	4.5	12.8	42.1
Owners, managers of small companies	23.3	5.2	8.0	3.5	7.7	43.1
White-collar employees	28.5	4.3	4.6	4.0	9.1	42.0
Primary sector workers	14.7	0.4	1.9	2.7	5.0	40.4
Students	28.1	4.2	6.4	5.1	10.4	52.9
Retired persons	15.7	6.7	3.9	3.5	9.9	20.5

Frequency: At Least Once a Year (%)

Regular season theatre	Opera	Classical dance	Modern dance	Classical concert	Sports match
24.4	5.3	5.1	4.3	10.6	37.4

Source:Ministère de la Culture et des Communications du Québec. 1996. *Pleins feux sur les publics de spectables.* Québec : MAC, Direction des communications.

Plan

CHAPTER 4
Consumer Behaviours

by Jacques Nantel

OBJECTIVES

- Describe in detail the various decision-making processes that form the basis of consumer behaviours
- Present the main variables that influence the structure and nature of decision-making processes
- Highlight the connection between decision-making processes and the information that consumers use
- Link the information used by consumers to various corporate marketing strategies
- Discuss these concepts within the context of arts management

INTRODUCTION

Why is it important to look at consumer studies and behaviour? Why is describing the consumers within a market in sociodemographic terms alone not enough? The answer to these questions is found in the very essence of marketing. One of the basic functions of marketing is meeting consumer needs. A marketing manager must accurately identify and fully understand these needs in order to create a product that fulfils a specific need or to position a product in terms of a specific segment of the population. This is, however, easier said than done. The manager who wants to position a product properly must have a good description of the consumers targetted by the company and must also know why these consumers will or will not buy a cultural product.

This chapter is entitled "Consumer Behaviours" – that is, behaviour in the plural rather than in the singular, as it is found in most marketing reference books. We have deliberately chosen the plural for two basic reasons.

First, behaviour in marketing cannot be expressed in the singular as if the only act were that of purchasing. There are many important questions left unanswered if we do not ask who goes to the opera or the theatre, and why; who goes to the movies, and why; who buys books, and why. Second, even though the behaviour adopted at the time of making a decision is extremely important, the manager who does not go beyond this point forgets the equally important and varied behaviours surrounding the decision. This type of analysis can explain why a consumer chooses to go to the theatre rather than to a restaurant. This is an example of what is called "intertype competition."[1] Consumers who collect works of art and also buy spin-off products provide yet another example of different behaviours that merit further research.

We also prefer the term "consumers," in the plural, since markets are composed of consumers who do not have homogeneous needs. Speaking in the singular implies that somewhere there exists a single average consumer representative of the entire market. In music, for example, this average consumer would be a hybrid who loves chamber music, enjoys heavy metal, and hums along to the latest country-and-western tunes. In other words, speaking of one consumer amounts to talking about everyone and no one in one breath.

The analysis of consumer behaviour given here is based on the assumption that consumers always base their decisions on a certain amount of information. This information may be divided into two categories: internal (previous experience) and external (type of product, word of mouth, etc.). For example, consumers targetted for a seasonal opera subscription would base their decision on personal knowledge of operatic music (previous experience) and on information provided – choice of works, singers, price, reviews, friends' comments, and so on. According to this assumption, a company could not effectively market a product without a good understanding of the type of information consumers use to make purchasing decisions and the way in which the information is perceived and used – in other words, the decision-making processes.

The processes involved in making a decision are greatly influenced by three major types of variables: those related directly to consumers themselves; those related to the purchasing context or situation; and those concerning the products being considered. These three variables form the "basic triad." A large part of this chapter deals with the decision-making processes adopted by consumers and the many ways in which the information they are apt to use is actually processed.

Figure 4.1 illustrates the main elements used in analyzing consumer behaviours.

This chapter first explores the basic triad (individual–product–situation), which determines the consumer's motivation in purchasing a product. We then look more closely at the notion of motivation and the individual variables in the main decision-

Figure 4.1

The Main Elements Used to Analyze Consumer Behaviours

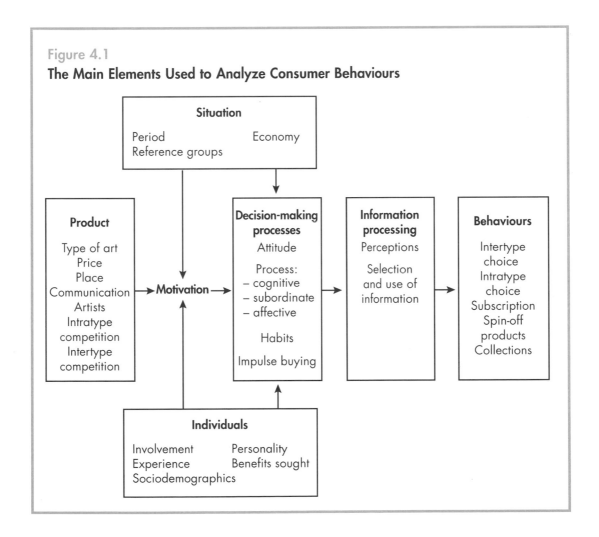

making processes. The variables related to the purchasing situation will follow, and, lastly, we will see how a consumer processes information before making a choice which then translates to a purchasing behaviour.

4.1 INDIVIDUAL–PRODUCT–SITUATION: THE BASIC TRIAD

One of the basic principles of consumer behaviour is the individual–product–situation triad. This principle stipulates that the dynamics of a market, or even a market segment, can be understood only if the consumer, the product purchased, and the purchasing situation are all taken into consideration. Only then can the tremendous wealth and complexity of consumer behaviours be appreciated. If two consumers, for example, are long-time subscribers to a theatre company, it would obviously be tempting to think that they are similar and that their future behaviours will also be similar. Yet, what if the first consumer is a loyal subscriber because she likes the repertoire presented and the other subscribes simply to keep up with the Joneses? In the first case, the consumer's decision-making process is closely related to the selection of plays offered. If many consumers are sensitive to this factor, the manager of the theatre company will focus on the season's selection in order to retain the theatre's clientele. If, however, as in the second case, the decision-making process is related to the consumer's social group, then the marketing strategy would have less to do with the choice of plays than with the medium and style of the message.

These two cases reveal how the consumer-product relationship can be different. As a result, any corporate strategy drawing on consumer loyalty would necessarily be different for each case. Based on the information provided, is the first subscriber less affected by social influences than the second? Such a conclusion would be rather hasty, if not dangerous, without a glance at the bigger picture. It may well be that theatre-goer 1 based her decision to subscribe exclusively on the repertoire offered, with no peer pressure whatsoever, yet will blindly accept a friend's opinion when buying a compact disk.

In short, to understand how and why consumers behave as they do, their decision-making processes and the various criteria they use must be studied. Indeed, these processes would be difficult to understand without looking at the individual product and purchasing situation. These two elements will be studied more closely below. Figure 4.1 outlines the main elements used in analyzing consumer behaviours and may clarify the many ideas presented in the next few pages.

4.2 MOTIVATION

It should be remembered when studying consumer behaviours that consumers will not consider buying a product unless they are strongly motivated to do so. Although this may seem like plain common sense, when forgotten it causes grief and frustration among managers and artists alike. Motivation lies at the very heart of consumer behaviours.

Lewin[2] probably describes motivation best. He considers it an imbalance between the consumer's current and desired states. The wider the gap between the two states, the stronger the consumer's motivation will be. This imbalance may stem from the consumer (e.g., an older consumer may want to read poetry or spend more time on leisure activities) or arise in a particular situation (e.g., at Christmas time, listening to holiday music in the mall encourages shoppers to buy). It may also be the result of promotion (e.g., advertising for *Phantom of the Opera* encourages the consumer to buy a ticket). More often than not, the consumer will not be influenced by any stimulus, regardless of the pressures applied. Consumer motivation to buy a product is largely related to previous experience and level of product involvement. These two variables have a tremendous influence on the nature of the decision-making process consumers use.

Whether the product is a cultural product, a consumer good, or a service, the complexity of the decision-making process varies according to the individual–product–situation triad. It should be emphasized that in most cases[3] there is a close link between how complex the decision-making process is and how extensively the information is processed. In other words, the more complex the decision-making process, the more diversified the consumer's information. For marketing managers, this statement is crucial, since it suggests that their marketing mix is analyzed more closely when the consumer is involved and the decision-making process is complex. In some situations, however, the marketing manager is better off if the consumer does not want too much information. This would be the case for a company that has a clientele with well-entrenched habits. On the other hand, a company might want consumers to have as much information as possible in order to understand why the product offered is superior to the competition's. In this case, customer involvement, if present, becomes a real advantage.

4.3 INDIVIDUAL VARIABLES

This section focusses on an analysis of five individual variables: consumer involvement in the product offered, consumer experience, consumer sociodemographic profile, consumer personality, and product features considered desirable by consumers.

4.3.1 Involvement

Of all the consumer variables, product involvement is by far the most important.[4] Even though researchers[5] in this area have defined involvement in different ways over the years according to research trends popular at the time, the consensus is that the term may be understood as the feeling of importance or personal interest associated with the product in a given situation. Rothschild[6] suggests the following definition: "Involvement is a state of motivation, arousal, or interest. This state exists in a process. It is driven by current external variables (the situation; the product; the communications) and past internal variables (enduring; ego; control valves). Its consequents are types of searching, information processing and decision making."

Involvement may therefore be considered a reflection of the importance of a specific product for an individual in a given situation. Involvement may be structural or conjunctural – that is, linked to the situation. One consumer may, for example, perceive theatre as a product with a constantly high level of involvement, whereas another may feel that level of involvement only in a situation – for example, when choosing the only play to see this year.

Whether involvement is related to an individual's interest in one product or an entire category of products,[7] involvement is largely a function of the risk that consumers associate with the purchase or use of a product or service. The riskier the purchase or use of the product, the greater the consumer's involvement.[8] There are several types of consumer risks.[9] They are not mutually exclusive, although they may well exist independently. The main risks influencing the purchase of a product are functional, economical, psychological, and social.

Functional Risk

In terms of cultural products, functional risk has the most impact on consumer behaviour. This type of risk may be defined as the possibility that the product does not meet the consumer's expectations. This risk is common in the service and cultural sectors, which usually do not allow consumers to test the product before buying. A consumer can, however, reduce functional risk dramatically by seeking as much information as possible on the play to be seen or the book to be bought. Critics' reviews, advertising (which often repeats positive reviews), or friends' opinions may also reduce functional risk. Another way to reduce functional risk is to go for "safe bets" or "sure things." The most recent Spielberg film, the new novel by Margaret Atwood, or the currently playing Neil Simon comedy do not require a very complex decision-making process simply because they are considered "safe bets." As cultural products, they do not represent a high functional risk. These examples reveal how a functional risk can influence the consumer's decision-making process. The consumer can reduce the risk either by seeking a lot of information or by turning to a known entity that requires less information. In short, the higher the perceived risk, the greater the degree of involvement, and, as a result, the more likely it is that the consumer will choose a decision-making process that lowers the risk.

Economic Risk

This risk is the easiest to understand: the more expensive the product, the more complicated the decision-making process. This relationship may be greatly attenuated by the consumer's income level, but it may also be affected by the total expense – for example, parking and babysitting. Together with functional risk, economic risk explains, at least partially, why some consumers prefer to rent a video rather than go out to a play or a movie.

Psychological Risk

This risk is frequently experienced in the consumption of cultural products. It may be defined as the risk related to the purchase or consumption of a product that does not correspond to the consumer's desired self-image. Perhaps a consumer is afraid to confront latent inner feelings and elects to not see violent scenes in a movie theatre. Another consumer who feels physically inadequate may prefer not to attend the ballet. Like other forms of risk, psychological risk increases the complexity of the consumer's decision-making processes.

Social Risk

Psychological risk is related to the individual consumer's self-image, whereas social risk is related to the image others have of the individual. Some people may subscribe to the opera to be part of a particular reference group rather than to enjoy the music. Conversely, some consumers may forgo the pleasure of a cultural event simply to avoid their friends' or colleagues' disapproval. Naturally, this risk is not present for all consumers. In fact, social risk is present only in cases in which the form of consumption is visible or the consumers are sensitive to their environment.

4.3.2 Experience

Experience, like involvement, has an important impact on the complexity of the consumer's decision-making processes. The broader the experience, the shorter the decision-making process. For a fan of Woody Allen films or of pop star Céline Dion, a new release translates to a new purchase. Of course, this equation is automatic only if the previous experience was satisfactory. A negative experience can also accelerate the decision-making process, albeit negatively. Experience in terms of cultural products, which are often quite different

from one another, may not be transferable. Moreover, many consumers look for something different, a novelty. In this case, previous experience would play a minor role. Nonetheless, when a consumer seeks out the work of a certain painter, playwright, or film-maker, that consumer expects some form of continuity. *Misery*, the movie based on Stephen King's novel of the same name, illustrates this phenomenon quite well.[10] How many authors trying to change genre have suffered because of the audience's need for continuity?

Experience affects the complexity of the decision-making processes that consumers use, because consumers categorize their previous experiences into subsets of possibilities that are known, unknown, retained, or rejected. Figure 4.2 shows this classification process according to the model presented by Brisoux and Laroche.[11]

This model is particularly interesting in that it illustrates how consumers form their consumption habits in the category of cultural products. Some producers are past masters in evoking the notion of possibilities through time-tested recipes, as seen in a series like *Star Trek* or the Harlequin romance-novel library. This type of product classification lets consumers manage their decision-making processes more effectively and reach a decision more quickly and efficiently. Not all consumers prefer known to unknown products, but the number of consumers who do make their decision to purchase this way is high enough to explain how some cultural products endure.

If, however, a product requires a high degree of involvement and the consumer's experience is both substantial and

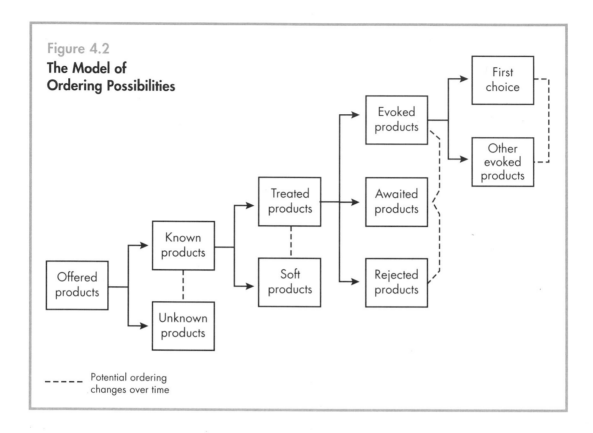

Figure 4.2
**The Model of
Ordering Possibilities**

- - - - - Potential ordering
changes over time

satisfactory, the consumer develops a strong affective predisposition[12] that acts upon his or her perceptions. The product will have more merit than can be attributed to it objectively. This predisposition explains the phenomenon of groupies and die-hard fans. In section 4.4, on the details of the decision-making process, these affective predispositions will resurface as part of the notion of attitude.

4.3.3 Sociodemographic Variables

Among the variables influencing the decision-making process, sociodemographic variables are probably the best known. In chapter 3, the relationship between these variables and the type of cultural product consumed was discussed. The same topic will be further described as part of market segmentation in chapter 5.

Sociodemographic variables have an impact on consumer behaviours because they determine the intensity of existing risks – for example, the influence of income on perceived economic risk. Similarly, the degree of experience may be linked to age. In other words, although sociodemographic variables do reveal consumer preferences for specific cultural products, it is often necessary to go beyond these variables for a full explanation.

4.3.4 Personality

Personality is the most intriguing yet least conclusive variable of all in terms of consumer behaviours. Marketing experts would like to believe that a single consumer, given his or her personality, will prefer rock to opera, or that some consumers like safe bets while others prefer innovation and novelty. However, these hypotheses are rarely backed by empirical research.[13]

Even though personality traits do not provide an exhaustive explanation of consumer behaviours, they can be of some interest. Snyder[14] suggests that some consumers tend to imitate peer behaviour while others tend to behave according to their own predispositions. This trait, called "self-monitoring," has a significant effect on the perceived social risk and, as a result, influences the type of decision-making processes the consumer will use.

4.3.5 Benefits Sought

A consumer may wish to purchase or consume a cultural product for various reasons, including exoticism, relaxation, enrichment, or escapism. For many products, the nature of the decision-making process is largely a function of the benefits sought. The consumer deciding among four films and one play could simply compare the five possibilities by looking at the various attributes of each one as well as the benefits of going out. This example will be seen again in detail in the next section, on decision-making processes. The benefits gained through the use of a product may vary from one consumer to the next. In this sense, they are closely linked to the functional risk. Steinberg et al.[15] have suggested a typology of the main benefits of the performing arts, including cultural enrichment, stimulation, peer approval, excitement, entertainment, education, social prestige, and child development, to name but a few. Other authors have proposed their own typology.[16] For example, studies by Gainer[17] show that the choice of a specific theatre may correspond, for some consumers, to a ritual of consumption linked to the creation of "small worlds"; the consumer's choice of a theatre may be influenced by the desire to please a loved one or by the fact that the venue is frequented by people of similar social standing; in such cases, the consumer's choice is not motivated by the product itself.

The concept of benefits sought enables managers to understand the structure of the decision-making process consumers use and thus how to select the elements of their marketing mix. Nevertheless, an analysis of consumer benefits is valid only if consumers do actually consider such benefits. This last statement may seem self-evident, but decision-making processes do not necessarily derive from the consideration of their benefits. Moreover, consumers may not even be able to express the benefits they want.

As a general rule, consumers consider the benefits offered by a cultural activity when their level of product involvement is high. For these benefits to be considered, consumers must have both the time and the ability to process information related to the decision. The customer must decide in a cognitive and structured manner. This last point is particularly important in marketing cultural products, which are very often unlike other products in that they target the sensorial, hedonistic, and emotional side of the consumer, rather than the cognitive side. The decision-making process is therefore more holistic, since it involves an overall evaluation of the cultural product and relies upon benefits that are often difficult to identify, let alone measure. Holbrook and Schindler[18] provide an interesting musical example. They proved that, regardless of cognitive judgment applied to different genres, consumers prefer the type of music that they liked during their adolescence (ages 15–20). In short, one of the major challenges of marketing culture and the arts lies in the fact that the decision-making process used by consumers is often coloured by highly emotional factors.

4.4. THE MAIN DECISION-MAKING PROCESSES

The different elements examined so far provide the framework for an intelligent discussion of the types of decision-making processes that might explain a consumer's decision to purchase or consume a cultural product. It cannot be emphasized enough that a marketing manager must understand the processes used by consumers in evaluating the many products a company may offer. The better the marketing manager's grasp of these processes, the better the company's marketing strategies will be. Figure 4.3 details the main decision-making processes used and some of the variables that characterize them.

In order to put all the pieces of the processes together, each one is described individually below.

4.4.1 Attitude

A decision-making process based on attitude requires both experience and involvement in the particular cultural product or category of cultural products. Die-hard fans and groupies are created through this process, which only appears if a product implies a high level of involvement,[19] if the attitude is based on either very satisfying or very unsatisfying experiences, and if the social context and the consumer's personality[20] allow this attitude to affect the decision-making process. Attitude represents a particularly effective mechanism, allowing the consumer to reach a decision simply, quickly, and effectively using positive past experiences and the ensuing personal judgment.[21]

The consumer's positive attitude is a precious asset to the organization or artist involved. Since it is difficult to change an attitude based on previous experience, this mechanism can be a double-edged sword that favours the organization or artist benefitting from the attitude and actually blocks other groups. The long-lasting influence of attitude as a mechanism can be explained by the bias it creates in the individual's perceptions.

There are attitudes toward products perceived as a whole (symphony orchestras, repertory theatres, etc.) and attitudes toward the components of a cultural product (a particular actor, author, or director). This nuance is vital to a full understanding of an attitude and how it was formed. Most attitudes are based on previous experiences, which may originate in a subordinate process, a cognitive process, or an affective process. In fact, these processes are rarely of

Figure 4.3
The Main Decision-Making Processes

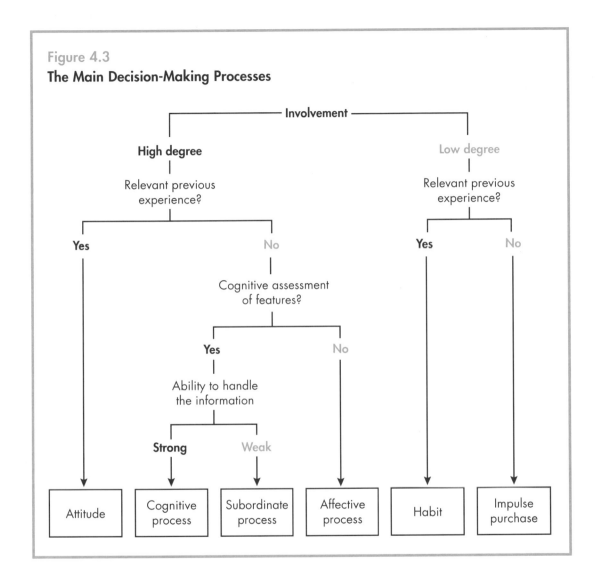

one single type; usually, they represent a combination of types. Often, an attitude is related to a learned mechanism of unknown origin. For example, why does a shopper not like yellow? One of these mechanisms is classic conditioning, through which a neutral stimulus becomes associated with an emotionally charged one. This concept is readily employed in advertising, especially when a celebrity is used to sell a product. The emotional charge associated with the star is transferred to the product or neutral stimulus. In cultural products, this type of association is at the core of many attitudes. Products associated with special events (the Christmas season, traditional celebrations, an outing with a loved one) are an excellent example of this use of attitude to earn prestige or fame.

4.4.2 Cognitive Processes

In the case of products that require a high degree of involvement, the inexperienced consumer tends to use cognitive decision-making processes. Both more lengthy and more complex, these processes require some judging of the various attributes of the product offered. The example in section 4.3.5 of a consumer choosing among four films and a play exemplifies the cognitive process at work. In making her choice, the would-be spectator considered the various benefits she judged important for this particular outing. By weighing each attribute in terms of importance and by judging each choice according to these attributes, the arts lover could objectively and rationally make an optimal choice. This approach, largely based on the work of Fishbein,[22] is known in marketing as the "linear compensatory model of decision-making."[23] As table 4.1 shows, this approach requires a technique that is both accurate and exhaustive.

If the consumer used this decision-making process, her decision would be formulated as follows:

$$A_{ijk} = \sum_{i=1}^{m} B_{ijk} I_{ik}$$

where
$i =$ Attribute of show characteristic
$j =$ Show
$k =$ Consumer
such that
$A =$ Consumer k's attitude score for brand j
$I =$ The importance or weight given attribute i by consumer k

Table 4.1

Example of a Linear Compensatory Decision-Making Model

	Ticket price	Actors' reputation	Funniness	Location of theatre
Relative importance of criteria	2	4	5	3
Movie 1	3	1	2	5
Movie 2	3	2	5	3
Movie 3	3	5	1	4
Movie 4	3	3	3	3
Theatre	1	4	3	1

1 = little importance – very bad   5 = very important – very good

B = Consumer k's belief as to the extent to which a satisfactory level of attribute i is offered by brand j

Using this model, the final choice would be the one that maximized the value of A_{ijk}. In this case, the results obtained using the model are the following:

Film 1 = 6 + 4 + 10 + 15 = 35
Film 2 = 6 + 8 + 25 + 9 = 48
Film 3 = 6 + 20 + 5 + 12 = 43
Film 4 = 6 + 12 + 15 + 9 = 42
Theatre – 2 + 16 + 15 + 13 – 36

Based on these results, this consumer should choose the second movie. Her choice can be explained in large part by the film's ability to make her laugh, a benefit particularly sought after on this occasion.

The conjunctive model, like the linear compensatory model, is a simple one designed to describe the structure of decision-making processes used by consumers. In this model, the consumer sets a minimally acceptable threshold for each criterion considered. If one of the options remains under par, it is automatically rejected. If, for example, the ticket to a show is over $50, it is instantly rejected, regardless of any other qualities within the range of criteria considered. The same rejection process occurs if the consumer cannot stand a certain actor. This consumer may refuse to see a film in which that actor plays, regardless of the story line, the director, or positive reviews.

The marketing manager would certainly benefit from knowing whether the target consumer used the conjunctive rather than the linear compensatory model, especially if the manager knows that a large number of consumers use the compensatory model and a $50 ticket would dissuade them. The "savvy" marketing manager could then try, if possible, to modify the structure of the decision-making process or lower the admission to under $50. In the first case, the manager would encourage the entire clientele to adopt the linear compensatory model by trying to persuade consumers that watching a famous actor or actress live on stage is worth the ticket price (compensation). Nonetheless, a consumer's decision-making processes are particularly difficult to bend, so the smart marketing manager might be better off giving this type of client a discount – for example, a seat in a lower-priced section. Of course, decision-making processes are rarely completely linear compensatory, conjunctive, or otherwise. Rather, they tend to be hybrids. Frequently, a consumer will start using a conjunctive model with a view to eliminating some options, then continue with a linear compensatory model to reach the final decision.

Identifying and understanding these processes are key steps for any manager targeting a specific clientele. By knowing the benefits or attributes desired or considered important by the consumer, a marketing manager can adjust the current marketing mix accordingly.

Naturally, understanding sophisticated cognitive processes is useful only if consumers actually use the same processes. Interestingly, this is not always the case in cultural products or the arts.[24] Given the unique, innovative quality of some cultural products, the trouble many consumers have in judging cultural products cognitively, and the very emotional component characteristic of the decision-making process, marketing managers should consider additional decision-making mechanisms in order to understand consumer behaviours. These additional mechanisms are called subordinate processes and affective processes.

4.4.3 Subordinate Processes

A consumer with a high level of involvement in a cultural product yet very little experience may use a cognitive decision-making process. But if the consumer either lacks or feels lacking in time or ability to absorb product information, this consumer will usually opt for a subordinate process.[25] Decisions will then be based on imitation, recommendation, or compliance. In all of the above cases, the decision-making process (or a part of it) is subordinated to a third party. If this mechanism is to work, the third party must be credible from the consumer's point of view. Often, the source of compliance or imitation is a friend or relative; hence, the determining influence of the reference group in terms of buying consumer or cultural products.

In other cases, the source of influence is an individual considered an "expert" in the field. For cultural products and the arts, the critic plays this role.[26] Sometimes the consumer will base a decision solely on the authority of a critic perceived as an expert in a particular area. Although this kind of behaviour may seem rather extreme, it does exist. For example, the bestseller list regularly published in major newspapers almost guarantees a book a longer life span. Many consumers, however, do not rely so heavily on the critics' opinions. In some cases, the critics' reviews are only one aspect or ele-

ment in a complex cognitive process. In other cases, critics' recommendations can be used only to limit the consumer's choice to fewer cultural activities, while the final choice depends on other considerations. The hybrid mechanism may operate in reverse by pushing consumers to judge for themselves the many possibilities in order to retain only a few. In this case, the final choice depends on the review.

In comparison with other types of products that have a high level of involvement (such as a car or house) as well as experts or specialized reporters, the critic's review is very important in the arts. The importance of the critic may be explained by the very nature of cultural products, which are harder to judge and riskier to consume.

4.4.4 Affective Processes

The decision-making processes presented thus far are based upon consumers as cognitive beings who analyze the various characteristics of a product to optimize their consumption of that product. This concept, based on a utilitarian view of the decision-making processes used by consumers, dominates marketing theory, but there are other approaches as well. Holbrook and Hirschman[27] have suggested that some products are not bought on the basis of objectively viewed features or specific functions; rather, their purchase forms a total experience. This is the experiential view. That experience is an attempt at hedonistic gratification. As a decision-making process, the total experience relies heavily on emotional elements (love, hate, joy, boredom, fatigue, etc.) rather than on the cognitive elements of product features and benefits.

According to Holbrook and Hirschman, these decision-making processes are particularly common among consumers of cultural products. In fact, Becker[28] suggests that in terms of the evaluation mechanisms consumers use, the affective processes are more typical in the purchase of works of art, whereas the cognitive processes are more common in the purchase of crafts. Most decision-making processes are neither entirely cognitive nor entirely affective. Instead, they are a blend of both processes.[29] In any event, a marketer should be well aware of this affective dimension.

Zajonc and Markus[30] have probably analyzed the affective decision-making process more thoroughly than any other researchers. An example of the affective process would be Mrs. Smith rushing out to buy the latest Michael Bolton recording because he is her favourite singer. In this case, the acquisition of preferences is based on a series of fairly deliberate experiences that give the consumer pleasure. Of course, the marketing manager must deal with the parameters used in this process. This task is all the more demanding because consumers have trouble explaining their own preferences. Managers targeting a group of pleasure-seeking consumers are often obliged to rely on a "trial and error" marketing strategy. In this sense, marketing strategy appears to be more of an art than a science.

4.4.5 Habit

Habit is another decision-making mechanism used by consumers. A little like attitude, habit allows a consumer to decide on a product quickly. Unlike attitude, habit is characterized by a low level of involvement. The following example highlights this distinction. Mrs. Smith has a strong positive attitude toward Minute Maid® frozen orange juice; she buys it automatically every week. Mrs. Jones does the same, although with a lesser degree of involvement. One day, the grocery store where both women shop stops carrying Minute Maid® orange juice. Given Mrs. Smith's high level of involvement, she might decide to shop elsewhere, not to buy orange juice, or to pick another brand after analyzing the features of similar products. On the other hand, Mrs. Jones is likely to substitute another brand of orange juice much more mechanically.

In short, habit provides consumers with an easy, routine way of selecting a product or category of products whose purchase or consumption represents very little risk. Since most cultural products, however, represent a high level of involvement, habit is a less frequent decision-making mechanism.

4.4.6 Impulse Purchasing

The decision-making process used by the consumer purchasing on impulse is characterized by a low degree of involvement and experience. These purchases are generally unplanned and of little consequence. Sometimes, product placement or the colours on the packaging are enough to prompt the consumer to buy. Some video-club members use this process. For these consumers, renting a video requires little involvement; hence, their decision-making process may entail simply taking the most familiar title they find among the recent releases.

4.5 SITUATIONAL VARIABLES

As seen in figure 4.1, the decision-making processes, along with the related information-processing strategies, are influenced by certain situational variables. The main situational variables are the period (month, day, season) when the purchase is made, the time available to the consumer to shop for the purchase, the presence or absence of reference groups, the economic climate, and the place where the decision is made.

4.5.1 Period

The period during which a purchase is made influences the decision-making process. A snowfall in early December, for instance, encourages consumers to do Christmas shopping. Tchaikovsky's *The Nutcracker* may be a holiday season favourite, but would it be sold out or held over in July?

4.5.2 Time Available

The amount of time a consumer has to make a decision also influences the decision-making process adopted. If there is little time, the consumer will rely more on subordinate processes and processes based on past experience.

4.5.3 Reference Groups

The presence or absence of reference groups also influences the decision-making process. If a consumer is aware of signals in his or her environment and must make a decision, the presence of a reference group or person of influence will increase the tendency to use a subordinate process.

4.5.4 Economic Climate

The economic climate also plays an important role. If the consumer is living through a recession or is keenly aware of the economic situation, he or she will tend to use a cognitive decision-making process in which price becomes more significant.

4.5.5 Place

The physical environment is another element influencing the consumer's choice of decision-making process. This factor is especially important, since the presence or absence of affective or cognitive stimuli would determine the process used.

4.6 INFORMATION PROCESSING

As mentioned at the beginning of this chapter, every decision-making process is based on a minimum amount of information. Consequently, a key function of marketing is to provide consumers with information[31] that may be adapted to either the type or the structure of the decision-making process selected. Naturally, the more experience related to the purchase of this product or category of products a consumer has, the less interested that consumer will be in seeking information from outside sources and in responding to a marketing appeal. This is exactly what a new theatre company faces when it targets the subscribers of an already established theatre.

Table 4.2 describes the links connecting the various decision-making processes discussed above, the different ways of processing information, and the main marketing strategies that could be applied.

4.7 CONCLUSION

As shown in table 4.1, a good grasp of the decision-making processes used by consumers in the act of purchasing a product gives a marketing manager information about how the consumer processes the information gathered. The manager is thus equipped to choose more suitable marketing strategies for the particular product.

Table 4.2   **The Main Forms of Information Processing and Resultant Strategies**

Decision-making process	Extent of information processing	Nature of the information	Type of outside information sought	Main marketing strategies
Attitude	Limited	Mostly internal, based on experience	Product qualities and features that reinforce consumer's attitude (perceptual bias)	For the company that benefits from this positive attitude: reinforce it and work to maintain satisfaction level. For other companies: introduce something startling in the consumer's process to focus on perceived risk. For the consumer, this strategy entails the use of one of the other decision-making processes. This should help the manager develop a more appropriate strategy.
Cognitive process	Vast	Mostly external	Qualities that maximize the practicality of the service or product desired	Provide the consumer with information on the features mentioned in the order that these features are used.
Subordinate process	Limited	Mostly external	Reference or opinion from source consumer considers credible	Count on imitation, reference or deference mechanisms (e.g., 10,000 viewers have already applauded).
Affective process	Limited	External	Impressions and emotions to produce a sensorial reaction (fear, joy, pleasure, etc.)	Use primarily a communications strategy based on the symbolic value of the product and the emotions involved (e.g., film clips presented at the beginning of a program).

(continued)

Table 4.2 (continued) **The Main Forms of Information Processing and Resultant Strategies**

Decision-making process	Extent of information processing	Nature of the information	Type of outside information sought	Main marketing strategies
Habit	Restricted	Internal, based mainly on experience	Passive searching for information; consumer does not look for it	For the company whose product has become a habit: try to keep the consumer passive and ensure that the product or service is available; certain radio or TV programs rely on habit. For other companies: introduce something startling in the consumer's process to focus on perceived risks. For the consumer, this strategy entails the use of one of the other decision-making processes. This should help the manager develop a more appropriate strategy.
Impulse purchase	Limited	External	Information not actively sought	The information given must attract the consumer, who may not be actively seeking it. Here the marketing manager must create an event of sorts.

Naturally, any understanding of the decision-making processes used by consumers can be gained only through analysis of the different variables that influence the processes; these variables have been described throughout this chapter and are illustrated in figure 4.1. Only the variables shown in the first box of figure 4.1, the product-related variables, have not been covered. These variables, which may be linked to the company's or the competition's marketing strategies, certainly do influence consumer behaviours and will be analyzed in detail in later chapters. The elements listed in the behaviours box can be found in examples given throughout this chapter.

SUMMARY

Consumers, as human beings, base their behaviour on a certain amount of information, which has already been processed according to particular decision-making processes. These processes are, in turn, based on the basic triad of individual–product–situation. Notable among the variables influencing both the type and the structure of the decision-making processes are the consumer's previous experience and level of involvement with the product.

Marketing managers must have an excellent grasp of the information-processing system that a consumer uses when buying their company's product. A good understanding of the factors that make up these processes will enable managers to optimize their company's marketing strategy. This understanding will, in turn, enable the company to do the following:

1) better segment its markets;

2) better position the company's products vis-à-vis the competition and the segments targetted;

3) select more suitable distribution modes and networks;

4) set up a price structure based not only on costs or competitors' prices, but also on the target consumer's perception;

5) develop a communications strategy that provides consumers with the information they want in the most suitable form.

QUESTIONS

1. You are the new marketing director of a decorative-arts museum. Over the past two years, the number of museum visitors has dropped considerably. Given the degree of product involvement implied, what marketing action will you take to improve the museum's position in the market?

2. Compare the linear compensatory and the conjunctive processes.

3. Why is it important for a manager to be well acquainted with the decision-making process that targetted consumers are using?

4. What is the difference between a decision to buy with low product involvement and a decision to buy with high product involvement? Support your answer with examples of cultural products.

5. What are the advantages and disadvantages of using sociodemographic variables as determining factors in consumer behaviours?

6. Which elements explain the influence of reference groups on some consumers?

7. What role does attitude play in the decision-making process? Use an example to back up your answer.

8. How do situational variables influence the decision-making process and the processing of information?

9. What are the consequences of selective perception for a marketing manager designing an ad campaign for a new play?

Notes

1. Intratype competition includes all similar products that fulfil the same need. Intertype competition includes all products, similar or not, that fulfil the same need.

2. Lewin, K. 1951. "Field Theory and Learning," in *Field Theory and Social Science*. New York: Harper and Row.

3. Bettman, J., E.J. Johnson and J. Payne. 1991. "Consumer Decision Making," in *Handbook of Consumer Behavior*, T. Robertson and H. Kassardjian, eds. Englewood Cliffs, NJ: Prentice-Hall.

4. Park, C.W., and B. Mittal. 1985. "A Theory of Involvement in Consumer Behavior: Problems and Issues," in *Jagdish Sheth Research in Consumer Behavior*, Vol. 1, JAI Press, p. 201–232.

5. Nantel, J., and R. Robillard. 1990. "Le concept de l'implication dans l'étude des comportements des consommateurs : une revue de la littérature." Cahier de recherche 90-01. Montreal: École des HEC.

6. Rothschild, M.L. 1984. "Perspectives on Involvement: Current Problems and Future Directions," in *Advances in Consumer Research*, Vol. 11. T. Kinnear, ed. Provo, Utah: Association for Consumer Research, p. 216–217.

7. Laurent, G., and J.N. Kapferer. 1985. "Measuring Consumer Involvement Profiles." *Journal of Marketing Research*, Vol. 22 (February), p. 41–53.

8. Ingene, C., and M.A. Hughes. 1985. "Risk Management by Consumer," in *Jagdish Sheth Research in Consumer Behavior*, Vol. 1, JAI Press, p. 103–158; Cox, D.F. 1967. *Risk Taking and Information Handling in Consumer Behavior*. Boston: Harvard University.

9. Peter, P., and M. Ryan. 1976. "An Investigation of Perceived Risk and Brand Level." *Journal of Marketing Research*, Vol. 13 (May), p. 184–188.

10. King, S. 1989. *Misery*. Paris: Albin Michel.

11. Brisoux, J., and M. Laroche. 1980. "A Proposed Consumer Strategy of Simplification for Categorizing Brands," in *Evolving Marketing Thought for 1980, Proceedings of the Annual Meeting of the Southern Marketing Association*, J.D. Summer and R.D. Tay Louis, eds. Carbondale, p. 112–114.

12. This notion of affective predisposition is what Fazio implies in his definition of attitude. See Fazio, R.H. 1986. "How Do Attitudes Guide Behavior," in *Handbook of Motivation & Cognition, Foundations of Social Behavior*, S. Richard and H. Tory, eds. New York, NY: Guilford Press.

13. Kassardjian, H., and M.J. Sheffet. 1992. "Personality and Consumer Behavior," in *Perspectives in Consumer Behavior*, H. Kassardjian and T. Robertson, eds. Englewood Cliffs, NJ: Prentice-Hall.

14. Snyder, M. 1982. "When Believing Means Doing: Creating Links between Attitudes and Behavior," in *Consistency in Social Behavior*, M.P. Zanna et al., eds. The Ontario Symposium, Vol. 2. Hillsdale, NJ: LEA.

15. Steinberg, M., G. Miaoulis and L. David. 1982. "Benefit Segmentation Strategies for the Performing Arts," in *An Assessment of Marketing Thought and Practice*, E. Walker et al., eds. AMA Series, n° 48.

16. See for example: Cooper, P., and R. Tower. 1992. "Inside the Consumer Mind: Consumer Attitude to the Arts." *Journal of the Market Research Society*, Vol. 34, n° 4, p. 299–311; Bergadaà, M., and S. Nyeck. 1995. "Quel marketing pour les activités artistiques: une analyse qualitative comparée des motivations des consommateurs et des producteurs de théâtre." *Recherche et applications en marketing*, Vol. 10, n° 4, p. 27–45; Bouder-Pailler, D. 1999. "A Model for Measuring the Goals of Theatre Atendance." *International Journal of Arts Management*, Vol. 1, n° 2 (Winter), p. 4–16.

17. Gainer, B. 1995, "Ritual and Relationaships: Interpersonal Influences on Shared Consumption." *Journal of Business Research*, Vol. 32, p. 253–260.

18. Holbrook M., and R.M. Schindler. 1989. "Some Exploratory Findings on the Development of Musical Tastes." *Journal of Consumer Research*, Vol. 17 (June), p. 119–124.

19. Fazio, R.H. 1986. "How Do Attitudes Guide Behavior?" in *Handbook of Motivation & Cognition: Foundations of Social Behavior*, S. Richard and H. Tory, eds. New York, NY: Guilford Press.

20. Snyder, M. 1982. "When Believing Means Doing: Creating Links between Attitudes and Behavior," in *Consistency in Social Behavior*, M.P. Zanna et al., eds. The Ontario Symposium, Vol. 2. Hillsdale, NJ: LEA.

21. This mechanism, presented by Katz in "The Functional Approach to the Study." *Public Opinion Quarterly*, Vol. 24, 1960, p. 163–204, is discussed by Fazio (see note 19).

22. Fishbein M., and I. Ajzen. 1975. *Belief, Attitude, Intention, and Behavior: An Introduction to Theory and Research*. Reading, MA: Addison-Wesley.

23. Bettman, J., E.J. Johnson and J. Payne. 1991. "Consumer Decision Making," in *Handbook of Consumer Behavior*, T. Robertson and H. Kassardjian, eds. Englewood Cliffs, NJ: Prentice-Hall.

24. Holbrook, M.B., and E.C. Hirschman. 1982. "The Experiential Aspects of Consumption: Consumer Fantasies, Feeling, and Fun." *Journal of Consumer Research*, Vol. 9, p. 132–140.

25. Olshavsky, R.W. "Perceived Quality in Consumer Decision Making: An Integrated Theoretical Perspective," in *Perceived Quality – How Consumers View Stores and Merchandise*, J. Jacoby and J. Olson, eds. Lexington, MA: Lexington Books, p. 3–29.

26. Laplante, B., and P. Lavoie. 1988. "La critique et son public: enquêtes." *Jeu, Cahier de théâtre*, Vol. 48, n° 3, p. 94–110; Litman, B., and L. Kohl. 1989. "Predicting Financial Success of Motion Pictures: The 80's Experience." *Journal of Media Economics*, Vol. 2, p. 35–50; Wyatt, R., and D. Badger. 1990. "Effects of Information and Evaluation in Film Criticism." *Journalism Quaterly*, Vol. 67, p. 359–368; Larcenaux, F. 1999. "L'influence de la critique sur le point de vente : une approche exploratoire sur le marché du disque classique," in *Proceedings of the 5th International Conference on Arts and Cultural Management*, L. Uusitalo and J. Moisander, eds. Helsinki: Helsinki School of Economics and Business Administration, June 13-17, p. 738–748; Holbrook, M.B. 1982. "Popular Appeal Versus Expert Judgments of Motion Pictures." *Journal of Consumer Research*, Vol. 26 (September), p. 144–155.

27. Holbrook, M., and E.C. Hirschman. 1982. "The Experiential Aspects of Consumption: Consumer Fantasies, Feelings, and Fun." *Journal of Consumer Research*, Vol. 9, p. 132–140.

28. Becker, H. 1978. "Arts and Crafts." *American Journal of Sociology*, Vol. 83, n° 4, p. 862–889.

29. Anand, P., M. Holbrook and D. Stephen. 1988. "The Formation of Affective Judgments: The Cognitive-Affective Model Versus the Independence Hypothesis." *Journal of Consumer Research*, Vol. 15 (December), p. 386–391.

30. Zajonc, R.B., and H. Markus. 1982. "Affective and Cognitive Factors in Preferences." *Journal of Consumer Research*, Vol. 9 (September), p. 123–131.

31. "Information" is used here to refer to advertising as well as the nature of the product, its price, and its point of sale.

For Further Reference

Belk, R.W., and R. Groves. 1999. "Marketing and the Multiple Meanings of Australian Aboriginal Art." *Journal of Macromarketing*, (June).

Consumer Marketing Strategies. 1989. Harvard Business Review Special Collection (n° 90087). Boston: Harvard Business Review.

Fiore, A.M. 2000. "Effects of a Product Display and Environmental Fragrancing on Approach Responses and Pleasurable Experiences." *Psychology & Marketing*, Vol. 17, n° 1 (January), p. 27.

Hirshman, E. ed. 1989. *Interpretive Consumer Research*. Provo, Utah: Association for Consumer Research.

Kassarjian, H.H., and T.S. Robertson, eds. 1991. *Perspective in Consumer Behavior*, 4*th* ed. Englewood Cliffs, NJ: Prentice-Hall.

Paul, P., and J. Olson. 1992. *Consumer Behavior*. Homewood, Illinois: Irwin.

Pieters, R. 1999. "Visual Attention to Repeated Print Advertising: A Test of Scanpath Theory." *Journal of Marketing Research*, Vol. 36, n° 4 (November) p. 424-438.

Robertson, T.S., and H.H. Kassarjian. eds. 1991. *Handbook of Consumer Behavior*. Englewood Cliffs, NJ: Prentice-Hall.

Rust, R.T. 2000. "Should We Delight the Customer?" *Journal of the Academy of Marketing Science*, Vol. 28, n° 1 (Winter), p. 86–94.

Van Raaij, W.F., et al. 1988. *Handbook of Economic Psychology*. Dordrecht: Kluwer Academic Publishers.

Venkatesh, A. 1999. "Postmodernism Perspectives for Macromarketing: An Inquiry into the Global Information and Sign Economy." *Journal of Macromarketing*, Vol. 19, n° 2 (December), p. 153–169.

Wilkie, W. 1993. *Consumer Behavior*. New York: John Wiley & Sons.

Plan

5

CHAPTER 5
Segmentation and Positioning

by Jacques Nantel

OBJECTIVES

- Understand fully the concept of segmentation and its application within the context of arts management
- Distinguish between segmentation bases and descriptors
- Comprehend the importance of segmentation to a manager in the arts milieu
- Understand the concept of positioning in terms of both competitors and target segments

INTRODUCTION

Segmentation is probably the most basic yet most misunderstood marketing principle. As we have seen in the preceding chapters, an organization wants its product to correspond as closely as possible to market needs.

Several definitions of a market have been suggested so far, but they all include the following point: a market is composed of consumption units with similar needs. It should be noted that these needs are similar yet not the same. The book market, for example, could be considered a market made up of consumers who share an interest in reading. This interest is demonstrated by their buying books. Although accurate, this description clearly does not help the marketing manager very much. Indeed, the subgroups forming this market could be described using many different variables, including type of book wanted (novel, biography, sci-fi) and reason for purchase (studies, leisure, personal development, social visibility).

In short, it is always possible, although not necessarily desirable, to analyze a market by breaking it down into segments characterized by a homogeneous demand yet presenting a heterogeneous demand in terms of other segments. We could even define segmentation summarily as the action of separating into subgroups the units that make up the market. In this way, each group would be characterized by homogeneous need, whereas the various subgroups would be separated by their heterogeneous needs. The following examples illustrate the principle of segmentation.

Weekly newspapers and magazines do not target the same clientele, yet they all try to meet similar needs (information or entertainment). The common trait or common denominator for these publications is maximum adaptation to the different needs of specific segments of the population. Magazines such as *Time*, *Paris Match*, and *Maclean's* and weeklies such as Montreal's *Voir* or Toronto's *Now* do not necessarily reach the same readership. Intuitively, *Time*'s readership could be described as Anglophone and interested in international news; *Paris Match*'s readership, Francophone and interested in national news from France; *The Maclean's* readership, Anglophone and interested in national news. *Voir* and *Now* are designed for people interested in the cultural scenes of Montreal and Toronto, respectively. This thumbnail sketch helps us visualize what we mean by "market segmentation."

If we look at stage productions as a market, we see how it could be divided according to genre – for example, opera, ballet, and theatre. This classification may be justified from the producer's viewpoint, but it is not relevant in terms of target segments. Consumers will likely find Verdi's *La Traviata* more similar to a play such as *Romeo and Juliet* than to an opera such as *Wozzeck*! In other words, the first two works may target the same segment, which is different from the target segment of the third.

5.1 THE FUNCTIONS OF SEGMENTATION

Market segmentation is probably the most powerful weapon in the marketer's arsenal. It can fulfil two important functions. The application of the principle of segmentation forces any company to analyze systematically the different needs expressed by its markets. In other words, here the function of segmentation leads companies to perform in-depth market studies to determine to what degree the demand is really homogeneous. Using the results of this type of analysis, the marketing specialist may decide to attack one or several segments, or the market as a whole.

The second function of segmentation is to provide a strategy stemming from an analysis of the market structure. This strategy is called positioning the product. There are basically two types of positioning. The first is product differentiation, which seeks to define the position a company's product should have vis-à-vis the competitor's product. Quebec's summer-theatre market presents an interesting example of product differentiation. These theatres often perform the same repertoire yet are distinguishable by location or by special meal and/or accommodation packages. In this case, the target segment is often the same, so each company will try to outdo the others, even by just a little, to attract that clientele. The second type of positioning is of particular interest to us. This type of positioning is closely linked to the principle of segmentation and attempts to offer consumers within a particular segment a product that meets their needs as closely as possible. In short, this form of positioning strives to define its product(s) according to the demands expressed by one or several segments. An example of this form of positioning would be the variety and diversity of musical groups: a Baroque quartet, a cham-

ber orchestra, an electoacoustic ensemble, and a full symphony orchestra do not all target the same audience. In fact, a symphony will even offer several combinations of concerts in order to reach different segments.

5.2 MARKET STUDIES AND SEGMENTATION

Although conceptually the principle of market segmentation may seem simple, in practice defining the segments can be problematic. Much of this chapter is devoted to the various approaches used in defining a market segment. Of course, no one can simply decide to "segment" a market. All that any business can do is to see if the market is indeed segmented – that is, whether or not there are different types of needs. Only after the marketing manager has a good grasp of the company's market structure can decisions about appropriate marketing strategies be made. In this respect, an accurate reading of the market structure is vital, since a poor analysis may easily lead a company to two types of errors, which, if applied to a strategy, could spell corporate disaster.

The first error is to assume that the market is segmented when in reality it is not. This reading of the situation might prompt an organization to develop new products when the original product is sufficient.

The second error would be to consider the market as uniform when in reality it is made up of various segments. Under this impression, a company might offer a product designed to please everyone and no one. Since the product is not really suited to anyone, it would end up at the bottom of the heap under products better suited to the specific needs of target segments.

Conversely, an accurate definition of the target market structure will assist the manager in crafting the company's marketing strategy. The different strategies will be examined in some detail at the end of this chapter. What follows here is a brief description.

In the case of a market with homogeneous needs, a company may opt for an undifferentiated marketing strategy. The product offering would be limited to a single product or product type. This is the case for the Montreal Opera Company in Canada, which must limit its program to a portion of its repertoire so as to please most of the relatively small number of opera fans in the metropolitan area.

On the other hand, in a market where demand is not homogeneous, a company may adopt one of the following two strategies. It could decide to attack several segments by offering several products. This is called "multiple positioning marketing" or "differentiated marketing." Large publishers like Bertelsmann in Germany use multiple positioning. A company may also concentrate on one single segment and thus pick up a large portion of the market; this is the case, in the broadcasting market, of CNN, which specializes in twenty-four-hour international news. Many cultural organizations use this "concentrated marketing" strategy.

5.3 DEFINING SEGMENTS

It stands to reason that an effective marketing strategy must be based on an excellent understanding of the target market's structure. In other words, a marketing manager must ask the following questions in drafting the optimal strategy: Is the market segmented? If so, what are the segments? The answers to these questions should enable a manager to create better strategies.

There are five essential conditions to be met in defining segments:

1) The response to marketing pressures (current or potential) in the market must vary from one segment to the next.

2) The segment must be definable in such a way as to guide corporate strategies.

3) The segment must be quantifiable.

4) The segment must be profitable.

5) The segment must be relatively stable over time.

5.3.1 Variations in Response to Marketing Pressures from One Segment to Another

In order to test whether or not a market is composed of segments, a marketing manager must first ensure that all the consumers do not have the same needs and that these needs are expressed through different behaviours. In most markets, consumers react differently to the products offered. In this book, segmentation will be based on the different ways of dividing a market in order to group the varied consumer reactions to marketing pressures.[1] The more segmentation is based on consumer behaviours, the more strategically useful it becomes. There are five basic determinants of market segmentation: the purchaser/non-purchaser dichotomy, frequency, loyalty, satisfaction, and preferred brand or product.

The Purchaser/Non-purchaser Dichotomy

This dichotomy is the most basic way of categorizing consumers. In fact, the purchaser/non-purchaser dichotomy could be said to reflect two segments, each having a different response to market pressures. All markets would therefore be composed of at least two segments. This way of looking at a market may help a company create new products.

Frequency or Rate of Consumption

Like the purchaser/non-purchaser dichotomy, the market for a cultural product can be divided according to the relative rate of consumption. Table 5.1 illustrates this division in the Canadian theatre market.

As table 5.1 shows, there is a major difference in the demand among various competing products as well as within the demand for each product in terms of fre-

quency of purchase. We can thus say that in terms of volume (frequency) of purchase, the theatre market is segmented. This statement alone would be of little use, though, without data on who attended the theatre, which theatre, and why. As we will see below, there is a second component to segmentation – descriptors. This component is vital to any serious discussion of marketing strategy.

The Degree of Product or Brand Loyalty

The third way of dividing a market relates to the degree of loyalty consumers show for a specific cultural product – that is, for a particular company or troupe. The impulsiveness or consistency revealed by consumers through their purchasing behaviour often provides an excellent basis for segmentation, since it categorizes consumers according to their sensitivity to various marketing pressures. In terms of cultural products,

Table 5.1

Market Segmentation in Theatre Attendance in Canada

Type of cultural activity	Percentage of Canadians attending 1 play in the past 6 months	Percentage of Canadians attending more than 3 plays last season	Percentage of Canadians attending 1 or 2 plays last season	Percentage of Canadians having not attended any plays last season
Dramatic theatre	24	40	46	14
Comedic theatre	27	26	53	21
Avant-garde theatre	10	18	49	33

Source: Les Consultants Cultur' Inc. and Décima Research. 1992. *Canadian Arts Consumer Profile 1990–1991 – Findings* (May).

subscriptions, especially regular subscriptions, allow for a greater understanding of consumer behaviour. Table 5.2 gives the percentages of subscribers and loyal subscribers for different types of performing arts. As this table shows, consumer behaviour in this sector varies from one art form to the next. Opera, as a market, enjoys a particularly devoted segment of consumers: 62% of those attending are subscribers with a maximum annual turnover rate of about one third, or 21%. This is not the case in comedic theatre, where the subscription rate is 39%, with a turnover of two thirds, or 26%. Given the major differences in the structure of the segments forming the various markets, these two product types should not be managed in the same fashion. The marketing manager of an opera company should devote a great deal of time to ensuring that the subscribers are satisfied with the operas performed, while the wise marketing manager of a theatre company would spend a lot of time selling subscriptions.

The Consumer's Level of Satisfaction

A fourth way of looking at segments is to consider variations in the level of satisfaction expressed by the consumer. Naturally, this measurement is related to the first three, since the act of purchasing or not

---

Table 5.2
Subscriptions to the Performing Arts in Canada

Performing arts	Percentage of regular subscribers	Percentage of former subscribers	Percentage of non-subscribers
Ballet	42	26	32
Modern dance	37	26	37
Dramatic theatre	57	17	25
Comedic theatre	39	26	35
Avant-garde theatre	25	25	49
Symphonic music	67	16	17
Classical contemporary music	58	24	19
Opera	62	21	17
Chamber music	58	24	19

Source: Les Consultants Cultur' Inc. and Décima Research. 1992. *Canadian Arts Consumer Profile 1990–1991 – Findings* (May), p. 260.

purchasing, the volume or frequency of consumption, and brand or product loyalty are all directly or indirectly related to the level of satisfaction expressed by the consumer.[2] Indeed, this point is especially interesting when spin-off products are launched, since these products are designed first and foremost for consumers who are satisfied with the original product. An analysis of the clientele based on its level of satisfaction also allows for the creation and positioning of new products that meet the needs of consumers who are dissatisfied with products currently on the market.

The Preferred Brand or Type of Product

The last way of looking at market segmentation is to analyze variations in preference with regard to different products or brands. A study on preferences in musical styles (table 5.3) published in the United States provides a good example of segmentation

Table 5.3
Music Preferences (USA)

Type of music	Liked in 1997	Liked best in 1997
Country-Western	64.6%	20.7%
Rock	59.8	18.2
Hymns or gospel	57.6	13.8
No particular type	NA	7.7
Classical/chamber	47.5	6.7
Mood or easy listening	67.1	5.9
Jazz	48.4	4.9
Blues or rhythm & blues	62.7	4.8
Latin, Spanish, salsa	28.9	3.9
Big-band	45.0	2.8
Rap	16.8	1.9
Operetta or show tunes	44.2	1.8
New Age	30.9	1.5
Soul	40.0	1.4
Contemporary folk	37.6	1.1
Reggae	31.6	0.8
Ethnic/national traditional	30.6	0.8
Bluegrass	42.1	0.7
Opera	18.8	0.6
Parade or marching band	32.1	0.2
Barbershop	22.4	0.1
Choral or glee club	26.0	0.1

Source: National Endowment for the Arts. 1997. *Survey of Public Participation in the Arts: Summary Report.* p. 47.

according to the type of product. This approach is especially well suited to situations where there are several rival brands – for instance, many movie theatres or different theatre companies. Unlike other approaches, this one is not limited to existing products, but extends to variations in the demand for a hypothetical product. The market study could also introduce the new product (as an idea, a suggestion, or a fait accompli) to consumers so that they can give their opinions. If need be, the study could also compare similar cultural products already familiar to the consumers.

5.3.2 Segment Description

Defining a segment according to an existing variation in demand is an essential step in segmentation; however, if that variation is non-existent, segmentation is obviously impossible. Although defining a segment is essential, this operation is far from adequate. As a matter of fact, defining segments by consumer profile alone would be redundant in terms of strategy planning. In other words, saying that a market may be made up of non-purchasers, loyal purchasers, or large-volume purchasers is not wrong, but limiting the description to a single system of classification is of little practical use. It is far more important to find descriptors for the different segments.

A descriptor is a variable that essentially characterizes a segment. Its first purpose is to answer the key questions of who and why. In other words, who is or is not going to the theatre, and why? Who regularly buys a season subscription to the opera, and who only occasionally buys a single ticket, and why? Why do some people go to the theatre

often, whereas others go only once in a while? Which consumers are ready and which are not ready to take a risk by seeing an avant-garde work?

In short, descriptors help characterize and quantify segments. There are almost as many descriptors as there are adjectives in the dictionary; however, researchers tend to limit themselves to previously effective or revealing ones. These descriptors may be grouped as follows: geographic, sociodemographic, psychographic, and related to the benefits sought by consumers.

Geographic Descriptors

Geography is one of the most commonly used descriptors in market segmentation. Geographic differences often reflect cultural, climatic, or environmental differences. What makes geographic descriptors interesting is the fact that they enable marketing managers or researchers to develop and visualize the profile for various consumers. J.G. Garreau, former publisher of the *Washington Post*, divided North America into nine large regions, each of which he considered a nation.[3] He believed that the cultural differences from one region to the next influence consumer profiles. According to Garreau, the Maritimes including New England is a region that has little in common with the region he calls Ecotopia, located west of the Rocky Mountains, and the Sierra Nevada (going from Anchorage in the north to Point Conception in the south). One of Garreau's nine regions is Quebec province; another comprises the rest of Canada plus part of the United States (from the Canadian border in the north to the Mexican border in the south, and between

Denver in the east and the Sierra Nevada in the west).

Geographic descriptors are appropriate tools for defining and estimating the segments that make up a market. Although easy to use – perhaps too easy – geographic descriptors are not problem-free. The main problem lies in the fact that many executives assume that their market is segmented and that this segmentation may be best described using geographic variables. In the broad area of cultural products, the distinction between a large city and a region is commonly used. This distinction is accurate only if the urban market for the cultural product in question is characterized by a demand different from that in the surrounding region(s). Since many cultural organizations do not have the resources to undertake a study of geographic descriptors, they may fall into the trap of assuming that there is a distinction between a city and its surrounding region(s) and basing their marketing strategies on that unfounded assumption. This potentially serious error in judgment could result in a company limiting its marketing efforts to a specific part of the territory and thereby completely overlooking a potentially rewarding market segment.

Sociodemographic Descriptors

Sociodemographic descriptors are all the variables used to describe or quantify the composition of a society, including age, sex, level of education, income, ethnic background, number of children, language, religion, type of dwelling, and profession. These descriptors are probably the most frequently used in segmentation, since they enable a company to personalize its clientele more easily. Not only do they describe segments in easily understood terms, but they also rely on national census data, which means they can give an idea of a market's potential.

Although easy to use, sociodemographic descriptors are not without drawbacks. Some find that sociodemographic descriptors are inadequate in describing segments typical of certain markets, particularly in areas where inter-brand discrimination is involved. Winter[4] points out some of the main flaws in sociodemographic descriptors. First, many marketing managers rely on these easy-to-use descriptors, which do not always reflect the market. Second, sociodemographic descriptors only partially fulfil a descriptive function – that is, they explain only who buys. Since they cannot explain why a large segment adopts a certain behaviour, they are of limited use in developing a corporate marketing strategy. For example, regardless of whether the studies are conducted in North America, Eastern Europe, Western Europe, or Australia, their findings consistently show that consumers of high art are better educated and more affluent than the average consumer; thus, for a company operating in this market, segmentation based on sociodemographic descriptors is not, generally speaking, very helpful. All in all, sociodemographic descriptors are useful in "personifying" the targetted segment(s), but they often are unable to provide the marketing professional with all the information needed to develop a proper corporate marketing strategy. Other descriptors, such as psychographic ones, may fill in the gaps.

Psychographic Descriptors

Everyone knows someone who always buys the latest product (no matter what it is), or someone who worries about the social image he or she will project by attending certain events. Obviously, for some products these people have a consumer profile unlike any average. However, their consumer behaviour cannot be attributed to age, sex, income, or region. Variations in preference or choice for many products simply cannot be explained using sociodemographic or geographic descriptors alone, but are related to variables that involve values and opinions. These variables have been named "psychographic descriptors."

Lazer[5] first introduced the concept of psychographic descriptors, which was later developed by Weels.[6] This type of descriptor can be divided into two broad categories. The first is linked to personality and draws upon the psychological research performed by Allport,[7] Cattel,[8] and Murray.[9] Certain personality tests are used in marketing to categorize consumers according to differences in their behaviour. In fact, many studies have tried to link the use of certain products to specific personality traits. For example, Tucker and Painter[10] observed that men who easily adopted new fashions in clothing were more sociable and had more influence on their peers than average. Similarly, many studies, including that of Robertson and Myers,[11] have used personality traits to group individuals in terms of the speed with which they would adopt a new product.

The second category of psychographic descriptors includes life-style analysis, which assumes that individuals can be grouped according to the activities they undertake, opinions they hold, and interests they show. Consumers are usually asked a battery of questions on activities, opinions, and interests. In fact, this test is often called an AOI test or inventory. The questions touch upon many subjects, ranging from shopping and leisure to economic and political views. Through general or product-specific questionnaires, several life-style analyses have been performed. Using statistical analysis, consumers are grouped by relatively homogeneous AOI profiles. These profiles are then tested to see if they enable researchers to pinpoint accurately the differences in levels of demand. These levels are usually evaluated according to preference in terms of competing brands.

In most cases, psychographic profiles are based on questionnaires given or sent randomly to a sampling of consumers. These questionnaires are very long and usually include a section describing the consumer profile in terms of numerous products, a media-consumption profile, a sociodemographic profile, and a psychological profile based on a series of questions related to consumer values in terms of their activities, opinions, and interests.

Marketing professionals should always bear in mind that psychographic segmentation based on AOI and values does have certain weak points.[12] The first is a lack of clear definitions and an absence of a valid theoretical framework. The second lies in the fact that the questions asked are often formulated by the researchers. If the questions are changed, the profiles and groupings are automatically modified. The third can be found in the way these profiles are drawn up using cluster analysis. Of all the multidimensional techniques available, this one is the weakest. Just one blip in the algorithm or a difference in computer capacity may completely upset the configuration of the profiles. A fourth weak spot lies in the length of the questionnaires normally used. One questionnaire can ask over 300 questions in the psychographic section alone. Right away, the extent to which the respondents are representative is questionable, since the people who are prepared to spend over an hour on a survey may not reflect the general public. Although this last point may be said of all surveys, the problem becomes more serious if the researcher wants to establish a psychographic profile of the society. Last but not least, the fifth weakness is the survey's lack of discriminatory power. In this sense, the number of studies showing the rate of consumption for a product or brand as more or less equal from one life-style to another is especially important.

Descriptors Based on Benefits

Of all the descriptors, those based on benefits sought best describe buying patterns. These descriptors answer the question, Why are there different levels of demand in the same market? According to the principle that all consumers do not buy the same type of product for the same reason, this approach attempts to group consumers who want the same benefits in the same product. The market can therefore be divided into as many segments as there are benefits or combinations of benefits sought. From a strategic viewpoint, benefit segmentation is especially important since it often

gives some shape to the notion of market positioning.

In the area of cultural products, several studies have attempted to define art consumer segments. Steinberg, Miaoulis, and Lloyd[13] have set out seven segments, four of which describe consumers who do not go to shows (consumers concerned about safety, consumers more involved with their children, hedonists, and pragmatists). The other three segments describe consumers who do go to shows ("culture vultures," those seeking entertainment, those looking for an aesthetic experience). A similar Canadian study[14] grouped consumers into eight segments according to benefits sought. The eight groups are as follows: devotees (8%); believers (17%); practising believers (14%); die-hard fans (18%); undecided (14%); uninvolved (17%); care-free pop-rockers (6%); and "out of it" (6%). In terms of cultural and artistic products, the greater the benefit segmentation, the more useful the segmentation is to marketing managers. In other words, a better grasp of the specific benefits that consumers want leads to better marketing strategies.

This form of segmentation, first introduced by Haley,[15] remains useful to companies looking for their own niche in the marketplace. The main advantage of this form of segmentation is that it sets out the reasons behind different levels of preference in a market. Once a corporation has this kind of reading of its market, it can try to enhance its product so that it corresponds better to the benefits sought by consumers.

This chapter covers the most important ways of describing segments. Naturally, there are other descriptors, but those presented here are the most pertinent to any analysis of the cultural-product market. Of course, market segmentation may use a combination of descriptors. In practice, the most important decision is the choice of descriptors. Why is one type of descriptor selected rather than another? At first glance, the answer appears simple, since a marketing manager could simply choose the descriptors that describe most effectively the different levels of demand found in the particular market. In practice, however, choosing descriptors is not always so easy. An excellent knowledge of the target market is vital to any segmentation study. On the basis of this study, a company can always try to divide its market using specific descriptors and thereby try to discover the structure of the market and profitable market opportunities.

Many companies seem to work backwards in their segmentation studies. Rather than start by analyzing the various levels of demand for their product, they start by segmenting their market based on descriptors in order to see if the groups offer different levels of demand. There is nothing really wrong with this approach as long as real differences in the levels of demand are found. In many cases, intuitive knowledge of the market may make this kind of approach desirable. However, it is fraught with weaknesses if there is no real difference in the level of demand. An executive may try out a lot of descriptors before realizing that not one of them actually reveals noteworthy differences in consumer behaviour. Moreover, some managers might even be convinced that the descriptors used are adequate when they do not describe the reality of the market at all. In these cases, companies often adapt their product to segments that are basically similar.

In terms of cultural products, creation plays a key role; as a result, a product can rarely be adapted to the needs or demands of a segment, and even less often to some average of several segments. Yet, it is important for a marketing manager to look at the finished cultural product and consider the characteristics of whatever segment might be most interested in the product.

5.3.3 Quantifying Segments

Describing the profile of each segment within a market is not enough; the size of each segment is also needed. Quantifying segments – in other words, determining the exact number of people per segment and the potential revenue per segment – is the third prerequisite for effective segmentation. Evaluating segments is easier if segmentation is based on sociodemographic descriptors. Once the segments are defined in these terms, it is relatively easy to use secondary sources, such as a national statistics bureau (Statistics Canada, US Census Bureau, Australian Bureau of Statistics), to analyze the number of individuals or companies that make up the segments. On the other hand, it is a different story when starting with psychographic variables, which often require the marketing specialist to do market studies based on scientific samplings to determine the number of individuals in any given segment.

The segments formed must be not only quantifiable but also useful. Segmentation is only effective inasmuch as it enables a marketing manager to create a different and effective marketing plan for each segment. In this respect, sociodemographic variables are not particularly useful. Even though they may help to put a human face on a segment, they are limited in their ability to explain behaviour. Hence, descriptors related to benefits and to usage are probably the most useful.

The combination of the last two criteria demonstrates one of the paradoxes of segmentation studies. Often, a descriptor enables the researcher to quantify segments quite easily, but these segments are not always useful in developing sophisticated strategies. This is often true of sociodemographic descriptors. Conversely, descriptors related to the benefits sought may pinpoint accurate segments, yet they do not quantify these segments. Ideally, segmentation is based on a blend of several descriptors.

5.3.4 Profitability of Segments

An effective segment is a profitable segment. Profitability is the fourth essential condition for effective segmentation. As a rule, if a company is interested in a specific segment, it has seen some potential profit there. As already mentioned, segments are useful only if groups with different needs can be identified. These needs are usually expressed by varying degrees of product consumption, interest, preference, or satisfaction. These varying levels of demand may, in turn, be expressed in terms of the probability of buying. Through a formula that multiplies the probability of purchase by the number of individuals per segment and by the expected average purchase, the marketing manager obtains the expected revenue per segment. Since adaptation of a corporate marketing strategy to a specific segment normally entails additional expense, product or service redesign, and adaptation of advertising and possibly distribution, the company must ensure that the earnings generated by that segment will indeed exceed those expenses. Companies may occasionally integrate fairly similar segments in order to ensure profitability. Of course, the dynamics of cultural markets are slightly different since corporate earnings do not come from consumers only, but also come from sponsors and government granting agencies.

5.3.5 Segment Stability over Time

The fifth and last condition for effective segmentation is the assurance (albeit relative) that the segments will remain stable long enough for the company to turn a profit on the additional investment that an adopted marketing strategy may imply. If market needs evolve quickly, some forms of segmentation may no longer be suitable. This is often the case with segmentation that relies upon descriptors related to benefits, especially in rapidly growing sectors like the fashion world. In these cases, a marketing manager must not only ensure that the segments do exist and are indeed profitable, but also try to determine their life span.

5.4 SEGMENTATION TECHNIQUES

How do marketing professionals use the five essential conditions described above to define which segments make up their market? In this section on segmentation techniques, it is important to remember that there are two broad categories: "a priori" and "cluster-based."

5.4.1 A Priori Segmentation

Using the a priori technique, a manager assumes that one or several descriptors may be adequate to explain variations in needs, preferences, or behaviours observed. In the market, the hypotheses behind these assumptions may stem from a range of sources that include gut feelings, secondary sources, and focus-group sessions. The marketing manager will use the results gathered during this first stage to determine whether or not the market is segmented and whether or not these segments may be described using the variables chosen. A scientific analysis of the market is necessary. Once the market has been divided according to the descriptors selected, the marketing manager can see if there really are different levels of demand. Should this be the case, the manager can decide which segment(s) to attack according to the five conditions presented above.

The advantage of this approach to segmentation is that it is analytically simple. In fact, it tests only specific hypotheses. For example, if a company believes that the levels of demand for a new symphony orchestra in a given city could vary according to age, benefits, and the novelty of the repertoire offered, the company could test its hypothesis before proceeding. The disadvantage inherent in this approach lies, however, in the fact that different levels of demand may be recognized but not explained by the descriptors the marketing manager has chosen, in which case the manager must develop new hypotheses regarding the descriptors which could explain these differences. The resulting hypothesis would then have to be tested, just as the previous one was.

5.4.2 Cluster-Based Segmentation

A manager using this type of segmentation must have some knowledge of the market structure, knowledge that is still based on either research or intuition. Nevertheless, it does not require strictly formulated hypotheses in terms of the nature of the descriptors that might help explain segment formation. In this approach, a market study is carried out to survey consumers on many aspects, including most of the segmentation bases and descriptors. Multidimensional techniques, such as cluster analysis or correspondence analysis, are then applied to define groups of individuals (thus the term cluster-based). Each group presents a certain internal homogeneity in terms of its level of demand, as well as a certain heterogeneity in terms of the other groups. Analysis follows, with some comparison of the groups that enables the marketing manager to ascertain whether these needs and behaviours are indeed different. If they are, some of the descriptors used in the market study are reused to further describe these needs and behaviours. The advantage of this approach is that it allows the marketing manager to discover innovative ways of defining segments without being restricted by predetermined patterns. The disadvantage lies in its length and cost in comparison with the first approach, which may give convincing results in the initial stages. Nevertheless, the cluster-based approach is particularly useful when applied to segmentation according to psychographic descriptors and descriptors related to benefits or usage.

5.5 FUNCTIONAL SEGMENT PROFILES

No matter which approach is used, the segments defined by a segmentation study must meet the five conditions given in section 5.3. Once a market is broken down into segments that (1) represent different levels of demand, (2) may be described using the questions "who" and "what," (3) are or may prove useful and quantifiable, (4) are or may be profitable, and (5) offer some temporal stability, those segments may be discussed in terms of their functional profiles. As a result, the challenges a manager in the cultural milieu must face are not in defining segments, but in finding segments for a particular cultural product. Once this has been accomplished, the wise marketing manager will use positioning to implement a successful marketing strategy.

5.6. POSITIONING IN MARKETING

While market segmentation may be considered an analytical concept, positioning a product is seen as a strategic concept. In other words, once a market structure is well understood, a company may decide on its strategic positioning. Two types of positioning are possible and not mutually exclusive. The first is positioning in terms of one or more segments; the second is positioning against the competition.

Figure 5.1 illustrates the way in which a company decides on the strategic positioning of its product. As we can see, the two principal factors guiding the company's decision are the structure of the market – the segments of which it is composed – and the positioning already held by the competition.

5.6.1 Positioning by Segment

As suggested above, a company may choose to adapt its strategy to the needs of one segment only. This kind of strategy, also known as the "concentrated marketing strategy," is highly recommended for cultural

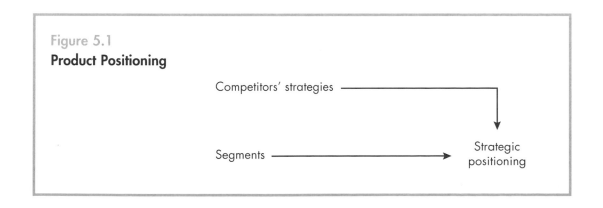

Figure 5.1
Product Positioning

Competitors' strategies

Segments

Strategic positioning

organizations, which, given their limited resources and unique mission, are well advised to target one particular segment. This type of positioning requires an excellent understanding of the segmentation descriptors that explain consumer preferences and behaviours. In some instances, this type of positioning uses segments defined through sociodemographic variables, as is the case for troupes specializing in children's or teens' theatre. In other cases, this positioning is based on geographical variables. In fact, the term "off-Broadway" means just that. (This is in contrast to the notion of a "fringe festival," which implies that the artistic product is at the margin or edge of mainstream theatre in a given city.) In most cases, though, cultural organizations are positioned by segments defined according to the benefits sought by consumers. For example, a survey conducted by the management of Powerhouse Museum in Sydney, Australia, led it to discover that the public perceived the Powerhouse as not a traditional museum but a place of discovery offering exciting, hands-on experiences; [16] to the extent that these attributes correspond to the benefits sought by consumers, they can be used in positioning the museum.

Using the data from a study of various cultural products, Nantel and Colbert[17] revealed the key benefits consumers sought from this type of product. Their research involved consumers matching up sixteen cultural products and thirteen adjectives commonly employed by theatre and art critics in the press. Figure 5.2 gives a perceptual map of the key benefits sought by show-going consumers. As we can see, the benefits selected have been divided into four broad categories along two main axes. The horizontal axis lists benefits sought along a continuum ranging from "entertaining" and "escapism" to "adds to my cultural knowledge," "enriching," "prestigious." The continuum on the vertical axis runs from "relaxing" to "exciting." It is no accident that "change of pace" lies in the centre of this graphic illustration. This benefit is common and essential to every type of cultural product. This classification of benefits allows a marketing manager to define, albeit roughly, four segments based on the benefits sought. There are consumers who want relaxing and enriching activities and others who want relaxing yet entertaining activities. Still other consumers seek exciting and enriching activities, whereas others want exciting and entertaining activities. Of course, a single consumer may look for one benefit in one circumstance and another benefit in other circumstances. Some consumers may prefer to limit their choice systematically to activities offering the same benefits, while other consumers may want a variety of benefits. All of these possibilities reveal the sometimes complementary, sometimes competitive nature of various cultural products. Different producers offering similar benefits could unite or form an association to provide a combination of activities for consumers wishing to concentrate their cultural activities in one area. Conversely, an association of products with different benefits would be more suitable for a segment of consumers seeking to diversify their range of cultural outings.

The sixteen products analyzed were then positioned according to these benefits and the four segments described in the preced-

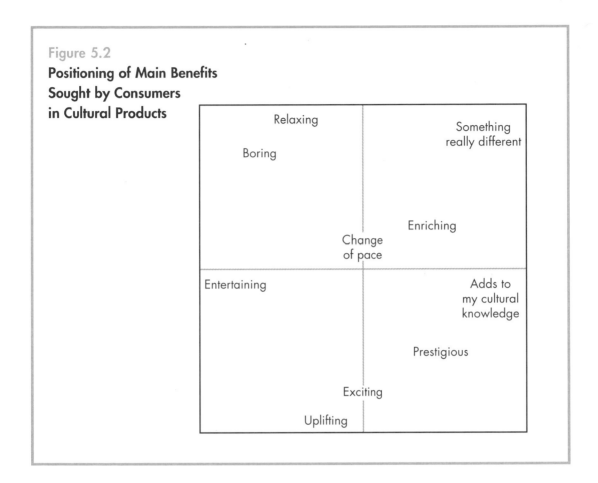

Figure 5.2

Positioning of Main Benefits Sought by Consumers in Cultural Products

ing paragraph. Figure 5.3 illustrates their positioning. Obviously, certain products, such as pop music and musical comedy, seem to offer similar benefits. On the other hand, ballet and stand-up comedy shows are in opposite corners, so to speak.

The positioning of a cultural product according to the benefits offered and, initially, the segments targetted enables a marketing manager to pinpoint which products are key competitors and potential allies. These examples reveal just how much any positioning strategy is the result of a keen

understanding of the features and benefits consumers want. Without this knowledge, positioning becomes a theoretical exercise of little use in shaping corporate strategy. Once again, as seen in chapter 4, it is very important to know which criteria consumers actually use in making their choices.

Once product attributes have been determined, positioning may take place using perception, preference, or behaviour. From a technical point of view, this type of positioning may be based on various strategic approaches. However, a manager must go

Figure 5.3

Positioning of 16 Cultural Products According to the Main Benefits Sought by Montreal Consumers

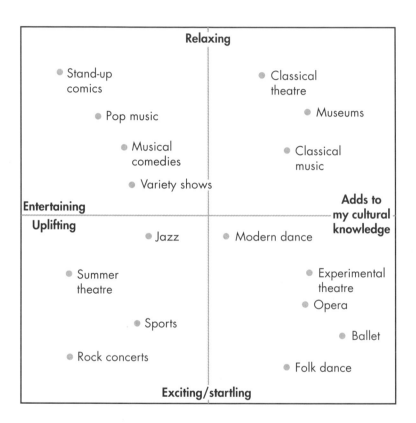

Source: Nantel, J., and F. Colbert. 1992. "Positioning Cultural Arts Products in the Market." *Journal of Cultural Economics*, Vol. 16, n° 2, p. 69.

beyond the type of positioning selected and remember that this exercise can be profitable only if it indicates the optimal way to market the product. This optimization can only occur if the manager knows which attributes or benefits require action.

5.6.2 Competitive Positioning

A good grasp of the segments targetted by a cultural product increases a manager's ability to position the product. Nevertheless, in many cases, several cultural products may serve and target the same segments, hence the same benefits, at the same time. Here is where competitive positioning, also called "product differentiation," proves invaluable. In such cases, the regular consumer must be offered an additional benefit that sets the product purchased apart from the competition. This is a major reason for the success of the BBC Proms Concert, a festival founded in 1895 at London's Royal Albert Hall. From the beginning, the Proms have always focussed on both aspects of a concert: the music and the social content. One of the things the spectators surveyed appreciate most about the Proms is the low-cost standing room for the audience in the arena and the gallery. The arena is the space in front of the orchestra pit where the most expensive seats are usually located. For the Proms, the seats are removed from this area and people are free to sit on the floor or remain standing. The seats are also removed from the gallery, which is located above the balcony and offers the advantage of allowing the consumption of food and beverages before the concert and during the intermission. "The Proms provide the audience with a high quality musical experience, but also an occasion for 'fun'."[18]

Some companies take the opposite tack: instead of trying to differentiate their products, they try to associate them with an existing product. This strategy enables them to benefit from the competitor's image. Movies with titles such as *Fatal Attraction* have bred "me-too" products such as *Fatal Seduction*. In a recent study[19] on positioning in major Montreal theatres, the average consumer's perception was that two companies, the Rideau Vert and the Théâtre du Nouveau Monde, were very close. This kind of positioning is not necessarily bad if it serves the needs of most consumers and the market can support two competitors considered fairly similar by the average consumer.

SUMMARY

Segmentation plays a pivotal role in the marketing strategy of a cultural organization. Given that a market is not segmented but a market's segments are defined, the role of the segmentation bases and descriptors used should be carefully considered.

"A priori" and "cluster-based" are two broad categories of segmentation techniques.

On a more practical level, segmentation involves the description of operational profiles of segments and the adaptation of segmentation theory to marketing strategy. Here, the notion of positioning is brought into play.

In short, segmentation is an ideal conceptual starting point for the strategy-planning process. It is, however, the result of serious, in-depth market analysis, and not a strategy in itself.

QUESTIONS

1. What are the two main functions of segmentation?
2. What are the consequences for a company of a poor analysis of market structure?
3. Why would a new theatre troupe be interested in the concepts of segmentation and positioning?
4. What does "multiple positioning" mean?
5. Describe briefly the five conditions needed to define segments.
6. Describe briefly the six segmentation bases used in marketing.
7. As the marketing director of a new symphony orchestra in your city, you identify several segments in the market. If you decide to adopt a multiple-positioning strategy, how will it affect your marketing decisions?
8. What are the limitations to using sociodemographic descriptors in marketing?
9. What advantages are there for a publisher in using benefit descriptors?
10. Why is it often preferable to use a blend of descriptors when describing a market segment?
11. What is the difference between "a priori" and "cluster-based" segmentation? What are the advantages and disadvantages of each type of segmentation?
12. Under which circumstances is it better to use one over-all marketing strategy? Use an example to support your answer.

Notes

1. Wind, Y. 1978. "Issues and Advances in Segmentation Research." *Journal of Marketing Research*, (August), p. 317–337; Lilien, G.L., and P. Kotler. 1983. *Marketing Decision Making: A Model Building Approach.* New York: Harper and Row.

2. Churchill, G.A., and C. Surprenant. 1982. "An Investigation into the Determinants of Consumer Satisfaction." *Journal of Marketing Research*, n° 19 (November), p. 491–504.

3. Garreau, J. 1981. *The Nine Nations of North America.* New York: Avon.

4. Winter, F.W. 1987. "Market Segmentation: A Tactical Approach." *Business Horizon* (January–February), p. 57–63.

5. Lazer, W. 1963. "Life Style Concepts and Marketing: Toward Scientific Marketing," in *Proceedings of the AMA Winter Conference.* Boston, p. 130–139.

6. Weels, W.D. 1974. "Life Style and Psychographics: Definitions, Uses and Problems," in *Life Style and Psychographics.* Chicago: American Marketing Association, p. 317–363.

7. Allport, G.W. 1961. *Pattern and Growth in Personality.* New York: Rinehart and Winston.

8. Cattel, R.B. 1973. *Personality and Mood.* San Francisco: Jossey Bass Publishers.

9. Murray, H.A. 1960. "Historical Trends in Personality Research," in *Perspectives in Personality Research*, H.P. Davis and J.C. Brengelman, eds. New York: Springer.

10. Tucker, W.T., and J.J. Painter. 1961. "Personality and Product Use." *Journal of Applied Psychology*, Vol. 45 (October), p. 325–339.

11. Robertson, T.S., and J.J. Myers. 1969. "Personality Correlates of Opinion Leadership and Innovative Buying Behavior." *Journal of Marketing Research*, Vol. 6 (May), p. 164–168.

12. See "The Blood Bath in Market Research," *Business Week*, February 1991, p. 72–74; Nantel, J. 1989. "La segmentation, un concept analytique plutôt que stratégique." *Gestion, revue internationale de gestion*, Vol. 14, n° 3 (September), p. 76–82; Kassardjian, H.H., and M.J. Sheffet. "Personality and Consumer Behavior: An Update," in *Perspectives in Consumer Behaviors*, 4th edition, T. Robertson and H.H. Kassardjian, eds. Glenview, IL: Scott, Foresman and Company.

13. Steinberg, M., G. Miaoulis and D. Lloyd. 1982. "Benefit Segmentation Strategies for the Performing Arts," in *An Assessment of Marketing Thought and Practices*. B.J. Walker, ed. Chicago: American Marketing Association, p. 289–293.

14. Les Consultants Cultur'Inc. and Décima Research. 1992. *Canadian Arts Consumer Profile 1990-1991 – Findings* (May).

15. Haley, R.I. 1968. "Benefit Segmentation: A Decision Oriented Research Tool." *Journal of Marketing*, Vol. 32 (July) p. 30–35.

16. Scott, C. 2000. "Branding: Positioning Museums in the 21st Century." *International Journal of Arts Management*, Vol. 2, n° 3 (Spring), p. 35–39.

17. Nantel, J., and F. Colbert. 1992. "Positioning Cultural Arts Products in the Market." *Journal of Cultural Economics*, Vol. 16, n° 2, p. 63–71.

18. Kolb, B.M. 1998. "Classical Music Concerts Can Be Fun: The Success of BBC Proms." *International Journal of Arts Management*, Vol. 1, n° 1 (Fall), p. 16–24.

19. Nantel, J., and F. Colbert. 1991. "Le positionnement d'une compagnie de théâtre et les actions stratégiques pouvant en découler," in *Proceedings of the First International Conference on Arts Management*, F. Colbert and C. Mitchell, eds. Montreal: Chaire de gestion des arts, École des HEC (August), p. 301–310.

For Further Reference

Athanassopoulos, A.D. 2000 "Customer Satisfaction Cues to Support Market Segmentation and Explain Switching Behavior." *Journal of Business Research*, Vol. 47, n° 3 (March), p. 191–207.

Dussart, C. 1986. *Stratégie de marketing*. Boucherville, Quebec: Gaëtan Morin Éditeur.

Kaufman, L., and P.J. Rousseeuv. 1990. *Finding Groups in Data: An Introduction to Cluster Analysis*. New York: John Wiley & Sons.

Kozinets, R.V. 1999. "E-tribalized Marketing? The Strategic Implications of Virtual Communities of Consumption." *European Management Journal*, Vol. 17, n° 3 (June), p. 252–264.

Nantel, J. 1989. "La segmentation : un concept analytique plutôt que stratégique." *Gestion, revue internationale de gestion*, Vol. 14, n° 3 (September), p. 76–82.

Statistique Canada. *Recueil statistique des études de marché*. Catalogue 63-224 (annuel).

Struhl, S.M. 1992. *Market Segmentation*. Chicago: American Marketing Association, Market Research Division.

Waggoner, R. 1999. "Have You Made a Wrong Turn in Your Approach to Market?" *Journal of Business Strategy*, Vol. 20, n° 6 (November–December), p. 16–21.

Weitz, B.A., and R. Wensley. 1988. *Readings in Strategic Marketing: Analysis, Planning and Implementation*. Chicago: Dryden Press.

Wind, Y. 1978. "Issues and Advances in Segmentation Research." *Journal of Marketing Research*, 15 (August), p. 317–337.

Wu, S-I. 2000. "A New Market Segmentation Variable for Product Design – Functional Requirements." *Journal of International Marketing and Marketing Research*, Vol. 25, n° 1 (February), p. 35–48.

Plan

CHAPTER 6
The Price Variable

OBJECTIVES

- Understand the components of the price variable
- Examine the objectives related to this variable
- Describe the main methods of price setting
- Understand the notion of elasticity
- Discuss the most common pricing strategies
- Introduce Baumol's Law

6

INTRODUCTION

In this chapter, we define price as a variable from the consumer's vantage point. We then look at how companies determine the prices of their products by considering the factors involved in the decision-making process, corporate price objectives, and certain methods that facilitate the decision-making process.

A brief review of the various ways of calculating product costs and profitability follows, with special emphasis on the highly specific context of the arts sector. The majority of artistic enterprises are, of course, non-profit organizations receiving financial assistance from the government and sponsors. We will stress here the role played by the state in setting the price that consumers pay for cultural products.

We then explain the economic notion of elasticity, which establishes a link between the variation in demand and price, and apply it to other variables within the marketing mix.

If we accept that the demand curve for a product is a combination of smaller curves, each one representing a market segment, we can relate the price variable to market segmentation. At the end of this chapter, the most common pricing strategies, along with the well-known paradox called Baumol's Law, will be presented.

6.1 DEFINITION

At first glance, price appears to be the sum a consumer must pay to purchase a product. For the purposes of this book, all applicable taxes are included. From the consumer's perspective, price is not necessarily limited to the above definition. The effort a consumer expends to obtain the product, plus any expenses related either to that effort or to consumption of the product, must be calculated. A night at the opera, for instance, involves not only the purchase price of a ticket, but also the effort expended in picking up that ticket prior to the show, in arriving on time at the theatre, and in spending the entire evening there. The opera-lover might pay for parking or public transit, have a drink at intermission or a meal after the show, and then go home and pay the babysitter! Studies[1] on this topic show how the costs associated with a cultural outing are generally double the actual ticket price.

The price of a cultural activity attended by the average consumer includes the three elements shown in figure 6.1. The wise marketing manager will keep this reality in mind when formulating and implementing any pricing strategy.

The notion of effort expended by the consumer – for example, time involved, duration of event, travelling – dovetails with

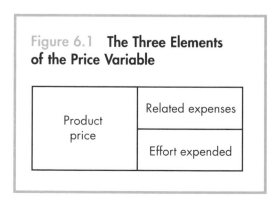

Figure 6.1 **The Three Elements of the Price Variable**

Product price	Related expenses

	Effort expended

that of the psychological effort. The first dimension is objective; the second, subjective. Psychological effort in making a purchase is similar to risk – for example, the social risk of being identified with a certain group; the risk of not understanding or not liking the product; the risk of being upset. As such, risk is the lack of certainty that desires or expectations will be met. It is therefore based on personal perception, which varies from one individual to the next.

The better consumers know and understand a product, the less their risk, since they can use their own judgment. Conversely, the less consumers know, the more they must trust external sources of information in order to judge the amount of risk involved. For instance, a classical play directed and performed by well-known professionals at the Stratford Festival in Stratford, Canada or the Lincoln Center in New York, two prestigious venues, represents less risk than an unreviewed avant-garde or alternative production that none of the consumer's peers has seen. Yet personal taste may prevent the same consumer from appreciating the less risky, better-known classic, while the riskier unknown entity might turn out to be a pleasant surprise.

Risk, both as a psychological dimension in terms of effort and as a component of price, is an important aspect to be considered in the marketing strategy for any cultural product.

6.2 PRICE SETTING

From the corporate viewpoint, setting a price is akin to sending a signal about product value to the marketplace. Price setting also determines the amount of effort an organization must supply to reach the break-even point and the acceptable level of financial risk.

The sometimes tricky task of price setting varies in difficulty from one corporation to the next and depends on market conditions. There are essentially three levels of difficulty. The first level involves a fairly easy decision, as in the case of a company whose product prices are regulated by an external authority – for example, a government agency – or a company that has no choice but to follow the market leader's pricing policy.

There are also instances in which price variances are restricted to an extremely limited spread. This situation occurs when consumers are up to date on competitors' prices and keenly aware of any shift in price.

The most complex situation arises when the marketing manager must choose among many options. This pricing decision requires detailed analysis and considerable reflection.

6.2.1 The Corporate Players

The final decision must take into consideration all those involved: consumers, competitors, distributors, various levels of government, and, in some instances, sponsors. The reaction of each of these players can be hard to predict. Therefore, the price of a product cannot be set according to one simple formula, but is the result of many compromises. The set price may be called "the best possible price under the circumstances."[2]

If some players react strongly, control of the price variable is crucial. If consumers or distributors can shift their allegiance in great numbers or competitors can turn to "dangerous" retaliation tactics, price as a variable must be considered carefully.

The same may be said of modifying a price. Although a reduction in price may be popular with shoppers, it may not be popular with the distributors who see their potential profits plummet.

A government may react to a price variation, or even impose one. A memorable example is the action taken by the Quebec department of cultural affairs, Canada, which abolished the municipal entertainment tax of 10% at the same time that the provincial sales tax (4%) came into effect. The entertainment tax had long been incorporated into ticket prices, so when replacing the 10% tax with the 4% one, cultural companies had the chance to keep the slight yet tempting difference.

Media pressures, however, soon prompted the Quebec department of cultural affairs to encourage the organizations it subsidized to lower ticket prices so that the ultimate consumer would benefit from the lower tax. In the end, price itself sends a message and undeniably contributes to a company's image. Before considering a price change, a company should always determine whether its goal could be better reached by changing another variable in the marketing mix.

6.2.2 Objectives Targetted

If the objective of the price variable is supposed to fit well with the other variables in the marketing mix, it must be based upon a corporate policy drawn from more general over-all goals. Filion[3] lists these objectives in four main categories, as they relate to profits, sales, competitive balance, or corporate image (see figure 6.2).

Profit-Based Objectives

As a rule, arts groups strive to set their prices as low as possible in order to encourage consumption. Many try to balance their revenues and expenses without necessarily seeking any surplus. On the other hand, money-making, profit-driven corporations must generate a certain level of profit to satisfy their shareholders.

One way to set a price is to calculate the return on investment (ROI) that the company wants to achieve. This amount is calculated by dividing the capital invested by the profit. For example, $25,000 in profit from $100,000 invested capital yields a return of 25%. This way of setting a profit goal allows the executive to choose which products should be launched in terms of the potential profit each one represents. The ROI calculation also allows for comparison of the return generated by different divisions in a large corporation. The same figures may be used by potential investors, corporate or individual, to select an investment vehicle.

Sales-Based Objectives

One corporate goal may be to expand the company's market share. By lowering its prices and thus reducing its profit margin, a company may expect to capture a percentage of the competitor's clientele and increase sales – and, hence, market share. This strategy may, of course, trigger salvos from the competition, which then lowers its

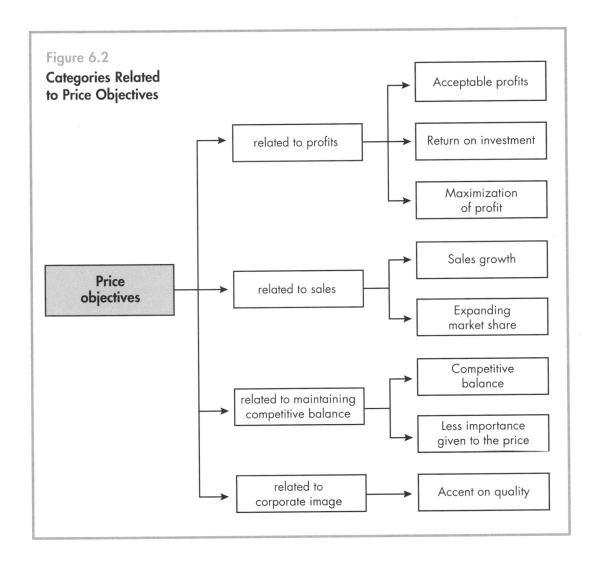

Figure 6.2

Categories Related to Price Objectives

prices too. In keenly competitive sectors in which the consumer remains indifferent to brands, this strategy may start an all-out price war that, in the end, benefits only the consumer.

Goals Related to Competitive Balance

In sectors at the maturity stage in their life cycle, companies may at times wish to maintain the competitive balance and avoid a price war. The competitors within the market then align their prices behind the market leader and rely on strategies related to other variables in the marketing mix to hold on to their market share.

The performing arts are currently in this situation. Companies in this sector set ticket prices at the same level as others in the same category. The maximum price is generally that of the company considered the biggest or most prestigious.

Goals Related to Corporate Image

A company may set its prices according to the image it wishes to project. As mentioned earlier, price may represent a highly symbolic dimension in the consumer's eyes. The firm wishing to project a quality image may set its price accordingly, whereas another firm trying to project the fact that its product is accessible to most people will set its price lower. Naturally, in all of these examples, the objective will be reached only if the price corresponds to the policies applied to other variables in the marketing mix and if the consumer sees this price in the same way as the manufacturer does.

6.2.3 Method Used

The goals related to price setting dovetail with the various methods that may assist the marketing manager in making a decision. Three methods are given in this chapter. The first method is based on consumers; the second on competition; the third on costs.

The Consumer-Based Method

According to traditional marketing theory, the best price is the one the consumer is willing to pay. The consumer is, in fact, the ultimate judge of price-related matters. Setting a price lower than that which the customer is willing to pay means losing potential profits; however, setting a price higher than that which the consumer will pay may actually mean lost sales. The most reliable way to know the consumer's price

threshold is to ask. Since there are various ways of asking, marketing-research techniques can be very helpful.

It should be noted that the consumer-based method suffers from one major limitation: prices set by the competition rein in a company's freedom in this area. Even if a consumer claims to be prepared to pay more for a company's product, if competitors set their prices considerably lower, that company must take note or risk losing sales and reducing its market share.

The Competition-Based Method

In opting for this method, a company sets its prices according to the competition's. Since no marketing research is required, this method is simple and inexpensive. Unfortunately, it lets others decide how much the consumer is willing to pay for the product. In other words, the distinctive features that a company's product may have are ignored, and any potential for positioning through price is lost. If consumers perceive competing products as similar and their perception cannot be changed, basing a price on the competition's price is the most appropriate method, since shoppers are sensitive to price changes. It is therefore important to monitor prices on the market in order to react swiftly to a competitor's price change.

The Cost-Based Method

The cost-based method is simple, since it involves setting a price which enables manufacturers to generate what they consider to be a fair profit. Setting this price requires some calculation of the cost price per unit produced. Another amount, or profit margin, is then added.

The main advantage of this method lies in its simplicity. There are, however, two disadvantages. First, the method does not take into account consumers' reactions. Second, it may be awkward to apply if unit costs vary in direct reaction to the product level (economies of scale based on the amount produced) or if it is difficult to spread out certain costs absorbed by the company through the manufacture of other products.

Executives usually use one of the three methods described above to set their prices, while keeping in mind the general principles underlying the other two methods. For example, a pricing decision is not made solely on the basis of the competitor's price; a firm must examine its costs and anticipate the consumer's reaction.

There are no exhaustive research studies proving which method is the most commonly used in the cultural sector. One study of the museum sector[4] indicates that the competition-based method is the most popular (approximately 50% of all respondents); however, the other two methods are used almost equally (25% each). The study also reveals that even if an organization opts for one method in particular, factors drawn from the other two methods are also taken into consideration.

6.3 CALCULATING COSTS AND PROFITABILITY

Regardless of the method used, corporate executives must always take into account the total of all costs incurred in manufacturing a product.

There are, to put it simply, two types of cost calculated in the total cost of any product: fixed costs and variable costs. Fixed costs remain unaffected by the number of units produced. Such costs include rent, permanent payroll, general insurance, and any costs unrelated to the company's production level. Variable costs are directly and proportionally related to the number or units manufactured. These costs include primary materials (e.g., the paper used to print a book) or transportation costs (e.g., additional transport costs for cities added to a theatre company's tour).

Classifying costs may prove difficult, however. Some costs do not vary proportionally according to the level of corporate activity, but vary according to the steps reached in the manufacturing of product units. The movie-theatre owner may assign additional staff to the ticket booth not on a per-customer basis but once a certain number of spectators is reached. For example, only one person may be necessary to look after the ticket booth as long as the number of patrons per evening is fewer than 500, two people once the number ranges from 500 to 1,000, and three people when the number rises above 1,000.

Once the fixed and variable costs which make up the total production cost are known, the break-even point can be calculated. The break-even point is an important concept in any pricing decision. Breaking even depends on the number of units sold, the selling price per unit, and the level and distribution of fixed and variable costs. This figure can be obtained by dividing the total of fixed costs by the gross margin or marginal contribution, which simply represents the selling price per unit minus the variable costs per unit. This concept is expressed in graphic form in figure 6.3.

Break-even point =
$$\frac{\text{Fixed costs}}{\text{Gross margin}} = \frac{\$50,000}{\$50 - \$25} = 2,000 \text{ units}$$

In this example, if the total of all fixed costs is $50,000, the selling price is $50, and the variable cost per unit is $25, the break-even point is reached when 2,000 units are sold. This means that the company will face a deficit if fewer than 2,000 units are sold, and will make a profit if sales exceed 2,000 units.

An executive may use this technique to appraise the risk of launching a new product according to some hypothesis related to different price levels. The risk is then expressed in terms of the number of units that have to be sold to reach the break-even point, as illustrated in capsule 6.1.

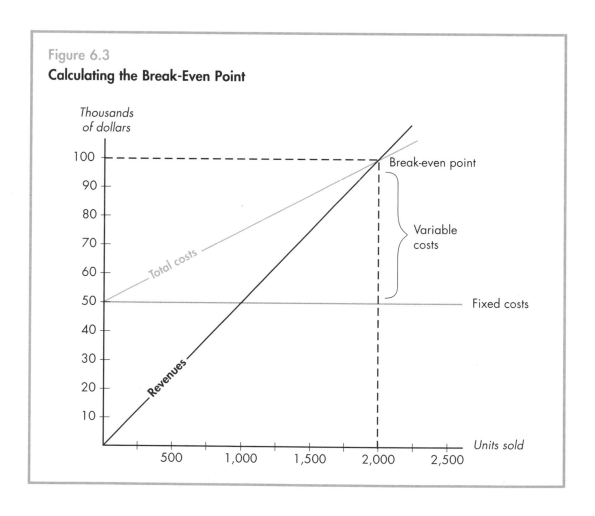

Figure 6.3
Calculating the Break-Even Point

| CAPSULE 6.1 | **DIFFERENT BREAK-EVEN POINTS ACCORDING TO THE THEORY OF PRICE APPLIED** |

The promoter of a show knows that the fixed costs per performance are $10,000, including artists' salaries. It costs $2 per ticket in variable costs – program, insurance, ticket handling, and credit-card commissions. The average ticket price will be set at a level that, multiplied by the number of tickets to be sold, will cover all of the promoter's expenses. At $30 a ticket, 357 units must be sold; at $25 a ticket, 435 units must be sold; and at $20 a ticket, 555 units must be sold. If the venue seats 1,000 people, the minimum capacity to be reached would be 35% (350 seats occupied out of the 1,000 available), 43.5%, or 55.5%, based on the respective ticket price. If the promoter thinks that 1,200 seats could be sold at a ticket price of $20, the performer may appear for just one night. This means taking a loss on the potential 200 tickets that could only be sold on another night. Given the cost structure, the one-night-only theory would generate $8,000 in profit $[(($20/\text{ticket} - $2 \text{ variable costs/ticket}) \times 1,000 \text{ tickets}) - $10,000 \text{ in fixed costs}]$. The two-night theory generates a $1,600 profit $[(($20/\text{ticket} - $2 \text{ variable costs/ticket}) \times 1,200 \text{ tickets}) - 2 \times $10,000 \text{ in fixed costs}]$. The first theory, or one night only, turns out to be more profitable financially, not to mention the impact of a full house rather than a hall at only 60% capacity. The promoter could decide to raise prices so as to attract only 1,000 people and increase profits. On the other hand, by lowering the ticket price, it might be easier to attract more consumers. In any event, the lowest possible price would be $12, since that is the break-even point for a 1,000-seat hall $[(($12/\text{ticket} - $2 \text{ in variable costs/ticket}) \times 1,000 \text{ tickets}) - $10,000 \text{ in fixed costs}]$.

6.4 STATE AND SPONSOR FINANCIAL CONTRIBUTIONS

The earnings generated through the sale of the basic product and spin-off products are generally considered to be only one of the company's three sources of revenue. The state (government) and sponsors also contribute financially. Through grants or subsidies, sponsors and the state finance a decrease in the price paid by the consumer. The purchaser of a ticket to a performance pays only a fraction of the real cost of the product purchased. State support and sponsorship are designed to encourage price-sensitive consumers to buy a product that interests them.

An increase in market demand, as the result of an over-all reduction in price, may be seen as one of the feasible goals of state participation in the arts. There are, however, limits to its effectiveness, as the next section will show, since the demand for cultural products is generally inelastic in terms of price.

6.5 THE NOTION OF ELASTICITY

Economists were the first to try to explain variations in demand. They created sophisticated models at the end of the nineteenth century to prove that there was a relationship of cause and effect between the set price of a product and the number of units sold. In a nutshell, the higher the price, the smaller the number of units sold. Conversely, the lower the price, the higher the number of units sold.

In simple terms, this theory maintains that the consumer wants to buy an article for the lowest price possible. On the other hand, a firm is inclined to produce an amount as large as the price is high (see figure 6.4). Obviously, for the firm, mass production allows for significant economies of scale that will increase the profit margin per unit. Not only do the sales figures increase, but also the profit margin per sale.

In figure 6.4, equilibrium is achieved where the curves representing supply and demand intersect. If, in fact, the price that consumers are willing to pay is very high, manufacturers are ready to produce more.

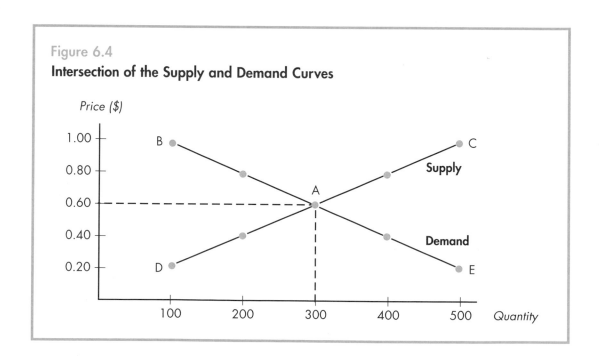

Figure 6.4
Intersection of the Supply and Demand Curves

Conversely, if the price were lower, manufacturers would be less interested in making the product, even though more consumers would be prepared to buy it.

Equilibrium is reached at point A, the intersection of the curves in the example illustrated in figure 6.4. The $1 selling price translates to the consumption of 100 units (point B) and leads to a supply of 500 units (point C); in other words, the companies are prepared to manufacture this number of units, given the profit potential. Conversely, a selling price of 20¢ would generate a supply equal to 100 units (point D), whereas consumer interest could generate demand equal to 500 units (point E). Equilibrium corresponds to the optimal point at which the greatest number of companies and the highest number of consumers are satisfied. In this case, that would be 300 units at 60¢.

Price elasticity is the term used to describe the relationship between the price and the quantity purchased. Since the quantity or amount purchased varies inversely and proportionally to the price, demand is considered elastic if, after a price change, the number of units or products consumed varies more than proportionally to this price change. Conversely, demand is considered inelastic if, in the case of a price change, consumption varies less than proportionally to the price. Ideally, perfect elasticity implies that even a minimal price shift would generate an infinite increase in the amount consumed. A perfectly inelastic demand would imply that for any price variation, the demand remains the same (see figure 6.5). Demand can be either elastic or inelastic to varying degrees. Elasticity may even be neutral, if the change in price and in quantity are equal.

According to one of the first studies on the subject, made by the Ford Foundation in 1974,[5] cultural products usually have an inelastic demand. This applies particularly to cultural events that become "must-sees" in a given season. In this case, consumers rush to attend no matter what the price.

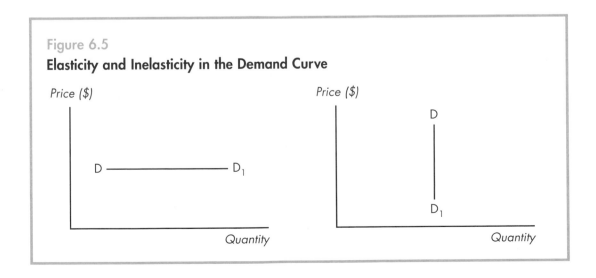

Figure 6.5
Elasticity and Inelasticity in the Demand Curve

The Ford Foundation study revealed that in the performing arts, a price hike from $5 to $10, or a 100% increase, translated to a drop in attendance of 20% to 30%. If the price was quadrupled, from $5 to $20, demand dropped by 35% to 45%. There is no doubt that a price increase exerts pressure on the demand, yet the difference in attendance is less than proportional to the price increase. It seems consumers are little affected by price changes as long as the prices stay below a certain threshold.

The example from the Ford Foundation study shows how elasticity in terms of price (although the same applies to other variables in the marketing mix) may translate to different levels of consumption. In other words, consumers may be quite indifferent to price shifts as long as they remain within a certain range that they consider acceptable. Beyond a certain point, even a slight difference in price will trigger a sudden drop in the number of units sold.

The model of price elasticity was well suited to the reality of the nineteenth century and early twentieth century, when most people experienced poverty and the slightest reduction in price increased consumption. After World War Two, however, incomes rose over all. This increase created a greatly expanded middle class, and consumers could then buy products using criteria other than price. At the same time, people's values changed. They became interested in wearing more stylish clothing, eating better food, and, more recently, protecting the environment and trying new leisure activities. Today, price is still an important factor in the decision to buy a product, but there are now variations in the type of product and the individual consumer's financial status and comfort, and so it is useful to apply the concept of elasticity to other variables in the marketing mix in order to explain variations in demand – product elasticity, promotion elasticity, and distribution elasticity. Indeed, an advertising campaign, an improved service, or a more suitable distribution network can affect demand. It is therefore possible to increase product sales by providing more points of sale, halls, or travelling exhibits, or by improving sales techniques such as accepting credit cards or selling through automatic tellers, by telephone, or by catalogue. Another way of attracting customers is to offer complementary products of a cultural or educational nature (children's workshops, guided tours, lectures, conferences, membership cards), as most museums now do. These examples show how modifying a particular variable can have a positive effect on the quantity consumed. On the other hand, it is obvious that a decrease in promotion or in the number of points of sale will lower product demand.

Unlike their commercial counterparts, artistic enterprises usually choose not to modify the product as a strategy to increase demand. This way, artists retain their creative (artistic) integrity, or the unique quality that makes them interesting. This is not necessarily true of the cultural industries, in which product elasticity may be used as a strategic variable. Of course, this presumes that modifying the product will indeed bring positive consumer reaction. In the cultural milieu, the product is at the core of the act of purchasing (see chapter 2). The level of demand is above all a result of the product offered. In this sense, product elasticity is greater than price or promotion elasticity. Furthermore, the degree of elasticity of the three other variables is a result of the product's elasticity. The best promotion or the greatest price reduction will not convince a consumer who has no interest whatsoever in the product.

Elasticity in terms of demand, according to the different variables of the marketing mix, varies with the product and target market. Ads or critics may rave about the virtues of a symphony orchestra, but not everyone will be interested in the benefits described. An opera company may offer student prices, but not all students will be interested in attending. A recording or a handcrafted object may be displayed at several points of sale with little increase in consumption.

In fact, the variables of the marketing mix must form an extremely coherent whole. As

previously stated, a poor choice regarding one variable can jeopardize an entire strategy. Demand for a given product may be elastic according to some variables in the marketing mix and inelastic according to others. Moreover, some markets, such as those comprising students and senior citizens, react more to the price variable than others.

In short, any attempt to estimate the demand or explain variations in past sales must take into account the effects of elasticity on the four variables that make up the marketing mix. If companies in a specific sector – for example, the association of performing-arts presenters in a certain region – want to increase over-all attendance in a market sensitive to the promotion variable, they could calculate the increase in demand generated by different levels of advertising expenditures. Figure 6.6 shows how, with a constant price, an increase in the advertising

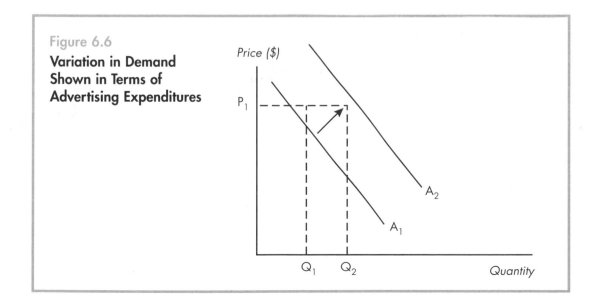

Figure 6.6

Variation in Demand Shown in Terms of Advertising Expenditures

budget from Pu_1 to Pu_2 translates to an increase in the quantity sold, from Q_1 to Q_2. The effect on demand of a change in each variable, individually or combined, could also be determined.

6.6 PRICE AND MARKET SEGMENTATION

So far, demand has been represented here as a continuous curve. In reality, however, it is a set of several small curves representing the demand for each segment of a market. Figure 6.7 illustrates this concept.

The car provides an excellent example. If there were such a thing as a generic car, there would be three market segments based on price: one segment wishing to buy a top-of-the-line car (segment 1); another segment wanting a moderately priced vehicle (segment 3); and, between these two, another segment (segment 2). A slight increase in price may not lead to lost sales in any particular segment. Beyond a certain point, however, the consumer may decide to forget about buying the product (segment 3) or may find the product at a lower price (segments 1 and 2).

The same pattern appears in the theatre market. Some people are prepared to pay a high price for an orchestra seat (segment 1), some are looking for low-cost tickets anywhere in the theatre (segment 3), and some want a moderately priced ticket (segment 2). For each segment, the price may vary slightly without necessarily translating to lost sales. Beyond a certain point, however, theatre-goers may opt for a lower-priced ticket for a lesser seat rather than miss enjoying the product completely. This would explain the variation in demand by price bracket in the Ford Foundation example.

The link between the notion of segmentation and the price variable helps explain certain results obtained by surveys focusing

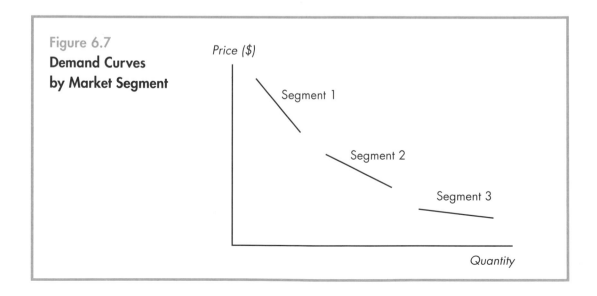

Figure 6.7
Demand Curves by Market Segment

on barriers to attendance at arts events. A study conducted in the United States,[6] for example, reveals that 64.2% of respondents cited "difficult to make time to go out" as their reason for not going out more often, while 53.2% said that "tickets are too expensive." An Australian study[7] arrives at similar results (lack of time/too busy 31%, cost/ too expensive 19%). In fact, these two reasons correspond to two different market segments.[8] On the one hand, the professionals and white-collar workers who account for a large proportion of performing arts audiences lack the time to attend the shows they would like to see and are even willing to pay more for a flexible subscription or for the guarantee that they will enjoy the show they attend (as in the case of shows given an extended run); on the other hand, students and retirees are interested in obtaining cheaper tickets because they are often on a tight budget. A strategy that would offer an across-the-board price reduction to all audience categories would translate into the company unnecessarily depriving itself of revenue without obtaining the desired effect, since a segment of the company's audience is insensitive to price.

The demand curve actually represents the over-all demand for a given product, considering each segment of the market and thus the average trend in terms of demand for that product.

6.7 PRICING STRATEGIES

In setting prices, a company must choose among several strategies, each one likely to influence consumer perceptions and, hence, the level of product consumption.

6.7.1 Skimming and Penetration

Skimming and penetration strategies are used primarily in the launching of new products.

The company that opts for the skimming strategy is introducing its product at a high price in order to earn the maximum profits per unit sold. This strategy targets a public prepared to pay a high price to consume a specific product. The vendor sells fewer units but at a higher price, in order to benefit from the substantial earnings generated initially by skimming. The company may later lower its prices gradually in order to reach more price-sensitive consumers. This strategy can be applied if the product is unique, has unique attributes, projects prestige, or enjoys a near monopoly. Obviously a market segment that is not price-sensitive yet likely to buy the product is essential.

The market-penetration strategy, on the other hand, consists of selling as many units as possible by setting the price as low as possible. The company realizes a relatively small profit per unit, but counts on the number of units sold to generate substantial profits. This strategy targets large market segments and budget-conscious consumers. The penetration strategy usually allows a company to cover its product design and launching costs more slowly than does the skimming strategy.

Although these strategies are usually applied to the launching of new products, skimming may sometimes also apply in the growth stage of a product. For example, a new show may be so popular that it is held over. In this case, when announcing extra dates, the company may choose to increase its ticket prices, since the show's popularity makes the audience less price-conscious.

Table 6.1 compares these two strategies.

6.7.2 Price Reductions

Rarely is a product sold at the same price to all consumers. All companies define policies to encourage consumption, reward loyalty, or adapt temporarily to the market environment.

According to Filion,[9] the price reductions most frequently applied by commercial enterprises are functional reductions, quantity discounts, seasonal reductions, discounts, and indemnities. These strategies are also used in the cultural milieu. Below is a brief description of each type.

The manager of a distribution channel may use functional reductions to encourage retailer loyalty. The manager lowers the price for the wholesaler, which actually increases the wholesaler's profit margin – for example, 40% rather than 30% – assuming that the wholesaler will then reduce the price the retailer pays.

Quantity discounts work to encourage those along the distribution channel to buy more each time so that they increase their inventory, which helps the manufacturer gain space. This type of reduction also allows companies to lower their handling and delivery costs. The same principle applies to the arts. The subscription customer pays a reduced admission fee by buying tickets to a series of shows. In return, the promoter is guaranteed a minimum

---

Table 6.1

Comparison of Two Strategies: Skimming and Penetration

	Skimming	Penetration
Definition	High initial price Step-by-step decreases to reach more segments	Initially low price keeps competition to a minimum and allows for long-term profits
Objective	Maximization of short-term profits	Maximization of long-term profits
Advantages	Costs soon absorbed Profit from the start	Rapid market penetration Large market share Reduced competition
Prior conditions	Superior product, difficult to copy Segment relatively indifferent to price	Price-conscious market Potential for long-term economies of scale

earning per production – in other words, less risk and a better take, since some revenue is collected in advance.

Seasonal reductions are used to encourage members of the distribution channel to order merchandise in advance – that is, before the season actually starts. This form of reduction shifts the burden of storing or warehousing merchandise to the wholesaler and retailer.

A discount is a reduction in the selling price given by the vendor to a purchaser paying an invoice within a certain time frame.

Indemnities are granted to distribution-channel members to encourage them to promote the company's product – for instance, refunding part of the retailers' promotional efforts to encourage them to make such efforts.

6.7.3 Prestige Pricing

Price has a psychological influence on the consumer's evaluation of the product. A high price tag raises expectations and, paradoxically, reduces the perceived risk. In fact, a high price usually reassures shoppers and even represents a "gold seal" of quality.

Although quality is almost always associated with high prices, the latter are not always associated with quality. At one time or another, every shopper learns this expensive lesson through personal experience. The association of high prices with quality is based only on subjective criteria and is not necessarily believed by all consumers. This association depends largely on their past experiences, their knowledge and awareness of the product, and their trust in the company promoting the product.

The link between quality and price does, however, enable a company to set relatively high prices by highlighting the prestige associated with the consumption of certain products. The world tour of the "Three Tenors" and the benefit galas frequently organized by museums are examples of strategies based on prestige pricing.

Prestige pricing actually increases the value associated with consuming a product, thus lending it an "added value" and reducing the perceived risk while generating greater profit for the company. The value-added component attracts a certain category of consumers who are label- or designer-conscious. This segment of the market may not have been tapped previously through strategies based on other variables in the marketing mix. In a strategy based on prestige pricing, real psychological or physical advantages sought by the targetted clientele must be offered. If not, the strategy may backfire. For example, the directors of the Ravinia Festival in the United States decided to open a private restaurant carrying a membership fee of $5,000 and offering members private parking near the main entrance to the Festival; company presidents can entertain guests at the restaurant prior to the concert and are offered a brief presentation of the evening's program; after the concert, members can mingle with the artists over dessert and refreshments.[10]

As figure 6.8 shows, the number of units consumed, or the demand, increases as the price decreases until point A is reached. After that, the relationship flips and the demand decreases along with the price. One explanation for this phenomenon lies in the

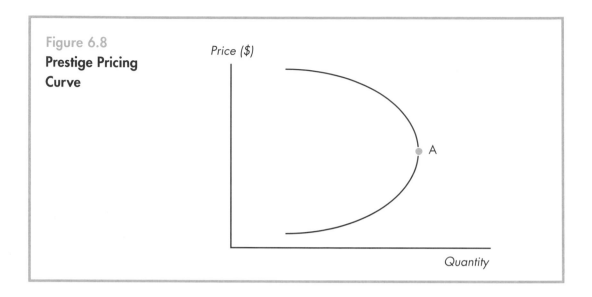

Figure 6.8
Prestige Pricing Curve

Price ($)

A

Quantity

fact that consumers seeking a prestige product want to stand out in a crowd. Of course, once all and sundry can have the product, the reason for buying it disappears. Conversely, those who do not want to be identified with another social class by their consumer behaviour may refuse to buy the same product even when it becomes readily affordable.

6.8 BAUMOL'S LAW

No chapter on price as a variable would be complete without some mention of what is now called Baumol's Law. Baumol is an American author whose seminal articles[11] (1967) examined the structural problems experienced by companies in the performing arts in terms of rising production costs. Baumol defines the problem as follows. First, performers' salaries rise more slowly than the wages earned by other workers

throughout the economy. Second, performers' salaries constitute the largest part of the production costs in the performing arts. Lastly and paradoxically, production costs for a live show increase faster than those in the over-all economy. Let us look at the reasons for this state of affairs.

Commercial enterprises set their prices according to the expenses they incur. In order to produce a good or a service, another amount, the mark-up, is then added to this price to ensure a profit. Mass production lets the commercial firm save substantially by spreading out its fixed costs and a percentage of the salaries over a larger number of units. This lowers unit costs considerably. What is more important, however, is that these firms are in a position to benefit from increased productivity through technological advances or reduced manufacturing times. By enhancing productivity, they can both lower their prices and raise their employees' salaries.

Salary increases do not raise total production costs; they simply spread the decrease in production costs between a price reduction and a salary increase.

Production costs for works in the performing arts cannot be lowered by increasing productivity, which is essentially linked to labour costs that cannot be shrunk any further. A Shakespearean tragedy requires the number of actors scripted. Beethoven's symphonies always require the same number of musicians playing for the same amount of time as when the symphonies were first composed. Logically, it would follow that an increase in salaries cannot be compensated for by a decrease in labour costs. Neither the number of employees nor the amount of time needed to assemble the product can be reduced. In other words, productivity cannot be improved. Therefore, a company in the performing arts cannot increase artists' salaries without increasing revenues. According to Baumol's research, American companies in the arts give lower pay increases than their counterparts in other sectors. Unlike other sectors, the arts see production costs rise more sharply, since artistic enterprises cannot take advantage of a gain in productivity.

This paradox helps to explain why the price of tickets to live performances must increase faster than the over-all consumer price index. Inflation actually represents the average of the prices asked by firms with high productivity gains and firms that cannot gain such productivity. The sectors that experience gains in productivity and lower their prices accordingly produce a decrease in the inflation rate, while others that cannot declare productivity improvements cannot lower their prices. But if the latter do not increase salaries, employees suffer a reduction of their revenues because of the increase in the cost of living. In order to be able to raise employees' salaries, these companies must increase their ticket prices to be able to cover these extra costs; in so doing, they put pressure on the price index. Organizations that can gain in productivity do not have to increase their prices in order to pay their staff better, since they can do that by sacrificing a portion of these productivity gains.

Baumol concludes that for companies in the performing arts to have the financial resources needed to increase performers' salaries at the same rate as organizations in other sectors, ticket prices – or public subsidies and private donations – would have to increase at a rate well above that of inflation.

In a nutshell, the greater the productivity gains in the over-all economy, the more the arts sector suffers. Conversely, the lower the productivity gains, the healthier the arts sector will be.

SUMMARY

For most pricing decisions concerning cultural products, the marketing manager or executive must consider not only the money associated with the good or service, but also the expenses related to the purchase and even the consumer's effort, which may be physical or psychological or both and includes the notion of perceived risk.

Price elasticity is a term used to describe the relationship between the set price and the quantity of goods bought by consumers. This relationship is elastic if, for a change in price, the number of products consumed varies more than proportionally to the change. The opposite occurs when, after a price change, the amount consumed is less than proportional to the price change. The notion of elasticity also applies to the other three variables in the marketing mix.

Consumers do not base their decision to buy a product on price alone. Other factors affect their thinking. These psychological factors influence the demand curve, which leads to different levels of demand according to market segment and product. In some extreme cases, this curve rebounds through "prestige pricing."

Pricing decisions must be made according to the objective a company targets through its pricing strategy. There are four main objectives. They are related to profits, sales, competitive balance, and corporate image.

There are also several price-setting methods available, including customer-based, competition-based, and cost-based pricing.

Price may be used as a strategic tool. A firm may use the skimming strategy (relatively high price, lower sales) or the penetration strategy (relatively low price, high number of units sold). There are a whole range of price-reduction strategies as well: functional reductions, quantity discounts, seasonal reductions, discounts, and indemnities. In the cultural sector, there are also reductions for seniors and for less desirable seats.

Lastly, the arts sector suffers from an inherent structural weakness expressed eloquently in Baumol's Law. Baumol showed why it is impossible to increase productivity and how labour costs dominate in the performing arts. As a result, commercial and non-commercial enterprises within the arts sector find themselves in a vicious circle in which admission fees must rise higher than the consumer price index.

QUESTIONS

1. Why should we associate the notion of risk with the price of a product?
2. Briefly explain the notion of elasticity in pricing.
3. How is the demand curve a combination of several curves related to different market segments?
4. What is the psychological price?
5. Compare and contrast the four categories of price-setting goals.
6. What are the advantages and disadvantages of each price-setting method?
7. What objectives does the penetration strategy target?
8. What roles do price-reduction strategies play?
9. Can you explain Baumol's Law?

Notes

1. Book S.H., and S. Globerman. 1974. *The Audience for the Performing Arts*. Toronto: Ontario Arts Council.

2. Oxenfeldt, A.R. 1975. *Pricing Strategies*. New York: AMACOM.

3. Filion, M. 1995. "Les décisions concernant le prix," in *Gestion du marketing, 2e édition*, F. Colbert and M. Filion, eds. Boucherville, Quebec: Gaëtan Morin Éditeur, chapter 7, p. 207–259.

4. Beaulac, M., and C. Duhaime. 1993. *Les droits d'entrée dans les institutions muséales: une recherche empirique*. Preliminary Report. Montreal: Chaire de gestion des arts, École des HEC.

5. Ford Foundation. 1974. *The Finances of the Performing Arts: Volume 2*. New York: Author.

6. National Endowment for the Arts. 1997. *Survey of Public Participation in the Arts: Summary Report*. Washington: Author, p. 26.

7. Roy Morgan Research. 1997. *Theatre Audience in Victoria*. South Melbourne, Australia (July), p. 6.

8. Colbert, F., C. Beauregard and L. Vallée. 1998. "The Importance of Ticket Prices for Theatre Patrons." *International Journal of Arts Management*, Vol. 1, n° 1 (Fall) p. 8–16. See also J. Scheff. 1999. "Factors Influencing Subscription and Single-Ticket Purchases at Performing Arts Organisations." *International Journal of Arts Management*, Vol. 1, n° 2 (Winter), p. 16–28.

9. Filion, M. 1995. "Les décisions concernant le prix," in *Gestion du marketing, 2e édition*, F. Colbert and M. Filion, eds. Boucherville, Quebec: Gaëtan Morin Éditeur, chapter 7, p. 207–259.

10. Cardinal, J., and L. Lapierre. 1999. "The Ravinia Festival Under the Direction of Zarin Metha." *International Journal of Arts Management*, Vol. 1, n° 3 (Spring), p. 70–84.

11. Baumol, W.J. 1967. "Performing Arts: The Permanent Crisis." *Business Horizons* (Autumn), p. 47–50.

For Further Reference

Dhalla, N.K. 1984. "A Guide to New Product Development Pricing Phase." *Canadian Business* (April).

Felton, M.V. 1989. "Major Influences on the Demand for Opera Tickets." *Journal of Cultural Economics*, Vol. 13, n° 1 (June), p. 53–64.

Ford, N.M., and B.J. Queram. 1984. *Pricing Strategies for the Performing Arts*. Madison, WI: Association of College, University and Community Arts Administrators.

Gabor, A., and C.W.J. Granger. 1966. "Price as an Indicator of Quality." *Economica* (February).

Plan

CHAPTER 7
The Place Variable

OBJECTIVES

- Know the three components of the place variable
- Describe the elements of a distribution channel
- Look at the main distribution strategies
- Define physical distribution
- Introduce the basic principles used in selecting a commercial location

INTRODUCTION

As we saw in chapter 3, the various intermediaries or agents handling a product along the channel from producer to consumer can be considered a fourth market for a cultural enterprise. The other markets are the state, consumers, sponsors, and distribution agents.

In the first section of this chapter, we define place as a variable and look closely at the distribution context for cultural products.

We start by studying the commercial ties among businesses and intermediaries along the distribution channel. Our focus then shifts slightly to the major strategies available to manufacturers whose marketing objectives are being met primarily through the place variable. We also examine the logistics involved in circulating goods within a network of "partners" – that is, physical distribution.

Lastly, we define the main elements to be considered in choosing the location of a business or cultural establishment.

The concepts discussed in this chapter apply to both the cultural industries and organizations active in the arts sector. In reality, application may vary according to the specific features of the products involved.

7.1   DEFINITION

7.1.1 The Three Elements of the Place Variable

The place variable includes three distinct elements: distribution channels, physical distribution, and commercial location.

Distribution channels or networks include all those who play a role in the flow of goods from producer to consumer.

Physical distribution refers to the fact that the product is offered to consumers according to decisions related to the logistics of distribution.

Store location is the choice of a physical site where the product can be bought or consumed – retail outlets, concert halls, museums, movie theatres, bookshops, or libraries.

7.1.2 Distribution of Cultural Products

In the cultural milieu, the consumer's form of consumption determines the product's mode of distribution.

There are products designed for collective consumption – products to which consumers gain access by gathering in one place for a set period of time. A show, an exhibition, and a film screened in a movie theatre are a few examples. There are also products designed for individual consumption, which consumers can enjoy whenever and wherever they desire. Recordings, books, and visual works of art owned by the consumer fall into this category. In the first category, there is a sequential distribution concept in touring shows and travelling exhibits. In the second category, the product may be distributed in the same fashion and even through the same network as any other consumer good.

This system for classifying products according to form of consumption reveals the important role played by the time, place, and duration of consumption (see table 7.1).

Table 7.1

The Consumer's Role in Determining the Place, Time, and Length of Consumption Activity

	Show	Exhibit	Film	Recording	Video-cassette	Book	Work of art
Place	−	−	±	+	+	+	+
Time	−	±	±	+	+	+	+
Length	−	+	−	−	−	+	+
Possession of technical dimension	−	−	−	+	+	+	+

Naturally, for some products the consumer has total control over when, where, and how long to consume. For example, a consumer may elect to read a novel at home, on the bus or subway, during lunchtime, and so on. The same consumer can decide when and how fast to read, whether to reread a passage, and so on. The theatre-goer, on the other hand, is not free to decide at any given time to attend a performance. For this consumer, travelling time, curtain time, and other factors must be known in advance.

There are also situations in which the consumer has a choice in two of the three aspects. For example, although a film may be presented for collective consumption, the same one may be playing simultaneously at several movie theatres, at different times. The consumer can thus pick the most convenient time and place. The museum-goer must visit the museum while it is open, but, with the possible exception of blockbuster exhibits, the exact day, time,

and length of the visit remain individual choices.

Besides place, time, and duration of consumption, there is the aspect of possession. Possession of the technical dimension of a product obviously gives an individual consumer greater flexibility.

From a managerial viewpoint, these different situations affect the pressures that a cultural organization experiences. In fact, the greater the consumer's choice in terms of place and time of consumption for a cultural product, the broader the marketing manager's range of distribution possibilities. Conversely, if product features restrict consumption, the manufacturer has less room to manoeuvre. For example, a publishing house can vary distribution routes or use more bookshops in order to offer its product to the widest possible potential readership. The promoter of a stage show, on the other hand, must necessarily tour regions in a certain order with a single version of the product. Since the latter situation often means being in the right place at the right time, a promoter's or marketing director's error in judgment is difficult to correct.

Risk also varies according to whether the choice of place and time depends on the consumer or the producer. When the consumer has some control, as is the case for recordings, books, or videos, the product can be consumed after purchase. This is not the case for products whose consumption cannot be postponed, such as stage shows or exhibits. In this case, consumers must choose among the products offered at that time. This distribution restriction increases the risk for live-performance products.

In short, the form of consumption unique to many different cultural products necessarily implies management of the place variable, which, in turn, is affected by the product. Hence distribution channels, physical distribution, and the location where customers buy or consume the product may need to be adapted to the product.

7.2   DISTRIBUTION CHANNELS

A distribution channel includes all of the different agents who bridge the gap between the producer, or manufacturer, and the end consumer. These are paid intermediaries who may never actually take possession of the product yet intervene in the production and consumption process. In the cultural milieu, this description would apply to all the intermediaries who make works accessible to the consumer. The producer of a good or a service and the consumer are part of this channel. The total number of agents, and hence their func-

tions, may vary from one company to the next.

Any decision related to the choice of a distribution channel and the various agents involved is important, since the company is simultaneously establishing business relationships with a number of "partners," and the quality of those relationships can spell the success or failure of future marketing strategies. Moreover, once a company signs a distribution agreement with agents, it loses some flexibility, so that modifying marketing strategies later on becomes more difficult. On the other hand, the choice of distribution channel influences the other variables of the marketing mix. Pricing, for instance, is a result of the number, quality, and size of the distribution agents used. The type of promotion required also depends on the channel selected. Of course, manufacturers cannot always choose their intermediaries. Food producers, for example, cannot always convince supermarket owners to stock their products. In the arts, it is often the presenter who decides on the show to be presented in a particular theatre, rather than the reverse. Similarly, bookshop owners may refuse to put certain novels on their shelves.

Naturally, a manufacturer is not forced to use agents and intermediaries. There is always the possibility of selling directly to the end consumer. Direct distribution is not always feasible, however, in the performing arts. A touring company, for example, rarely has the human and financial resources required to produce its show in all the cities visited. Record companies and publishing firms face the same situation. Put simply, intermediaries fulfil a number of key functions. This explains why producers entrust intermediaries with the distribution of their product. In doing so, however, producers relinquish a share of their power over the actual sale of the product and also distance themselves from their clientele. This loss of power may create friction among the various members of the distribution network.

7.2.1 The Functions of an Intermediary

The intermediary's primary function is to reduce the number of contacts the producer or manufacturer must maintain to reach a given number of customers. The simple example shown in figure 7.1 illustrates this idea. Without an intermediary,

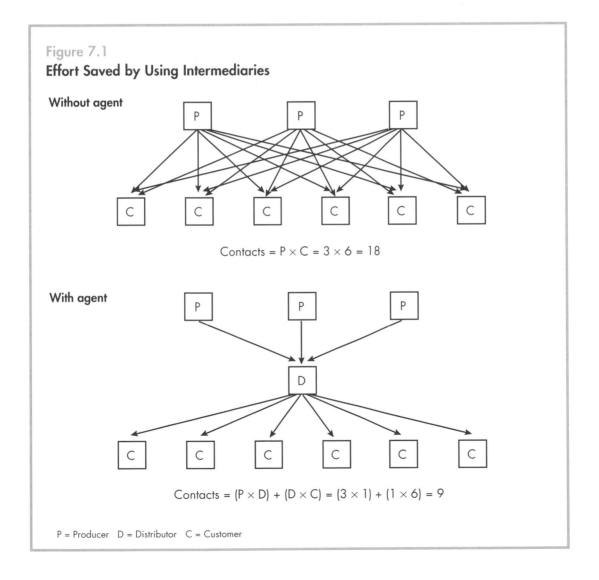

Figure 7.1
Effort Saved by Using Intermediaries

Without agent

Contacts = P × C = 3 × 6 = 18

With agent

Contacts = (P × D) + (D × C) = (3 × 1) + (1 × 6) = 9

P = Producer   D = Distributor   C = Customer

the manufacturer in this example must make eighteen contacts to reach six customers, whereas with an intermediary the number is cut in half. Applied across any country, given the number of consumers and manufacturers plus the distances from one community to the next, this pattern could easily multiply into millions of contacts.

Intermediaries do more than reduce the number of contacts among the various players within a market; they perform several other important functions. Table 7.2 presents these functions in three categories: logistics, commercial, and support.

All along the distribution channel, various agents handle some of the logistics involved in distributing a product. Not only do they look after transportation and warehousing, but, more importantly, they enable a company to adjust the quantity and variety of the product. This point is significant, since consumers usually buy small quantities of products produced by different manufacturers – for example, one or two compact disks, a couple of novels. Manufacturers may, however, release a large quantity of a few products so as to benefit from the economies of scale described in chapter 6. As mentioned above, intermediaries allow a company to make adjustments in the quantity and selection of products sold by offering a specific number of products from different companies. As a result, consumers can find what they want in one place and manufacturers or producers can respect their standards of quality.

The distribution channel is valuable in terms of commercial as well as logistical functions. When agents negotiate and sign agreements, they take possession of the product – if not physically, at least legally. They also handle product promotion and deal with customers. The producer of a show, for example, may provide some of the advertising material needed but also assigns to the presenter or theatre owner the task of advertising the artists performing that season. The presenter actually communicates with the consumer and provides customer services, such as reservations, tickets, and coat check. The producer benefits from the presenter's experience, knowledge of the local market, and corporate image. The producer who does not use the services of an intermediary must take on all these responsibilities and tasks without necessarily having the appropriate infrastructure.

Support services allow a company to delegate other important responsibilities to an intermediary. In agreeing to sign a contract with a producer, the presenter takes on

Table 7.2	
The Functions of a Distribution Channel	
Logistic function	Changes • in quality • in variety
Commercial function	Product purchasing Negotiations Promotions Contacts
Support function	Risk-taking Financing Research

some of the risk associated with an artist's performance and, at the same time, assumes some of the financing involved – for example, promotional expenditures. Usually more "in touch" with the consumer, the presenter can often provide a wealth of information.

Obviously, the different functions carried out by intermediaries vary according to the type of distribution channel used. In some cases, intermediaries assume all the functions described above, while in other cases these functions are shared by different partners along the channel.

7.2.2 Types of Distribution Channels

The number of different intermediaries per level along the distribution channel determines whether it can be called complex or not. Figure 7.2 describes the different types of distribution channels. The simplest is obviously the producer selling directly to the consumer. In the arts, this form of distribution could be a theatre company that owns its own venue. Longer channels could be the film producer using a distributor who deals with movie theatres or a string quartet using an agent to find a presenter.

The use of a direct distribution channel does not necessarily mean, however, that the company is content to distribute its product at a single venue. For example, the Royal Armouries Museum in London, England, which has been housed in the Tower of London since its founding in the fifteenth century, decided to adopt an alternative approach to reaching a broader public.[1] In partnership with private enterprise,

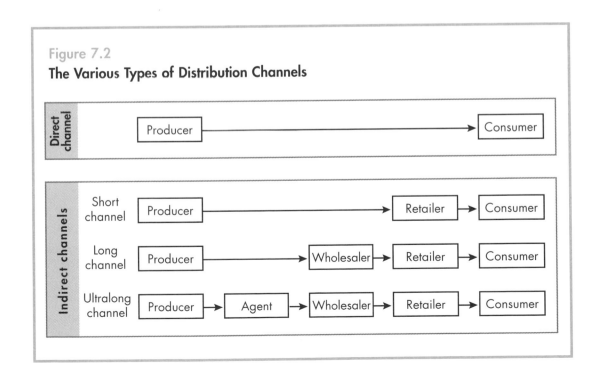

Figure 7.2
The Various Types of Distribution Channels

Direct channel
Producer → Consumer

Indirect channels
Short channel: Producer → Retailer → Consumer
Long channel: Producer → Wholesaler → Retailer → Consumer
Ultralong channel: Producer → Agent → Wholesaler → Retailer → Consumer

the Museum opened two additional sites, one in Portsmouth and the other in Leeds. This expansion has allowed the museum to display more of its collection while reaching a wider audience.

Figure 7.2 covers all the realities of the cultural milieu; it should be noted that the partners at each stage of distribution may be assigned different titles and functions in specific sectors. In the performing arts, for example, there are often a producer, an agent, and a presenter; however, this is not the only network possible. A producer may decide to deal directly with the presenter without an agent. In fact, a firm may decide to distribute its product via several different distribution channels. In the publishing world, for instance, books are sold through at least three different channels: retailers, schools and libraries, and direct sales. In the film industry, it is only when the end consumer is about to view the product that distribution becomes fragmented. Distributors receive the film from the producer, then use one of five different ways to reach the consumer – movie theatre, video club, pay TV, traditional TV, or non-profit network. In the recording industry, consumers can turn to record shops, department stores, or mail-order clubs.

Even though a particular type of distribution network may dominate within a given sector, one firm may decide to turn to a different distribution system that suits its particular needs or products or takes advantage of its ability to take charge of certain functions performed by the distribution channel. The more intermediaries in the distribution network, the higher the price of the product, since each intermediary must cover costs; it follows logically that the firm that manages to take over one portion of the distribution process can increase profits while still offering customers highly competitive prices.

The main disadvantage of the long distribution channel is a lack of flexibility. This disadvantage is a result of the large number of intermediaries, which essentially reduces a manufacturer's ability to manoeuvre. Another disadvantage is a lack of control over the way the product is sold. The higher the number of intermediaries, the more distant and less influential a manufacturer becomes. On the other hand, the producer's costs are lower with a long channel. For example, the sales force is generally reduced to a minimum, since the company deals with a limited number of agents.

In short, the advantages of a long distribution channel correspond to the disadvantages of a short one, and vice versa. The smaller the number of intermediaries, the greater a company's influence on the marketing of its product. On the other hand, the shorter the channel, the higher the producer's costs.

The manufacturer's choice of distributors, distribution route, and order of distribution can be highly strategic. In the case of the movie E.T., the film's producer chose to retain the distribution rights for the film in video format in order to maximize box-office sales before releasing the title to video clubs.

As already pointed out, a company cannot always choose its distribution route or even the distribution agents who actually sell its product. Indeed, theatrical touring companies may find that there is only one presenter in town, with whom they must necessarily do business. As a monopoly, that presenter has a strategic advantage over the producer in negotiating contracts. The tables are turned, of course, once a star is involved. A well-known entertainer represents a safe bet, or known commodity, for the local promoter, who must include a few low- or no-risk productions in any given season to offset the risks associated with lesser-known performers or harder-to-sell shows. The agent of a well-known artist has the upper hand in negotiating the performer's contract.

In the world of Canadian film production, many entrepreneurs have been frustrated by their inability to have their films adequately distributed in their own country. This has resulted from Hollywood's historical domination of the distribution outlets – cinemas in every Canadian city and town from coast to coast. Thus, the problem for many Canadian film-makers is a problem of access to the channel; in 1994-1995, while 59% of the total number of theatres, including drive-ins, were chain theatres, they accounted for 85% of total attendance.[2] By way of comparison, American films account for only 57.4% of total attendance in France.[3]

7.2.3 Managing the Distribution Channel

Mallen[4] outlines the main aspects of distribution management using four objectives and six strategic decisions.

In general, manufacturers use a distribution channel to maximize their profits. In order to do so, they must keep the various intermediaries along the channel motivated.

Maximizing profits means first maximizing sales (objective 1), then minimizing costs (objective 2). A firm must consider its maximum profit margin over both the long and the short terms, since in some situations it may be preferable to sacrifice immediate profits for the long-term betterment of the firm. Hence the firm's destiny is tied to that of the intermediaries. Since the intermediaries have a stake in the company's future, they develop a relationship similar to a partnership. Here the idea of maximizing motivation takes on its full meaning, since motivating the distribution agents, or "partners," has a definite impact on the manufacturer's financial health. A bookseller, for example, may decide to showcase one particular publisher's books. Similarly, a distributor may promote one artist more than another. In other words, maximizing motivation among the members of the distribution route meets two more of the manufacturer's objectives: maximize co-operation along the route (objective 3) and maximize the manufacturer's influence on the members (objective 4). If the manufacturer obtains maximum co-operation from each member, the place-variable functions are handled efficiently. Nevertheless, the manufacturer must maintain a healthy level of influence over the various partners.

The company seeking long-term maximum profits or the non-profit group striving for long-term financial stability must build up a distribution network that meets the following six criteria, presented here as a series of choices. These basic criteria deal with the choice and length of the distribution channel, and the distribution strategy (intensive, selective, exclusive), as well as the number and selection of intermediaries over-all and at each stage of distribution.

The first decision is exemplified by a classical-music ensemble that must choose between hiring an agent and using its own sales force to organize a tour. The choice depends on the sales objectives set by the ensemble, the costs involved, and the amount of co-operation and influence (real and desired) it expects. Obviously, it is easier to exert influence on an employee seen daily than on an outside agent with other clients. On the other hand, the set cost that an employee's salary represents is higher than an agent's commission, which often depends on that agent's productivity. In fact, distribution at the international level frequently requires using a foreign agent well acquainted with both the local market and potential customers.

A company must also decide on a distribution strategy: Is it better to use as many distribution partners as possible, or to select only those which meet specific criteria (see section 7.3)? The exact number of intermediaries (agent, wholesaler, retailer) at each of the different stages of distribution can then be set.

Once a company has decided on the distribution strategy, the length of the distribution channel, and the number of intermediaries at each level, it must decide which type of intermediary is most likely to meet corporate objectives. The ideal intermediary will fulfil the functions set out by the company. For example, a record company or book publisher may opt for distribution in department stores, where musical expertise or literary advice is almost non-existent, rather than be associated with a chain of specialized shops where sales clerks might advise the customer.

The producer must also decide how many routes to use. Should the latest film be marketed right away in movie theatres and in video clubs? Should another distribution possibility, such as pay TV, be included? All of these questions (and possibly more) should be answered in the decision-making process.

Once these four decisions have been made, the manufacturer or producer must decide how much help to give the various partners – for example: What kind of promotional material? How much material?

Lastly, the firm must decide on the individual intermediary. For example, if a large museum wishes to hold an exhibition in several different regions, it must select the appropriate venues with the necessary technical equipment or capacity (size of halls, standard display conditions, etc.). The firm can then decide on the various candidates according to whatever museological and marketing criteria it chooses.

7.2.4 The Behaviour of Distribution-Channel Members

One of the fundamentals of distribution management is controlling the behaviour of the members along the channel. The distribution channel should not be seen simply as the flow of merchandise from producer to consumer, since it is also a social network in which interpersonal relations play an important role in the over-all dynamics. Rosenbloom[5] describes four key dimensions in this social network: conflict, power, roles, and communication.

Misunderstandings in distribution should be considered normal, unless, of course, they turn into conflicts that could paralyze channel activities. Conflicts can arise in various ways – for instance, the parties may have poor communications, a different definition of each partner's role, diverging views on the responsibility inherent in certain decisions, or even contradictory objectives. The distribution manager must always be on the look-out for potential "hot spots," be able to judge their impact on the firm, and be able to decide how to resolve problematic situations in the best interest of all concerned.

Any company using partners to bring its product to market seeks to influence the different members of its distribution channel so that certain tasks are accomplished properly. The following means can be used to that end. Partners may be rewarded, monetarily or otherwise, or penalized, especially when the company is larger than the other members. Legitimacy granted by the members at the previous level is also required here; otherwise the whole system falters. Some agreement on the outcome is also needed so that everyone feels like a team player. Lastly, corporate expertise is needed so that the members conform to the company's will.

The knowledgeable distribution manager will also have a definite idea of the roles each member along the channel should play. Once each member knows what to expect from the others, relations generally run more smoothly. Naturally, the producer or manufacturer must also convince the various partners to accept their own role and that of the others.

As in any other human enterprise, communication and information are fundamental in distribution management. Conflicts between two different partners can arise from a simple difference of opinion caused solely by poor communication. The absence of vital information can actually poison the marketing of a product.

7.3 DISTRIBUTION STRATEGIES

Below is a description of two major types of distribution strategies: intensive, selective, and exclusive strategies, and push and pull strategies.

7.3.1 Intensive, Selective, and Exclusive Distribution Strategies

The intensive distribution strategy involves the maximum distribution of a product through as many points of sale as possible. In this strategy, the producer makes no selection among retailers interested in carrying its product. The recording and publishing industries provide numerous examples of intensive distribution.

Selective distribution involves selecting retailers according to specific criteria. This form of distribution prevents retailers from all offering the same product. The selection process corresponds to specific objectives often linked to corporate image. Companies using the selective distribution strategy are actually trying to control their image and ensure that their retailers or partners have a positive image or enjoy a reputation for credibility in the milieu. This strategy can also create a certain sense of product uniqueness or rarity by limiting the number of points of sale, so that the consumer must shop at specific, carefully chosen places to obtain or consume the product.

In the visual arts, some artists choose the galleries with which they wish to do business. In doing so, they exclude competing galleries that would like to sell their works. Once manufacturers select the retailers with whom they will do business and grant them exclusivity, they are said to be using the exclusive strategy. In this case, the retailer enjoys the monopoly for a given product within a specific territory. Film producers often use this strategy when granting exclusive distribution rights for a film to a distributor in a specific region or territory.

7.3.2 Push and Pull Strategies

The push strategy consists of offering a higher profit margin to retailers so that they will work harder to promote and sell a given product to their clientele. Manufacturers can offer this additional margin by reducing their advertising budget. They assume that a retailer earning higher profits on one brand will work harder to sell that brand.

The pull strategy, on the other hand, involves massive investments in advertising to generate sufficiently strong demand that will make retailers want to sell the product in order to please their customers.

Both strategies may be applied to cultural products. The pull strategy is used by some record distributors, such as K-Tel Records, or various American record companies handling stars like Michael Jackson. Most producers, however, tend to use the push strategy.

Many manufacturers have turned to push tactics by strategic default rather than

design. As a strategy, pull requires a hefty initial outlay, which small firms cannot always afford. In the performing arts, for example, touring companies usually do not have the resources to launch a vast promotional campaign to attract an audience. Only the company's renown or reputation earned through previous products may incite promoters to buy a product. It would seem that in the case of a well-known performer or group, the producer necessarily returns to the pull strategy. Major media coverage in a large city often acts as a pole attracting provincial or regional audiences. The success of a touring Broadway show, such as *Cats, Les Misérables,* or *Miss Saigon,* depends on both its Broadway success and its ongoing success.

7.3.3 How the Strategies Interrelate

The two main types of pricing strategy (chapter 6) and the two main types of distribution strategy (section 7.3) have been presented separately; however, in reality they are closely linked.

By using the skimming strategy, a company sells its product at a price higher than the competitor's. As a result, it sells fewer units yet generates a higher profit margin per unit. The strategy is successful only if the company earns a fine reputation or projects a prestigious image. This type of reputation or image is easier to achieve using selective or exclusive distribution strategies, which are generally associated with a push strategy. The penetration pricing strategy, which consists of selling as many units as possible at the lowest possible price, goes hand in hand with the pull strategy or the intensive distribution strategy.

7.4 PHYSICAL DISTRIBUTION

Physical distribution consists of all the logistics and transportation involved in bringing a product to market. Key distribution questions are: Where will the product be sold? How will it be shipped there? The various components of physical distribution are shipping, warehousing, inventory management, order processing, and merchandise handling and packaging.

The way in which a company manages its physical distribution is very important. Wise decisions involving the logistics of product distribution can reduce marketing costs significantly. Conversely, poor decisions can lead to major expenses and actually alter the image consumers have of the company. Distribution management is all the more delicate since the two physical distribution objectives – minimize costs and maximize customer service – are contradictory.

The general condition required to maximize customer service is a short ordering cycle with no product shortages and no shipping errors. This umbrella condition implies that a company must maintain a large inventory and therefore rent or own substantial warehousing facilities. Obviously, these facilities represent an equally substantial cost. Also needed are delivery facilities, qualified staff, and order and inventory-control systems capable of handling customer orders efficiently. Often, the corporate decision-making process hinges on the following two questions: What is the optimal inventory level required to avoid exceeding x number of shortages during a given period? What degree of quality is required, in terms of the labour and inventory-management systems, so that the ordering cycle does not exceed x number of days? Both questions are extremely important strategically, especially in a highly competitive market.

The conditions mentioned above are applicable in the cultural industries, in which a large number of physical units, such as records or books, are distributed. In other sectors, however, the idea of customer service, a fundamental aspect of physical distribution, applies even though stocking, warehousing, and ordering cycles are not involved.

Although their goods are not material, producers in the performing arts do have to determine how the product will be distributed to the public. The many parameters to consider include choice of cities on a tour, selection of venues, and ticket-sales techniques (mail order, automated ticket counter). These decisions must be made according to the company's distribution strategies. The company must strive for quality in suitable and diversified modes of distribution, such as ticket sales, since quality and diversity are two key aspects of customer service.

In large cities, where competition is fierce, the quality of customer service can play a crucial role. The potential audience member trying to reach a theatre company's box office may give up if the line is always busy, and may even call another theatre. If there is only one acceptable alternative, their second choice is obvious. However, if consumers can choose among three, four, or five acceptable theatres, they may hesitate, since they may well be indifferent to the alternatives. In this case, ease of ticket availability may be the determining factor. If tickets to their first choice are unavailable, they will opt for their second choice.

7.5 COMMERCIAL LOCATION

Physical distribution consists of making a product accessible to the consumer. Location is the physical site where the product is bought or consumed. Points of sale or showrooms must be accessible, since consumers' effort is directly proportional to their interest in the product. As seen in chapter 2, products may be divided into three categories – convenience goods, shopping goods, and specialty goods – according to the amount of effort the consumer is prepared to make in buying them. The cultural product is defined as a specialized purchase even if the consumer's behaviour may push a particular product into the "shopping goods" category.

In any event, the amount of effort a consumer will expend is limited. If the physical location is off the beaten path and difficult to reach or if the product is offered at inconvenient hours, the potential consumer will react. The Montreal Musée d'art contemporain provides an excellent example of the power of location. Until moving downtown and next to Place des Arts, this museum struggled at Cité du Havre, a location off the Island of Montreal, far from the city's other cultural venues and poorly served by the public transit system. Not long ago, most museums were open weekdays only from nine to five; now, museums cater to their clientele by remaining open evenings and weekends. Hours and parking have become key factors affecting attendance figures. Various geographical and physical features, such as a bridge, a railroad crossing, or an industrial park, can also play a psychological and decisive role in limiting a consumer's choice of leisure activities.

The status and size of a city also influence the consumer. Consumers living in a suburb of a large city and even in nearby towns will travel downtown to attend a show. The opposite, however, is not necessarily true.

Several factors come into play in choosing a location. Access by public transit, parking, food and beverage services, and other factors must all be considered.

In both retail and the arts, the best location is one near several other establishments. The appeal or attraction of a group of businesses has a synergizing effect that an isolated enterprise simply cannot achieve. Large shopping centres in North America rely on this principle to draw their clientele. The downtown Toronto lakefront area provides the example of Ontario Place and Harbourfront Centre, joined in summertime by the Canadian National Exhibition. Another obvious example is the concentration of theatres in the Broadway district of New York.

7.5.1 The Trading Area Principle

A trading area may be defined as "the geographical space from which a sales outlet draws its clientele and sales."[6]

The appeal of a particular point of sale is far from uniform within any territory. In fact, the farther away the consumer goes from the point of sale, the lesser the attraction of that location. This variation in intensity of attraction leads to a threefold division within a trading area. The three subdivisions are called primary, secondary, and tertiary trading areas.

7.5.2 Definition of the Three Trading Areas

The primary trading area includes customers from the main population served by the sales unit – in other words, the densest part of the overall area in terms of number of customers reached. Depending on the type of business, the geographic features of the location, or the sociodemographic profile of its residents, this area can represent up to 80% of the clientele. For a shop, the primary trading area is the most important geographic sector, since most of its business relies on the area that includes the most faithful customers.

The secondary trading area includes the second most important consumer population. Here, sales hover between 20% and 40% of the sales volume. This is the geographic sector in which a business is most vulnerable to aggressive competition.

The tertiary trading area is essentially a residual zone holding 10% to 20% of the clientele. These customers shop only occasionally at the store or visit it only by chance – for example, tourists. Every shop has a tertiary area, over which it has little or no influence.

Trading areas have irregular shapes, and competitors' areas may be superimposed according to the geographic features of a city or neighbourhood and the power of attraction of each competitor (see figure 7.3).

The configuration of a trading area depends largely on the type of product offered. A presenter with a varied program may find that some products reach a specific clientele and that a comparison by product category could reveal different contours for the trading areas.

Executives or managers who want to know what the trading area is for their sales unit need only take a sampling of their clientele, write down the addresses of their customers, and pinpoint them on a map of the city or area. The result is a cluster of points, each one representing a customer, as seen in figure 7.3. The next step is an analysis of the data gathered.

7.5.3 The Usefulness of the Trading Area Concept

The outline of a trading area is useful since it allows a business to accomplish the following eight goals.

1) Estimate the demand in dollars within the geographical territory covered and compare the demand to the sales figures already in hand. The resulting calculation is the firm's market share.

2) Estimate future demand and its impact on store sales figures, especially if residential construction is planned within the area.

3) Decide on long-, short-, and medium-term market shares and sales objectives.

4) Measure the impact of competition in the territory and within each of the three trading areas vis-à-vis the competition.

5) Seek to obtain a better grasp of the socio-economic profile of the population living in the "attraction" area of the sales unit in order to adapt the marketing mix to potential customers.

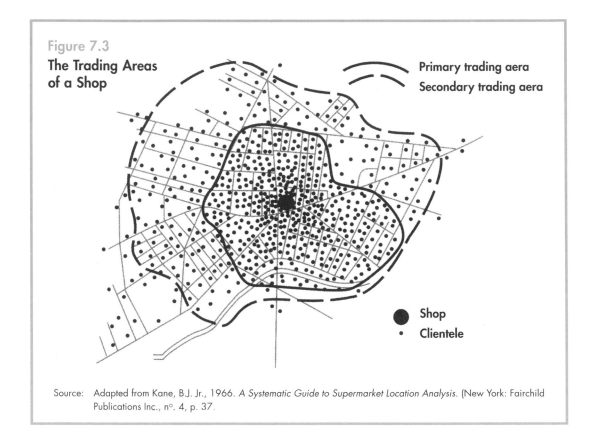

Figure 7.3

The Trading Areas of a Shop

— Primary trading aera

-- Secondary trading aera

● Shop

• Clientele

Source: Adapted from Kane, B.J. Jr., 1966. *A Systematic Guide to Supermarket Location Analysis.* (New York: Fairchild Publications Inc., n°. 4, p. 37.

6) Plan promotional campaigns according to potential consumers and the geographic limits of the attraction area. It could be that the firm is wasting time and money by distributing print ads in a territory larger than the trading area or, conversely, that the firm could improve its coverage.

7) Compare outlets of a chain and, through rigorous planning based on the potential trading area, open new units. If, for example, the future location has characteristics similar or identical to those of an existing outlet, a company might forecast its volume, the size of the territory, and even the size of the new store.

8) Plan expansion by either enlarging the current store or opening other outlets.

7.5.4 Factors Determining the Extent and Configuration of the Trading Area

The three main factors determining the extent and configuration of the trading area are the product, the company's marketing strategies, and the consumer's perception of the company or the product.

"Product" is used here in the generic sense, to connote all consumer goods. The commercial zone of shops selling convenience goods is normally limited to 2 kilometres, whereas the zone for shopping goods or specialty purchases may extend to 5, 10, or even 20 kilometres. Concert halls, museums, art galleries, bookstores, record shops, and movie theatres are all in the specialty or shopping-goods category and normally have extensive commercial zones.

The other variables in the marketing mix play a role in determining the extent and configuration of the trading area. A certain pricing policy or an exciting promotion may encourage some consumers to patronize one shop rather than another. The fact that one firm is targetting a specific market segment will bring a specific category of consumers who live in a certain neighbourhood and thus give the trading area its own particular shape. This is the case for most museums, art galleries, and concert halls, which generally attract an educated, well-heeled clientele. An analysis of where this clientele lives usually reveals a concentration within postal codes where the income is higher than average. The first three letters of the postal code are used in this type of analysis.

The extent and configuration of a trading area depends on how consumers perceive certain factors. Distance, for example, may be evaluated in terms of real or psycho-logical barriers found en route to the shop. The traffic, the number of traffic lights or stop signs, and even habit can make a consumer overestimate or underestimate the time and distance involved in going to a particular store. The real or physical path may be short, while the consumer is under the impression that the shop is far from home or another reference point. The opposite may also occur. Based on this perception, the trading area becomes rather elastic.

Some physical obstacles may actually change consumer behaviour. A river with a bridge, railway lines, highways, industrial parks, and public parks, to name a few obstacles, combine to shape the trading area. Shoppers will not cross a busy street, railway track, river, or industrial zone if they can avoid it. They will even travel a considerable distance farther to shop at a competitor's.

The type of street or the location of a shop influences the extent of the trading area. For example, a business situated within a subway station has a trading area which may be vast but remains limited to commuters. A business outside the subway entrance enjoys the attraction of the overall centre.

SUMMARY

The place variable includes three distinct elements: the distribution channel, the physical distribution, and commercial location.

Distribution channels include all those who play a role in the chain bringing the product from the manufacturer to the end consumer. A distribution channel can be short, as in the case of a museum dealing directly with the public without any intermediary whatsoever, or long, as in the case of a recording company using agents who sell to wholesalers who then sell to retailers. The distribution route enables a manufacturer to reduce the total number of operations it performs, by fulfilling a number of logistic functions, such as shipping and warehousing, and commercial functions, such as promotional support, financing, and inventory.

The main aspects involved in the management of a distribution channel correspond to four objectives and six strategic decisions. The four objectives are: maximize profit (or attain the break-even point) by maintaining maximum motivation within the distribution channel; maximizing profits means maximizing sales and minimizing costs. The six strategic decisions involve the length of the distribution channel, the distribution strategy deployed, the type of intermediaries, the ratio of routes to intermediaries, the degree of co-operation offered to intermediaries, and the selection of those intermediaries.

A distribution channel should not be considered simply the flow of merchandise from producer to end consumer. It is actually a social network in which interpersonal relationships play a role and influence the dynamics. The four key dimensions within this social network are: conflict, power, roles, and communication.

There are two broad types of distribution strategy: intensive, selective, and exclusive; and push and pull. The first type corresponds to the number of points of sale a firm wishes to use. If the firm is using the intensive distribution strategy, it wants to maximize the number of points of sale used. If the firm is using the selective distribution strategy, it chooses retailers according to specific criteria and, with an exclusive strategy, grants additional territorial protection. The second type of strategy involves the use of a profit margin earned by the intermediary and is based on the effort the manufacturer wants the intermediary to expend. If the agent or intermediary pushes the product, the margin will be greater, and vice versa. The producer or manufacturer uses this margin to balance the cost of an advertising or promotional campaign.

Physical distribution is made up of all the logistics and movements involved in bringing a product to market – that is, shipping, warehousing, inventory management, order processing, handling, and packaging. Physical distribution must meet two contradictory objectives: minimize costs and maximize customer service.

Location is the choice of a physical site where the product will be bought or consumed by the customer. By studying where consumers come from, it is possible to determine three trading areas based on the distance from the sales outlet and the concentration of the clientele. The extent and configuration of these trading areas are called primary, secondary, and tertiary. They are determined by the following factors: product (generic sense of term), corporate marketing strategies, and consumer perception.

QUESTIONS

1. The way a cultural product is consumed influences the distribution of that product. How?
2. What is a distribution channel?
3. Why are decisions about the choice of a distribution channel important?
4. What is the main reason for having intermediaries?
5. What are the main functions of a distribution channel?
6. What does complexity means in terms of a distribution channel?
7. Why must a company consider long-term maximum profits when managing its distribution channel?
8. What are the six basic questions a manufacturer must answer before setting up a distribution channel?
9. Explain the concept of a social network within a distribution channel.
10. Explain how the following strategies are interrelated: skimming and penetration; intensive, selective, and exclusive; push and pull.
11. Describe the different components of physical distribution.
12. What are the general factors to be considered in choosing a good location?
13. How is the concept of a trading area useful to a manager?

Notes

1. Roodhouse, S. 1999. "A Challenge to Cultural Sector Management Conventions – The Royal Armories Museum." *International Journal of Arts Management*, Vol. 1, n° 2 (Winter), p. 82–90.

2. Statistics Canada. 1997. *Canada's Culture, Heritage and Idetity: A Statistical Perspective*. Ottawa: Author.

3. Bégin, D., F. Colbert and R. Dupré. 2000. "Comparative Analysis of French and French-Canadian Willingness to Support the National Film Industry." *International Journal of Cultural Policy*, Vol. 7, n° 2 (December).

4. Mallen, B. 1977. *Principles of Marketing Channel Management*. Toronto: Lexington Books.

5. Rosenbloom, B. 1983. *Marketing Channels: A Management View, Second Edition*. Chicago: Dryden Press.

6. Colbert, F., and R. Côté. 1990. *Localisation commerciale*. Boucherville, Quebec: Gaëtan Morin Éditeur.

For Further Reference

McIntyre, C. 1985. *Carnet de route : guide de tournée à l'étranger*. Ottawa: Affaires extérieures, Services de la promotion artistique, Gouvernement du Canada.

Papadopoulos, N., L.A. Heslop and J.J. Marshall. 1990. "Domestic and International Marketing of Canadian Cultural Products: Some Questions and Some Directions for Research," in *ASAC Conference*, Whistler, British Columbia, p. 232–240.

Plan

CHAPTER 8
The Promotion Variable

8

OBJECTIVES

- Define promotion as a variable
- Identify the main functions of promotion
- Look at various promotional tools
- Learn how to select the most appropriate promotional tools
- Study a communications plan
- Explore the possibility of sponsorship as a promotional tool

INTRODUCTION

Promotion, the fourth variable in the marketing mix, is vital to the marketing strategy of any company. Promotion actually bridges the gap between the company and the marketplace.

In this chapter, we look at promotional tools, their functions, and selection criteria based on the objectives already set out. We then define the various components of a communications plan. Lastly, we look at sponsorship as part of the sponsor's arsenal and as a source of income that no cultural or artistic enterprise can afford to neglect.

8.1 DEFINITION

Marketing, advertising, and promotion are regularly confused. The following succinct definition should clarify matters. Advertising is actually a promotional tool, whereas promotion is a variable in the marketing mix. The marketing mix is one part of the overall marketing model.

Promotion is first and foremost a communications tool, an instrument transmitting the official corporate message and image. Companies have direct control over corporate communications and can decide how to manage their image and the content of their message. Of course, other variables within the marketing mix can also reflect the company's image, and, in the cultural milieu, the critics too send a message to the potential audience.

Cultural enterprises project an image to specialized publics as well as to the general public. Their image derives from consumer perceptions based on others' opinions, critics' reviews, experience, promotional campaigns, and so on. Although companies may not be able to control the consumer's perception based on messages received from other variables in the marketing mix, they can nonetheless influence public perception. In fact, pricing policy, choice of distributors, and promotional technique used can create or modify image. A high price level usually reflects a prestigious image, as in the case of a concert in a famous hall. Conversely, a concert advertised in the daily newspaper with a low ticket price reflects a more popular image.

Promotion is also a tool of change that enables a firm to modify perceptions, attitudes, knowledge, and awareness. As such, promotion can educate the consumer about a product in varying degrees. It can also adjust consumer attitudes by turning indifference into desire or transforming negative perceptions into positive ones.

Mokwa[1] lists the following three key promotional objectives:

1) Information: Let consumers know that the product exists and provide the essential details, such as time and place of performance, ticket prices, and forms of payment accepted.

2) Persuasion: Convince consumers to buy the product through additional motivations, such as quality of show, appearance of famous stars, unique nature of program, ease of access and payment, social prestige or recognition, and personal enrichment.

3) Education: Give consumers the tools and codes they need to evaluate the specific features of the product. This activity helps to expand the clientele for a particular

discipline, since consumers are better informed and thus prepared to consume the product. Children's educational programs in museums exemplify this objective.

8.2 PROMOTIONAL TOOLS

The four main tools used in promotion are advertising, personal selling, public relations, and sales promotion. The weight given to each one may depend on the company's budget or the traditions within a particular industry.

8.2.1 Advertising

Advertising may be defined as the impersonal means for which a company pays to communicate with its target market. Visibility obtained through press releases or media coverage is considered publicity rather than advertising. Publicity is one element of the public-relations function.

An advertising message may appear in different media, electronic and print. Common examples are TV and radio commercials, newspaper and magazine ads, posters, billboards, and advertising within the public-transit system.

Boisvert[2] points out that advertising "involves some payment to an advertising support vehicle, such as a radio or TV station, magazine, daily newspaper, or billboard, in order for the ad to appear."

The advertising message, whatever its medium, has a limited life span. In fact, ads are developed for a specific medium and may target both the general public (mass advertising) and a highly specific public (targetted advertising). The executive's

challenge is to find out which advertising vehicles are the most appropriate. Here, a profile of the public reached by the various media that the firm is considering would prove useful.[3]

The poster is used extensively by cultural enterprises. It is, however, merely a support for the other advertising tools used. In fact, potential customers may not always see a poster and, if driving, cannot stop to read the information given. Moreover, the average amount of time spent reading a poster is very short. The life span of a poster itself is brief, especially in large cities, where the practice of covering or removing posters has become fierce. As well, the amount of information that can fit on a poster is limited. A poster should be designed to attract attention and generate interest among prospective customers. Usually, it acts as a reminder of the message given in the main campaign.

8.2.2 Personal Selling

Personal selling consists of transmitting a message from one person to the next through direct contact. This technique enables the seller to deal with the customer's reasons for not buying. Personal selling may be face to face, over the telephone one on one, or in groups.

Advertising is an extremely potent means of persuasion if the message to be transmitted is simple. For more complicated messages, personal selling is more effective, since the representative of the company can adapt the advertising message to the consumer and respond to his or her questions or reasons for not buying.

Telemarketing is an example of personal selling that can be used either as the main tool when contacting a target market or as an additional tool when targetting groups that are more difficult to convince. Cultural and artistic enterprises are now using tele-marketing more frequently and successfully.[4]

Besides using persuasion to sell a product, a salesperson also performs research and provides information. Sales representatives learn all about customers' needs, problems, and reservations in order to respond to their expectations, and they supply services related to sales activities, maintain cordial interpersonal relationships with customers, and provide friendly assistance and advice during the purchasing process. They may also co-ordinate consumer needs with other company products or services.

The communication process follows a series of eight steps (see table 8.1), ranging from prospecting to following up.[5] Prospecting, or "qualifying," means judging the potential of new customers. Preparation

---

Table 8.1
The Eight Steps of Personal Selling

Step 1	Prospecting (Qualifying)
Step 2	Preparation
Step 3	Approach
Step 4	Diagnosis
Step 5	Presentation
Step 6	Dealing with objections
Step 7	Closing
Step 8	Following up

---

sets out the "attack" strategy and how to get an appointment with the customer. The approach includes both setting up the sales presentation most likely to trigger a positive response in the customer and, through the previous, preparation, stage, presenting the product. Diagnosis is the sales representative's analysis of the customer's needs. Presentation is the act of persuasion during which the salesperson introduces the product and tries to convince the potential customer to become a bona fide customer. Dealing with objections consists of drawing out the customer's objections and reservations so as to counter each one. This is no easy task, since a voiced objection may hide an even stronger silent one. A salesperson must expose the client's real objections and counter them using solid arguments. Closing involves actually finishing the selling process at the appropriate time – that is, when the customer seems ready to buy. Lastly, the follow-up step seeks to ensure that the client is satisfied and, if need be, to make adjustments in order to maintain the business relationship for future sales.

8.2.3 Public Relations

Public relations (PR) has been defined as "the management function that evaluates public attitudes, identifies and individual or an organization with the public interest, and plans and executes a program of action to earn public understanding and acceptance" (*Public Relations News*, October 27, 1947). One of the main weapons in the PR arsenal of a cultural organization is publicity, which serves to promote a product or company in the media without paying to advertise. Press releases and conferences, speeches and presentations, free air time on radio or TV, and general media coverage are all examples of publicity.

For financial reasons, many cultural or artistic groups are obliged to use publicity as their main vehicle to inform potential customers. Of course, the media also benefit from this relationship, since cultural activities interest and attract a sizable audience.

Cultural enterprises have tremendous power in terms of publicity, but the media do have the final say in deciding whether to air or print information and in which format. Hence, there is always some risk involved.

While it is important to distinguish clearly between the public-relations function, which deals with a variety of the organization's publics (employees, board members, volunteers, audience members, the media, governments, sponsors, and donors), and the publicity function, which deals almost exclusively with media relations, it should also be noted that since many cultural organizations focus the bulk of their PR activity on the media, they have a tendency to equate public relations with publicity.

8.2.4 Sales Promotion

Sales promotion can be divided into three sections: sales aids, motivational items or programs, and spin-off products.

First, there is the simple logo or relevant message printed on small objects (matchbox covers, pencils, pins), or sales aids, which are usually given away free of charge.

Second are motivational goods or services used to encourage customers to buy. Common examples include reduction coupons, contests, subscription gifts, and special offers typified by the "buy one, get one free" approach.

Spin-off products are yet another form of sales promotion. The term "spin-off products" denotes goods related to the company's main product yet generating a separate revenue. Typical examples include T-shirts, recordings, posters, mugs, and stationery. The primary objective of selling spin-off products is usually to increase the independent[6] revenue of the company. The products may act as almost an afterthought, sold to help project the company's image. Museums and large organizations in the performing arts often use this form of promotion.

Sales promotion is usually applied to consumers, but it may also be used with retailers and distributors. When sales promotion is used with consumers, reductions might be given on the purchase of a certain number of tickets, for example. The same reduction technique can be used to encourage retailers to offer the product or promote it more. Bonus points per unit sold, which can be exchanged for valuable prizes such as airline tickets or holiday packages, are typical sales promotions.

8.2.5 The Promotional Mix

As mentioned above, promotion uses four main tools: advertising, PR, sales promotion, and personal selling. Every organization has its own recipe or scale for deciding on how much of each ingredient is needed. Some groups may be able to afford only the free promotion PR/publicity offers. Small artistic enterprises fall into this category: they often run print ads or produce posters but concentrate their efforts on obtaining media coverage. The ad or poster thus supports the other promotional tools and projects the group's image. Other groups may base their promotional strategy on the purchase of advertising in media that target specific segments. Some try to strike a balance among the four tools available. In the end, the promotional mix depends on the organization's goals and means.

8.3   THE FUNCTIONS OF PROMOTION

Promotion has two main functions: to communicate a message and to produce a change in the consumer.

8.3.1 Communicating a Message

The message a company wants to communicate may use one or any number of codes (pictorial, visual, graphic, written, symbolic, or even colour), which must be properly perceived and understood by the consumer. Schramm[7] developed a communications model that applies to all messages (see figure 8.1).

Schramm's model breaks the communication process down into eight components.

1) Sender: the one who starts the act of communication. The sender may be an individual, an organization, or a group.

2) Encoding: the process by which certain symbols, signs, colours, and other visual, graphic, or written elements designed to convey the meaning of the message are combined and co-ordinated.

3) Message: the cornerstone of communication. It is composed of signs, symbols,

and other elements organized and transmitted to the receiver.

4) Decoding: the process by which the receiver attempts to understand the organization and meaning of the signs, symbols, colours, and any other elements used by the sender.

5) The receiver: this may be an individual, an organization, or a group who may or may not be predisposed to receive the message. A message may therefore be sent but not received if the targetted receiver is not "picking up" the signal.

6) Field of experience: the extent of experience in communication. There are in fact several fields of experience, not just one. For instance, there is the sender's experience, which includes his or her past experiences and knowledge of communication, and the receiver's experience, which unites all of his or her experiences in receiving messages and decoding them.

7) Point of reference: this includes all references used by the sender and the receiver to understand the act of communication. This framework or point of reference is the overall experience or general knowledge of individuals or groups interacting in the communication process.

8) Feedback: this is the receiver's reaction to the message as perceived by the sender. Feedback is important in that it enables the sender to adjust the communication process according to his or her perception of the receiver's response.

There is a ninth component not included formally in Schramm's model but nevertheless linked to the transmission of a message – the channel of communication. This is the means employed by the sender to get the

Figure 8.1

Schramm's Model of Communication

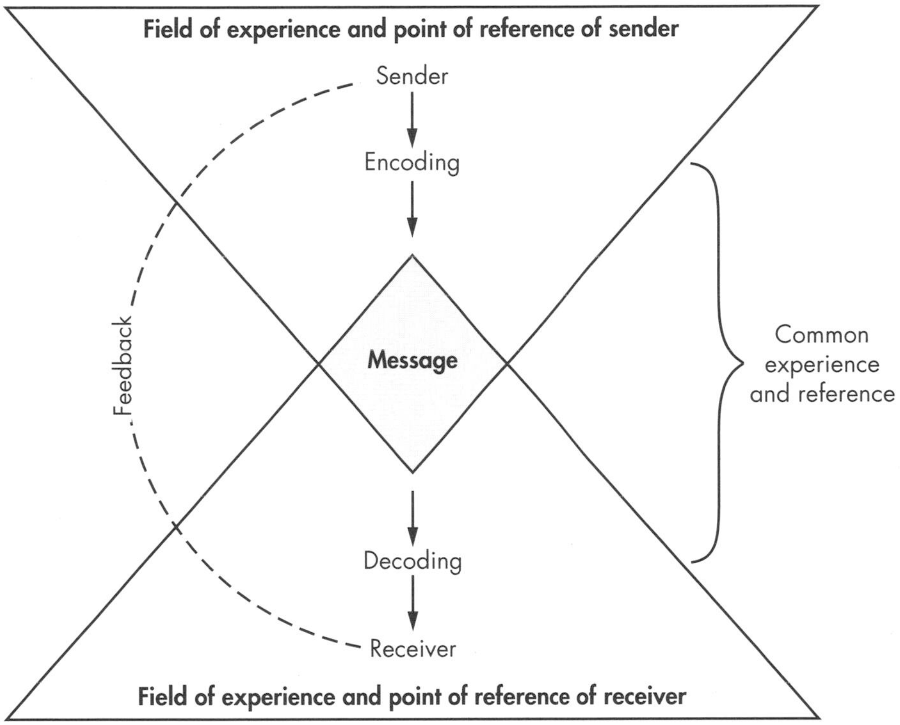

Field of experience and point of reference of sender

Sender

Encoding

Feedback

Message

Common experience and reference

Decoding

Receiver

Field of experience and point of reference of receiver

Source: Adapted from Schramm, W. 1960. "How Communication Works," in *The Process and Effects of Mass Communication*. Urbana, IL: University of Illinois Press.

message to the receiver. It may be electronic, written, or face to face.

The choice of channel is significant, because it determines how and how well a message reaches the target audience. A message broadcast on TV, for example, does not reach the receiver unless the receiver is watching the right channel at the right time.

Communication is truly a bilateral process that involves the active participation of both sender and receiver. It enables the sender to analyze gaps in understanding and to adjust accordingly so as to reach the receiver in a more efficient and suitable manner.

The communication process described here applies to individuals as well as to mass communication. In any event, for a message to be transmitted efficiently, the sender must know the identity of the receiver and which codes the receiver will understand.

Codes alone do not ensure the correct routing of a message. There are several possible disturbances, called interference, that can thwart the transmission of a message. The sender's image, or use of inappropriate codes or inadequate channels, may create interference. Environmental factors may also have a direct influence on the understanding of the message as biased favourably or unfavourably. The impact of critics' reviews provides an excellent example. The "noise" or interference from the critics modifies the content of an advertising message or influences the potential customer's perceptions and understanding, by intervening directly in the communication process without the sender being able to foresee the impact. By keeping in touch and reacting, the sender can adjust his or her promotional strategy according to the deviations perceived between the results expected and those obtained.

8.3.2 Producing a Change in the Customer

Besides conveying a message, promotion acts as an agent of change. As such, it tries to generate positive consumer attitudes toward the product and, ultimately, product sales.

The function of promotion may be defined as a series of four steps: attract attention, create interest, generate desire, provoke action. These four steps are known by their mnemonic name AIDA (attention, interest, desire, action), as shown in table 8.2.

Of course, promotional campaigns are not conducted in a vacuum. One company's message is in competition with a staggering number of other messages produced by a host of other companies throughout the dif-

| Table 8.2 | |
The AIDA Formula	
A	attract Attention
I	create Interest
D	generate Desire
A	provoke Action

ferent sectors of the economy. Estimates have shown that the average consumer is exposed, consciously or unconsciously, to somewhere between 250 and 3,000 messages daily. The exact number depends on the individual's media-consumption habits. These messages are received while the consumer reads the morning paper, listens to the car radio, watches TV, or glances at a poster or billboard. Out of all those messages, approximately seventy-five will actually be perceived and only twelve will be retained. In other words, there is a constant barrage of messages and stimuli coming from all directions, and the average consumer must develop various mechanisms to filter out some messages. Obviously, any company trying to attract the consumer's attention faces an arduous task, especially given the number of messages and of consumer defence mechanisms.

Defence Mechanisms

Psychological processes called "defence factors"[8] play a role in diminishing and even blocking messages transmitted by the mass media. These factors act as filters and enable the consumer to select messages.

The selection process is linked to exposure and attention as well as understanding or retention.

Consumers looking for a product choose the messages they want to see or hear (selective exposure). For example, a consumer who wants to see a play willingly looks at the ads placed by theatre companies in the daily newspaper.

Selective perception implies that the consumer notices only certain messages because of the urgency or importance of personal needs. If those needs are very strong, the customer will be more receptive and possibly interested in buying. This mechanism explains how a consumer seeking one title can find it in the window without even seeing the other books displayed there.

Selective comprehension is another filter that comes into play when decoding an ad. The consumer interprets the signs (colour, symbol, shape, etc.) according to his or her needs and values. For example, red or orange is usually associated with warmth in people's minds, whereas deep blue is associated with cold. Signs or symbols must be selected carefully or the potential customer might misunderstand the message.

Another mechanism is selective retention, which enables the consumer to retain only part of the message received and perceived. Novelty, repetition, and interest do have a significant influence on retention, but the consumer's needs and values also have a definite influence on which messages are actually retained.

Subliminal Advertising

The obstacles encountered in persuading consumers to buy have encouraged researchers to search for ways to avoid the filters described above. Their research has led to experiments in subliminal advertising. In theory, subliminal advertising allows a message to break through the consumer's defences and reach the subconscious without the consumer's knowledge. In the consumer's subconscious, the desire to buy the product is then provoked.

An early experiment in subliminal advertising carried out in 1959 at a movie theatre started the American trend of ads using elements of subliminal advertising. The principle behind the experiment was quite simple.[9] The researcher had inserted one image of Coca-Cola among the twenty-four images projected per second on the big screen.[10] As a result, viewers saw an unequivocal message, "Drink Coca-Cola," every second without knowing it. At intermission, sales of the famous soft drink rose by 52% over previous sales figures. The same experiment using popcorn generated an 18% increase in sales.

Further experimentation never yielded such convincing results, and nothing proved conclusively that the increase in sales during the 1959 experiment could be attributed solely to the subliminal messages projected on the movie screen. Other, external, factors not even considered by the researchers, such as room temperature, promotion at point of sale, and sheer chance, could have played a role.

Various individuals and lobby groups considered subliminal advertising dangerous and condemned it as a manipulative practice akin to brainwashing. As a precautionary measure, several countries have outlawed subliminal advertising.

8.4   THE CHOICE OF PROMOTIONAL TOOLS

8.4.1 The Parameters of Influence

The promotional tools a company chooses depend primarily on the company's choice from the following two parameters of influence: the complexity of the message and the target market's knowledge of the product.

Since the choice of promotional tools varies according to the complexity of the message, a simple message can be delivered easily through advertising, whereas a complex message requires a far more personal approach.

The complexity of the message is often related to the complexity of the product as perceived by the customer. For example, a true opera buff immediately sees a reason for buying tickets to *Madama Butterfly*, while someone who does not know opera or even has a negative bias toward opera might see no reason whatsoever to do so. Although an advertising campaign can encourage the opera fan to buy tickets, personal selling would be far more effective in interesting the potential opera-goer in tickets to a performance of *Madama Butterfly*, or could at least deal with the consumer's arguments or modify perceptions.

There are six stages in the process that leads a potential buyer from ignorance to action (see table 8.3).

The true opera devotee may be at stage 4, conviction. This is usually an individual who knows the repertoire, understands the significance of the works, can appreciate the content, and might be led to the deci-

Table 8.3

The Purchasing Process Based on the Consumer's Product Knowledge

Step 1	Ignorance
Step 2	Knowledge
Step 3	Understanding
Step 4	Conviction
Step 5	Decision
Step 6	Action

sion stage more easily than the consumer starting out at stage 1, ignorance.

The more advanced the consumer is along the ignorance-action continuum, the less complicated the promotional campaign. The faithful readers of an established author launching a new book or the current subscribers to a series of concerts are part of a market segment near the action stage. Conversely, promotion is more complex when the potential consumer hovers around the ignorance stage or has a negative bias toward the product.

A promotional campaign should therefore guide consumers from wherever they may be along the continuum through the stages of the buying process up to the actual purchase of the product.

8.4.2 A Practical Model

The model[11] presented in figure 8.2 shows how the complexity of the product, the market size, and the choice of promotional tools are related.

The model is presented as a series of pyramids that represent the product, the market, advertising, and personal selling. Each pyramid forms a continuum. The tip and base act as poles reflecting the importance of certain characteristics; for example, the tip of the product pyramid demonstrates a low level of complexity, while the base reflects a high level.

The tip of the consumer pyramid indicates that the consumer market is limited and not very extensive, while the base portrays a much larger market, often called the "mass market."

The personal selling and advertising pyramids illustrate the order of importance of one or the other of these tools based on the complexity of the product and the market segment. Thus, the tip indicates limited recourse to promotional tools, while the base corresponds to extensive use of promotional tools.

As a rule, complex products are designed for a limited market. A product may be complex in terms of its technical specifications or in terms of the customer's product knowledge. Similarly, if a market segment has a negative attitude toward a product, that product may be considered complex to the consumers within that segment. The more complex the product, the more detailed the sales pitch and the higher the level of information used to convince the consumer. In this instance, personal selling is the most suitable tool, since advertising does not convey very complex or dense information. For example, a concert of electro-acoustic music is a simple product for experts in this type of music. A poster will therefore be adequate to inform fans and encourage them to buy a ticket. On the other hand, the sales pitch will have to be stronger for the consumer who has never heard of this art form and is not even a

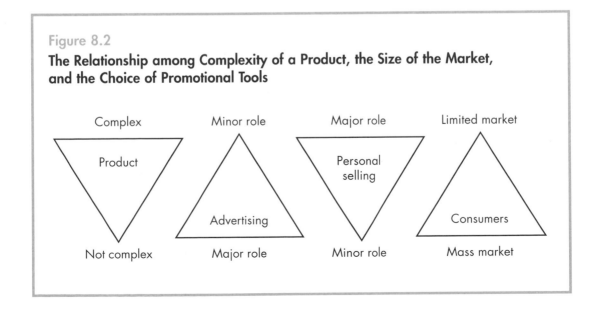

Figure 8.2

The Relationship among Complexity of a Product, the Size of the Market, and the Choice of Promotional Tools

music fan. A poster and a newspaper ad will not be powerful enough to convince the latter consumer to attend. Personal selling is needed in this instance.

Conversely, since there is a vast market for simple products, personal selling is not necessary or even desirable, given the high cost involved. Advertising as a promotional tool works better in this case, since it allows for much broader market coverage.

The model shows the relationship among product, market, and two promotional tools: personal selling and advertising. In simple terms, complex products usually target a limited market and personal selling is the favoured tool. In this case, advertising is used only to support the sales force. Conversely, in the case of simple products, the role of the sales force is very limited. In general, a simple product is destined for a broader public.

Organizations in the cultural milieu often have limited financial means and support their ads with an intensive publicity campaign. In fact, publicity frequently is the main promotional tool, with advertising relegated to a supporting role.

8.5 THE RECEIVER

Schramm's model, as shown in figure 8.1, shows the sender encoding and transmitting a message which is received and decoded by the receiver. The information sent may well be received but not actually used by the receiver. For example, some governments have legislated against advertising directed toward children. Advertisers are therefore obliged to reach children by targetting another group, usually the children's parents, who do not actually use the products themselves.

The process that consumers use to purchase a product may include several "players" who must be considered when developing a marketing strategy. They are the initiator, the influencer, the decision maker, the buyer, and the user. Several messages must be created to reach the various players intervening in the purchase process.

A study conducted in 1983 and updated in 1990 in Canada analyzed the market for children's theatre within the school system and then looked at the decision makers who have the final say as to whether the show will be presented or not.[12] There are many individuals involved, with varying roles in the decision-making process. The home and school association or parents' committee plays the role of influencer. The teaching staff is the initiator of the process, and the school principal usually plays the dual role of decision maker and buyer. Lastly, the pupils are the users of the product. Each individual school may have its own decision-making procedure, and the number of players and their corresponding roles may double or shift at different stages in the process. For example, sometimes the parents or the teaching staff will trigger the process.

Any artistic enterprise must know how the consumption units within the target market make decisions and examine the purchasing process. The company must consider not only the consumer public but also the various decision makers playing a role in the purchase process. As seen in chapter 7, the distribution channel may be considered a market in itself. A company producing children's shows must develop a sales pitch that convinces the presenter and, in turn, enables the presenter to convince parents to buy their children tickets.

8.6 THE COMMUNICATIONS PLAN

Once the marketing manager has determined which groups to target, it is time to develop a strategy based on the objectives set and the target segments to be reached.

8.6.1 The Basic Questions Any Communications Plan Must Answer

This plan is a practical tool used in reaching objectives and specific market segments. It forces a company to reflect upon which approach to adopt within several key parameters. In simpler terms, this plan can be considered an exercise that answers the questions Who? What? To whom? How? When? With what results? Table 8.4 lists the basic six questions.

Table 8.4

The Basic Questions of a Communications Plan

Question 1 – Who?

Question 2 – What?

Question 3 – To whom?

Question 4 – How?

Question 5 – When?

Question 6 – What results?

Who?

First, a company must know the image it projects – that is, the consumer's perception of the company – to run an effective promotional campaign. Questions that a marketing manager or team should ask include:
- How does the public perceive the company and the product?
- How does the company measure up in terms of the competition?
- Does the image projected accurately reflect the image desired?

What?

The company must then decide what kind of message to send. Key questions include the following:
- What advantages does the product have?
- What motivates the consumer to buy the product?
- What are the company's intentions in terms of communications?
- Can the image be changed?
- Is it enough just to make a product known, or do potential customers need to be led up to the buying stage?

To Whom?

The company must segment its market and decide who actually receives the message. In other words, the questions are as follows.
- Which segment should be targeted?
- Who are the decision makers?
- What is the profile of the target market?

How?

The company must then consider what is the optimal way of reaching the target segments. The following questions should be asked and answered:

· Which media are usually consulted by the target segment(s)?

· Should written or electronic media be favoured?

· Which media should be used to reach the over-all majority of target groups?

· Which promotional tools should be used most (personal selling, advertising, PR, or sales promotion)?

· Which codes should be used (colour, symbol, etc.)?

· Which appeals should be used (renown, prestige, accessibility, novelty, exclusivity)?

When?

Naturally, the company must decide when the message should be transmitted, given the various objectives and limits implied by the choice of a particular channel. A number of questions arise:

· When should the subscription campaign be launched?

· What are the media and ad-placement deadlines?

· Which day is best for advertising (Saturday, Thursday, or another day)?

· What are the target market's shopping or purchasing habits?

What Results?

The company must have measurable objectives that enable it to judge promotional efforts. The following questions should give an idea of how effective a communications plan has been.

· By what percentage did sales increase?

· How did attitudes change?

· Is there a gap between the objectives targetted and those achieved? If so, why?

· Did the company draw upon all the resources at its disposal?

· Did it overuse its resources?

· Did the communications plan reach the target groups who did not know the product existed?

· Finally, the bottom line: did the consumer actually buy the product?

8.6.2 The Content of a Communications Plan

Boisvert[13] defines a communications plan as "an ordered series of decisions and operations designed to structure the channel of communication, to determine which elements to include in a campaign, and to evaluate the amount of money needed." A communications plan requires some prior analysis to enlighten this ordered series of decisions. Chapter 10 shows how such a plan is integrated into a more comprehensive plan, the marketing plan, which combines in a coherent whole all plans and strategies affecting the marketing mix.

The Stages of a Communications Plan

After analyzing the situation, the marketing manager or team must set communications objectives, draft a budget, and create the over-all promotional strategy with specific strategies for each component of the marketing mix. Three key decisions must be made for each component: determine the concept, determine the means or tools, and determine the budget. Lastly, the strategies must be implemented and monitored.

Setting Communications Objectives

Any promotional campaign needs clearly

defined communications objectives, which must conform to the objectives of the marketing strategy. Marketing and communications objectives are somewhat different in nature.

Marketing objectives are expressed in terms of market share or sales volume. Communications objectives are related to changes that a company wishes to make in the customer's consumption process. Communications objectives usually include increasing awareness, maintaining the current rate of intention to buy, or modifying the consumer's preference.

In any event, these objectives have to be expressed quantitatively in order to facilitate measuring the results achieved. For example, a company might want to increase its market share by 10% (marketing objective). The company must therefore increase the intention of buying by 50% among potential consumers (communications objective).

Drawing up a Promotional Budget

Drafting a promotional budget is usually a delicate matter in any company. Unfortunately, there is no miracle cure or secret recipe that enables a marketing manager to determine the optimal amount to invest in a promotional campaign.

Boisvert[14] has suggested using the following three basic principles in order to set the upper limit of the amount to be invested:

1) Each additional dollar invested must contribute to corporate profits.

2) Each additional dollar that generates at least one cent of profit is worthwhile.

3) The cost of a sale must be less than the revenue generated by that sale.

These three principles are both economically and logically obvious, but rarely does a company have the information needed to calculate down to the penny a budget that corresponds to them.

Boisvert sets out five practical methods that enable a company to calculate a promotion budget:[15]

1) The Like Last Year (LLY) method consists of reviewing the promotional investment made the previous year and adjusting it according to the scope of activities planned over the current year as well as various environmental factors, such as inflation or a goods and services tax.

2) The Sales Percentage (SP) method consists of dividing previous budgets into periods according to the sales figures attained. Since this method is based on the past, it enables a manager to set a percentage that can be applied to a sales forecast as part of over-all projections.

3) The Everything Possible to Invest (EPTI) method may be applied in situations requiring a massive injection of funds to promote a product. Typical examples include the launching of a recording or the premiere of a movie. This method may also be used when attendance figures for an exhibition or box office sales for a musical comedy drop noticeably. Marketing managers usually try to create synergy through sustained and repetitive promotional efforts in the hope of increasing product consumption.

4) The Comparative Parity (CP) method consists of drawing up a communications budget based on industry or sector

standards. This type of information can normally be found in government publications, professional journals, and trade magazines, or obtained from private sources.

5) The Objectives and Tasks (OT) method consists of first performing an in-depth analysis of the target market, then setting out the communications objectives and means, and, lastly, calculating the approximate costs involved.

These five methods are but a few examples of how to calculate a promotional budget and are neither exhaustive nor exclusive. They are given here simply as guidelines. A company might draft a budget using a combination of all five methods or develop its own method.

8.7 SPONSORSHIP
(by J. Dennis Rich)

In the 1980s, corporate giving began to move more and more toward "strategic philanthropy" based on the old concept of "doing well by doing good." Corporations began to enter into collaborations and partnerships with non-profit organizations, which raised recognition for both parties and enhanced the corporation's image.

Today, cultural and artistic enterprises turn to the private sector for financial support. Sponsorship represents a major source of revenue well worth including in this chapter on promotion. Sponsorship is actually a promotional tool for the sponsor, whose presence has an impact on the content of the advertising material for an institution or event.

8.7.1 Defining Sponsorship

Sponsorship is the term for a relationship between a sponsor and an event, agency, or property in which the sponsor pays a cash or in-kind fee in return for access to the exploitable commercial potential associated with the event, agency, or property.[16] It is part of a strategically planned promotional effort.

A related term is *cause-related marketing*. This is a strategically planned *promotional* effort designed to increase a company's sales or improve its position in the marketplace through actions that also benefit a non-profit organization. Generally, this means that when consumers purchase the company's product or service, the company donates to the non-profit enterprise.[17]

Perhaps the first example of cause-related marketing occurred during the 1983 restoration of the Statue of Liberty. American Express worked with the Ellis Island Foundation to create a promotion encouraging both new card applications and frequent use of the card by donating to the Statue of Liberty restoration fund each time a new card was approved and each time a member used the card. The promotion raised $1.7 million for refurbishment of the statue and resulted in a 45% increase in new cardholders and a 28% increase in card usage.

Unlike in philanthropy, money spent on sponsorship and cause-related marketing is a business expense, not a donation, and is expected to contribute to the company's marketing communication and show a return on investment. Sponsorship involves interaction between two distinct parties: the sponsor, which provides funds, goods, or services, and the sponsored event or group, which receives the funds, goods, or services in return for certain considerations. The business relationship supposes that each party is satisfied with what it receives in return for what it gives.

8.7.2 The Need for Fundraising and Sponsorship

In 1966, William J. Baumol and William G. Bowen wrote *The Performing Arts: The Economic Dilemma*.[18] In this now-famous book, they developed what has come to be known as "Baumol's Law." Baumol and Bowen examined the challenges faced by performing arts companies in the United States in terms of rising production costs. They defined the problem using the laws of economic productivity. Throughout the economy, they reported, worker efficiency typically doubles every twenty-nine years. But, for the performing arts, this is not possible. A Beethoven symphony or a production of *Hamlet* require as many performers as they did when they were written. However, performers' salaries have not risen more slowly than those of other workers. At the same time, production costs have risen more quickly than the over-all economy. Thus, Baumol's Law accounts for the extraordinary rise in ticket prices and for the necessity of fundraising for cultural enterprises. Out of this need, cultural agencies have sought to reach donor markets.

8.7.3 The Importance of the Sponsorship Market

Saturation in the mass media has forced companies to seek other means of reaching the consumer. Sponsorship and cause-related marketing are among those means. Sponsorship is the fastest-growing medium in the market. When compared to advertising and sales promotion, sponsorship expenditures have grown 613% over the past sixteen years, from 103% and 127%, respectively. Total North American sponsorship spending in 1997 came to $5.9 billion. Worldwide, sponsorship in 1997 came to $15.3 billion.[19] Not surprisingly, most of the sponsorship money – 68% – goes to sports. However, the demand of corporations for a new and better way of communicating with their target audiences has benefitted every type of sponsorship.[20]

In the 1990s, a new concept of sponsorship and cause-related marketing began to emerge. Short-term sales-related promotional sponsorships began to be replaced by sponsorship and cause-related marketing being integrated into the very identity of companies. The new form of strategic philanthropy seeks to affiliate non-profit events, organizations, or causes with a particular brand [21] as part of a comprehensive, integrated marketing strategy.

For example, when the Field Museum in Chicago purchased Sue, the largest Tyrannosaurus Rex ever unearthed, in an auction, the museum put together a groundbreaking deal with McDonald's and Walt Disney World Resorts.

In return for helping the Field Museum purchase Sue, both corporations gained access to Sue's image for use in their own promotions. The deal will see the Field Museum's name mentioned in conjunction with customer-savvy public relations and marketing efforts by two of the world's largest corporations. All three entities have a similar, if not the same, customer base: children under the age of 13 and their families. At the time of Sue's purchase, the agreement reached by the Field, Disney, and McDonald's was heralded as innovative and was expected to be copied widely. The Field Museum's preparatory laboratory where Sue's bones are being cleaned has been named the "McDonald's Preparatory Laboratory," and at Disney the public will be able to watch as technicians and scientists work on Sue. A copy of Sue's skeleton will be provided to both Disney and McDonald's for use by the corporations. Because of these activities, the Field Museum will benefit from long-term relationships with each corporation.[22]

This sort of affiliation occurs regularly outside the realm of culture and the arts. Time will tell if this type of merger among commerce, education, and entertainment will be replicated.

8.7.4 The Decision-Makers

Cause-related marketing and sponsorship are not simple corporate contributions. Corporate contributions are donations not associated with any marketing program (see Table 8.5) and are generally handled by different people from those who make the decisions about sponsorship and cause-related marketing. Cause-related marketing and sponsorship involve the marketing, communications, promotion, or public relations functions of a company. Consider the definitions again. Both sponsorship and cause-related marketing are strategically planned *marketing* efforts designed to increase a company's sales or improve its position in the marketplace through actions

that also benefit a non-profit organization. The key idea here is *strategically planned marketing effort*. It means that sponsorship and cause-related marketing are based on a strategy and a plan – they are not just coincidental activities. No such effort should take place without a carefully constructed plan. Both partners – the sponsoring company and the non-profit agency or event – should create the plan together.

In the collaboration between cultural agencies and companies, arts managers need to bear in mind that the company is engaged in strategic philanthropy designed to improve its image or increase sales. Some arts and cultural agencies have a problem with this. Their leadership seems to believe that helping a company make money may not be consistent with their non-profit mission. However, as long as the activities of the sponsoring company are ethical and legitimate, and as long as the arts agency is doing nothing to violate its tax-exempt status, there is nothing wrong with participating in a partnership that benefits both partners. The definition of sponsorship suggests collaboration and makes it clear that the sponsorship and/or cause-related marketing must also benefit the non-profit agency. Whatever the form of support – it may be unrestricted funds, financial support for a particular program, in-kind contributions, or increased public awareness – it should be something that helps the arts agency advance its mission.

Successful corporate sponsorships are a little like successful marriages. Both depend on finding the right partner – one with similar interests and goals. The long-term success of a partnership requires hard work, to

Table 8.5

Comparison of Sponsorships and Charitable Contributions

	Sponsorship	Charitable Contribution
Publicity	Highly public	Usually, little fanfare
Source of funds	Typically, marketing, advertising, or communications budgets	Philanthropic or charitable contributions budgets
Accounting	Written off as a full business expense, similar to promotional or media placement expenses	Write-off is limited by tax laws regulating charitable contributions; as a result, accounting/tax considerations are less likely to influence the way a corporation designates funding of a non-profit organization
Objectives	To sell more products or services; to enhance corporate image in markets and among distant stakeholders (customers, potential customers, geographic community)	To be a good corporate citizen; to enhance corporate image among closest stakeholders (employees, shareholders, suppliers)
Partner/ Recipient	Events, teams, or cultural organizations, projects, or programs; a cause is sometimes associated with the undertaking	Larger donations are typically cause-related (education, health, disease, disasters, environmental), but contributions can also be cultural, artistic, or cause-related; at times, funding is designated for a particular project or program; at other times, it is provided for operating budgets

Source: *The Sponsorship Report.* (www.sponsorship.ca/p-issues-callit.)

ensure that each party's needs are met.

8.7.5 Benefits Sought by Companies

In 1990, V. Fisher and R. Brouillet discovered that companies seek the seven benefits when undertaking sponsorship (Table 8.8):

Today, companies all over the world are seeking such benefits. In Ireland, for example, companies revealed that they invest in sponsorship as a marketing tool for the following reasons (Table 8.9):

Table 8.6

The Corporate Sponsor's Decision-Making Process

Position/Department in the organization	Participation (% of cases)
Marketing director	46.4
President	45.7
Vice-president, marketing	45.7
General management	29.7
Sales department	29.7
PR department	26.1
Promotions department	23.9
Advertising department	21.0
Communications department	20.3

Source: Godbout, A. N. Turgeon and F. Colbert. 1991. *Pratique de la commandite commerciale au Québec: une étude empirique.* Montreal: Chaire de gestion des arts, École des HEC, cahier de recherche GA91-02 (September), p.25.

Table 8.7

Participation of Outside Agencies in the Decision-Making Process

Type of Outside Agency	% of cases
Advertising agency	51.4
PR agency	17.1
Sponsorship agency	8.5
Promotions agency	3.0
Multi-service agency/ More than one agency	20.0

Source: Godbout, A. N. Turgeon and F. Colbert. 1991. *Pratique de la commandite commerciale au Québec: une étude empirique.* Montreal: Chaire de gestion des arts, École des HEC, cahier de recherche GA91-02 (September), p.25.

Table 8.8

Benefits Sought in a Sponsorship Program

Better corporate image	37%
Increase in sales	22%
Greater visibility	15%
Social role	15%
Support for a cause	5%
Broader communications mix	4%
Specific target group sought	2%

Source: Fisher V., and R. Brouillet. 1990. *Les commandites: la pub de demain.* Montreal: Éditions Saint-Martin, p. 15.

Interestingly, neither study asked whether the company stood for anything.[23]

8.7.6 Sponsorship and the Consumer

Consumers understand that companies are in business to make a profit, but nowadays they also expect them to be involved. The Cone/Roper Cause-Related *Trends Report*[24] reveals that public acceptability of sponsorship is overwhelmingly positive. In addition, the report reveals sponsorship's ability to influence what and where consumers buy.

The report indicates that 74% of consumers now find it acceptable for companies to engage in cause-related marketing, up from 66% in 1993. Sixty-one percent of consumers believe cause-related marketing should be standard business practice. Eighty-three percent say they have a more positive image of a company that supports a cause they care about. Approximately two thirds of consumers – 130 million Americans – have declared that, price and quality being equal, they are likely to switch to a brand or retailer associated with a good cause.

Leaders in the sponsorship field interpret these data to mean that cause-related marketing and sponsorship have become necessary for brands seeking a strong relationship with customers and communities.

Table 8.9
Main Reasons for Undertaking Sponsorship

Rank	Current sponsorship objectives	% of Irish sponsorship managers
1	Improve community relations	59%
2	Promote corporate image	57%
3	Increase brand awareness	54%
4	Media exposure	39%
5	Increase brand image	37%
6	Improve PR	37%
7	Long-term sales	30%
8	Entertain customers	26%
9	Staff morale	2%
10	Other	6%

Source: "Sponsorship Outlook '99." *Sponsorship Strategies, 1998.* (www.amarach.com/amarach/sponsreports.htm)

The Cone/Roper report also shows that socially and politically active consumers – a key group for marketers – are especially receptive to companies that are supportive of social issues. Ninety-four percent of these socially aware Americans report having a more positive image of such companies. This group is also likely to switch brands or retailers to support a company associated with a good cause. Consumers also report that they expect companies to support a cause over time and in a substantive way. Almost 80% of Americans consistently report that they prefer companies to make a long-term commitment rather than focus on many different causes over shorter periods.

8.7.7 How Sponsorship Is Measured

Fisher and Brouillet[25] discovered that, for companies, the value of a sponsorship arrangement depends upon the number of visitors or participants, the location of the company's logo on promotional material for the event, the visibility of the sponsor at the event, potential media coverage, image, social impact, and the commercial potential of the event.

Sponsorship, then, can be measured with these criteria in mind. It can also be evaluated by measuring awareness or attitude changes toward the sponsor's product or services, by quantifying it in terms of sales results, or by comparing the value of sponsorship-generated media coverage to the cost of equivalent advertising space or time.[26]

8.7.8 Selection Criteria

Table 8.10 presents the criteria used by companies in selecting which events and organizations to sponsor.

8.7.9 Successful Sponsorship and Cause-Related Marketing Applications

Unless actually requesting contributions, a cultural or artistic enterprise should promote the win-win aspect of sponsorship. Requests or applications made to potential sponsors should take into account not only the need for the sponsorship, but also the benefits to the sponsor. To this end, it is important for cultural marketers to:

1) think like a marketer. This means it is important to identify the marketable assets of the cultural or artistic enterprise. These may include name, community, public awareness of the organization and its programs, and board members.

2) learn as much as possible about the companies being approached. Read the business press; check companies' annual reports; look at their ads and promotions.

3) try to figure out what a company's target market is before approaching it.

4) address the needs of the sponsor. Arts managers need to show companies that working with their organization will help them sell more products or services, and at the same time benefit the arts agency.

5) identify primary decision makers. For sponsorship and cause-related decisions, the person to approach is not the head of the foundation (if one exists); most often, it is an executive in marketing and/or sales.

While the amount of money put into sponsorship continues to grow, sponsors say the quality of sponsorship proposals is declining. And, increasingly, companies measure the impact of sponsorships with hard numbers. This means that sponsorships and cause-related marketing partnerships must be more carefully planned.[27] A

Table 8.10
Relative Importance of Selection Criteria

Selection criteria	Average*
Criteria related to the group sponsored	3.56
Skill of organizers	3.61
Potential success of event	3.52
Criteria related to the event	3.05
Ability to meet objective set	3.64
Potential media coverage	3.40
Popularity of event	3.39
Financing arrangements	3.39
Potential association by image	3.39
Type of audience	3.36
Type of sponsorship (arts, sports, etc.)	3.34
Compatibility with product/firm	3.28
Geographic reach of event coverage	3.18
Points in common with firm	3.12
Attention given by public/audience	3.10
Commitment required for event	3.08
Level of risk (financial, artistic)	3.02
Integration with other promotions	2.94
Possibility of having guests	2.51
Tax advantages	1.98
Sale of spin-off products (e.g., souvenirs)	1.73
Criteria related to the sponsor	2.89
Possibility of exclusive sponsorship	3.25
Managers know the project	2.83
Administration endorses the project	2.57
Criteria related to the market	2.58
Competition	2.89
Political or commercial pressures	2.29

*4 = very important   3 = important   2 = slightly important   1 = unimportant

Source: Godbout, A. N. Turgeon and F. Colbert. 1991. *Pratique de la commandite commerciale au Québec: une étude empirique.* Montreal: Chaire de gestion des arts, École des HEC, cahier de recherche GA91-02 (September), p.27.

successful proposal should take the following factors into account:

1) A good proposal *sells benefits, not features*. Cultural managers tend to be very proud of their program, venue, or event. As a result, their proposals often describe the opportunity – the merits of the cause, the artistic excellence of the festival, concert, or exhibit, the economic impact of the event – rather than the benefits to sponsors. Sponsors do not buy causes, events, exhibits, or performances. They buy promotional platforms to help them sell products or services.

2) The successful proposal addresses the sponsor's needs, not the needs of the cultural agency. It is common for sponsorship applications to emphasize the agency's need for money. However, companies with an interest in sponsorship are not motivated by a cultural agency's need for money. Companies want to know *what is in it for them*.

3) The successful proposal is tailored to the sponsor's business category. This means that different sponsors require different benefits. For example, a proposal to an insurance company might focus on access to the arts agency's mailing list or board of directors, while one to a soft-drink distributor might explain on-site visibility and sales rights.

4) The successful proposal includes promotional extensions. There are two types of sponsorship benefits. First, there are the automatic benefits that come with the deal and do not require the sponsor to do anything additional, such as sponsor identification in collateral materials and on-site signage. The second type of sponsorship benefit comes from the sponsor's ability to build upon the sponsored institution, event, performance, etc., through trade, retail, and sales extensions. Today, automatic benefits rarely provide enough return to justify the time and expense of sponsorship. An effective proposal shows how a cultural property or event can be used as the unifying element or theme for media advertising and sales promotion. It is not sufficient to give companies a checklist of automatic benefits. Proposals should also include a menu showing prospective sponsors how to capitalize on their investment.

5) The successful proposal minimizes the prospective sponsor's risk. It is much easier for a corporate marketing or communications executive to authorize a media buy than a sponsorship. A proposal can minimize risk by, for example, making guaranteed media a part of the package and listing reputable co-sponsors. Co-sponsors tell a prospective sponsor that the opportunity being offered has been favourably reviewed by other companies.

6) The successful proposal includes benefit. This means a cultural agency or event should present itself in terms of its total impact on achieving sponsor's objectives rather than isolating one element such as media coverage (see Table 8.11, The Relative Importance of Sponsors' Objectives). The idea here is that when it comes to the benefit for the sponsoring company, the whole should be greater than the sum of the parts.

7) Finally, sponsorship should offer a company the opportunity to form an alliance that brings it resources it could not otherwise access.

Table 8.11
The Relative Importance of Sponsors' Objectives

Objectives	Average*
Sales-related objectives	2.93
Increase sales	3.26
Make prospecting easier for sales force	2.58
Product-related objectives	2.90
Increase top-of-the-mind awareness of product	3.30
Identify a product with a market segment	3.07
Modify product image	2.67
Encourage customers to try product	2.50
Corporate objectives	2.65
Enhance corporate image	3.56
Increase awareness of firm	3.36
Increase long-term performance	3.34
Become involved in the community	3.13
Identify the company with a market segment	2.92
Impress opinion leaders favourably	2.88
Acquire new business contacts	2.81
Change public perception of firm	2.58
Improve employee relations	2.48
Keep up staff morale	2.37
Mark a special event	2.31
Counteract bad press (damage control)	1.98
Reassure shareholders	1.79
Facilitate recruitment of new employees	1.77
Personal objectives	2.09

*4 = very important, 3 = important, 2 = slightly important, 1 = unimportant

Source: Godbout, A. N. Turgeon and F. Colbert. 1991. *Pratique de la commandite commerciale au Québec: une étude empirique*. Montreal: Chaire de gestion des arts, École des HEC, cahier de recherche GA91-02 (September), p. 26.

8.7.10 Negotiating the Sponsorship Agreement

When negotiating a sponsorship agreement, the underlying business relationship established between the sponsor and the sponsored cultural/artistic enterprise must be kept in mind at all times. For the sponsor, the event or enterprise is primarily a promotional tool. For the sponsored organization, the sponsor is almost like a client who must receive certain benefits in exchange for money. Both parties need to feel they are getting their money's worth.

This means a written contract is imperative. The contract should include:[28]

1) corporate and arts agency goals

2) goods and services to be offered by both parties

3) the geographic area to be covered

4) dates for starting and ending

5) creative specifications, such as allowable usage of logos, names, and images of the partners – for example: Who controls advertising on broadcasts? What does the title "official sponsor" entail?

6) details on how funds will be accounted for and what portion of sales will be given to the arts enterprise

7) information on the legal/financial system in place to track and distribute funds.

8.7.11 During and After the Sponsorship

It is important for cultural managers to develop a system that examines and analyzes the sponsorship or cause-related marketing campaign from start to finish. The sponsored enterprise needs to keep track of the campaign goals and consumers' perceptions and communicate these to the sponsor. Remember that sponsors follow up to see if their communications objectives have been met. They want as much information as possible. By providing such information, an artistic enterprise enables the sponsor to evaluate whether its investment is worthwhile.

After the event or at agreed-upon intervals, evaluative meetings should be held with the sponsor to assess the results and benefits gained by both parties. Finally, it is also necessary to celebrate success and to thank the sponsor for their service in support of the arts enterprise and to the community.

8.7.12 Pitfalls and Dangers of Sponsorships: The Arts Agency's Perspective

It would be foolish to believe that sponsorship or a cause-related marketing campaign is without risk. Arts managers need to discuss sponsorship with their key stakeholders, including the board of trustees, staff, and artistic leadership. Possible negative repercussions need to be discussed. In any sponsorship or cause-related marketing venture, the arts enterprise must focus first on its mission. Sponsorship and cause-related marketing must, of course, generate income for the arts institution, while the corporate partner derives publicity, image enhancement, the assistance of volunteers from the arts agency to promote the venture, and increased sales.

The question most often raised about sponsorship and cause-related marketing is whether corporations profit unduly. Today, with the controversy surrounding exhibits and events such as the recent *Sensation* exhibition of works owned by Charles Saatchi at the Brooklyn Museum, there is much discussion about sponsorship and the possibility for conflict of interest. Simply stated, the issue is: Are sponsorships and cause-related marketing partnerships ethical?

From the cultural manager's perspective, the reputation of the arts enterprise is a fundamental concern. Managers must determine whether the mission and nature of the agency is diminished or changed in important ways by association with a for-profit company.[29] Whatever the circumstances, managers need to be careful not to affiliate with a sponsor who is a major competitor of a major stakeholder – for example, contributors. It is equally important to think through "exclusions" – that is, companies with products or services that may appear to conflict with the artistic enterprise's mission. For example, it would be advisable for a children's theatre to refuse a sponsorship from a tobacco company.

Cultural enterprises should consider developing and adopting a policy on sponsorship. Such a policy should do the following:[30]

1) Stress the partnership nature of sponsorship.

2) Define sponsorship as a business arrangement distinct from a contribution.

3) State the arts enterprise's commitment to the concept in positive terms. Companies like to know that arts agencies are enthusiastic about collaborating, as opposed to taking an approach that says, "We will take your money but we don't approve of you."

4) State exclusions clearly (i.e., who the agency will not do business with).

5) Spell out clearly the rights of the sponsor and those of the arts enterprise.

6) Provide an escape clause allowing the arts enterprise to cancel the arrangement should the sponsor's activities run counter to the cultural agency's mission.

The board of trustees should approve the policy. All sponsorship agreements should be in writing.

As governments throughout North America and much of Europe move to cut support to arts organizations, corporate sponsors are often seen moving in to fill the breach. In this context, several mega-sponsors have emerged. In some cases, this has even led to the actual renaming of cultural venues.

As competition for support heats up, corporations increasingly expect greater recognition for their efforts. More and more companies are, in fact, moving away from simple philanthropy to sponsorship with a marketing edge. Companies are taking greater care to target and select arts institutions that are well matched with their own demographics. In other words, sponsorship is not about having a good heart!

This does not mean that arts enterprises should respond by engraving the name of a sponsor on the stage floor or by referring to a sponsor during the course of a play. Rather, arts managers need to seek a balance between outright intrusion into the artistic product and mission, and tasteful recognition of a sponsor's contribution.

SUMMARY

Promotional tools are advertising, personal selling, PR (which includes publicity), and sales promotion.

The functions of promotion are essentially to communicate a message to the consumer and bring about a change in the consumer. The change is particularly important if the customer is near the ignorance stage. If a great deal of change is needed or the product is complex, personal selling is the most appropriate tool. On the other hand, if the change or product is relatively simple, advertising should be used, with the other tools used to support it. In the cultural milieu, limited budgets make PR/publicity the most widely used tool.

In any form of commercial communication, knowing the various players involved in the purchasing decision is important. There are normally five: initiator, influencer, decision maker, buyer, and user. The next step is to draw up a communications plan that answers the questions Who? To whom? What? How? When? With what results?

As a rule, there are eight steps to follow in drawing up a communications plan. The first three are related to the corporate marketing strategy: analysis of the situation, setting marketing goals, and developing the marketing strategy. The five steps specifically involving the communications plan are setting objectives, drawing up a budget, developing strategies, and implementing and then monitoring such strategies.

Corporate sponsorship in the cultural sector has become a part of the communications strategy of the cultural or artistic enterprise. Throughout the 1980s, the proportion of the budget allotted to sporting events was gradually transferred to cultural events. Sponsorship is strictly a business decision for executives who consider it a way to replace the traditional media as a promotional vehicle.

QUESTIONS

1. What is promotion?
2. What distinguishes the four promotional tools?
3. What are the main functions of the promotion variable?
4. When is personal selling better than advertising?
5. Where does public relations fit into the promotional strategy of an artistic enterprise?
6. Give examples of a situation in which the consumer is near the ignorance stage and a situation in which the consumer is closer to the action (buying) stage.
7. Who are the decision makers involved in buying a ticket for a children's show? Why?
8. What purpose do the basic questions behind a communications plan serve?
9. Do the critics play an important role in the cultural consumer's decision-making process?
10. What is the difference between a marketing objective and a communications objective?
11. Describe Boisvert's five methods for drafting a promotional budget.
12. What are a sponsor's objectives?
13. What are the main selection criteria for corporate sponsors?

Notes

1. Mokwa, M.P., W.M. Dawson and E.A. Prieve. 1980. *Marketing the Arts.* New York: Praeger.

2. Boisvert, J.-M. 1988. *Administration de la communication de masse.* Boucherville, Quebec: Gaëtan Morin Éditeur.

3. The consumer profile for any given media or specific program or for written press is relatively easy to obtain in almost all countries. There are several sources. In Canada for example, ratings and a sociodemographic profile of radio and TV audiences for different television networks may be obtained through the Bureau of Broadcast Measurement (BBM).

4. Weisberg, L. 1987. "Telemarketing, a Growing Art Form." *Advertising Age*, 27 July, p. 5–9.

5. Desormeaux, R. 1995. "L'équipe de vente," in *Gestion du marketing, 2e édition,* F. Colbert and M. Filion, eds. Boucherville, Quebec: Gaëtan Morin Éditeur, chapter 11, p. 415–458.

6. Here, "independent revenue" is used to denote the revenue generated by the company itself in the form of admission fees, the sale of tickets or spin-off products, etc. This type of revenue is exclusive of any grant or subsidy from either the public or the private sector.

7. Schramm, W. 1960. *The Process and Effects of Mass Communication.* Urbana, IL: University of Illinois Press.

8. Kotler, P. 1972. *Marketing Management.* Paris: Publi-Union.

9. McConnell, J.V., R.L. Cutter and E.B. McNeil. 1958. "Subliminal Stimulation: An Overview." *American Psychologist*, Vol. 13, n° 1, p. 229–242.

10. Twenty-four frames per second is the minimum speed at which the human eye can perceive movement or an image projected on screen.

11. Colbert, F. 1983. "La publicité, le marketing et le marché." *PME Gestion*, Vol. 3, n° 5 (January), p. 3–4.

12. Colbert, F. 1983. *Le théâtre pour enfants: marché en turbulence.* Montreal: École des HEC; Colbert, F. 1990. *Un marché en turbulence: huit ans plus tard.* Montreal: Groupe de recherche et de formation en gestion des arts, École des HEC.

13. Boisvert, J.-M. 1995. "La promotion et la composition promotionnelle," in *Gestion du marketing, 2e édition,* F. Colbert and M. Filion, eds. Boucherville, Quebec: Gaëtan Morin Éditeur, chapter 9, p. 315–359.

14. *Ibid.*

15. *Ibid.*

16. See IEG Network, http://www.sponsorship.com/forum/faq.html.

17. *Ibid.*

18. Baumol, W.J., and W.G. Bowen. 1966. *Performing Arts – The Economic Dilemma.* Cambridge, Massachusetts, and London: M.I.T. Press.

19. "Best Practices in Event Marketing and Sponsorship" (138 pages): associates.com/Publications_Reports/Event_Marketing_Report__Execut/event_mark eting_report__execut.html.

20. IEG Network, http://www.sponsorship.com/forum/faq.html.

21. Cone Cause Related Marketing, www.conenet.com/website/crm/index.htm.

22. Prologue, http:\\www.fundwell.com. See also the Field Museum website, www.fmnh.org/.

23. See Romesch, R. 1997. "Doing Well by Doing Good." *New Republic* (January 6), p. 4.

24. Cone/Roper Cause-Related. 1999. *Trends Report: The Evolution of Cause Branding.* www.roper.com

25. Fisher, V., and R. Brouillet. 1990. *Les commandites: la pub de demain.* Montreal: Éditions Saint-Martin, p. 15.

26. IEG Network, http://www.sponsorship.com/forum/ faq.html.

27. See Ukman, L. 1995. "Six Attributes of the Successful Proposal." *IEG Network*, December 4.

28. "How Social Responsibility Gets Results." Welland, Ontario: Tri-Media Marketing & Publicity Inc. www.tri-media.com/info-idx.html.

29. Hammack, D.C., and D. Young, eds. 1993. *Non-Profit Organizations in a Market Economy.* San Francisco: Jossey-Bass, p. 300–301.

30. McClintock, N. 1996. "Why You Need a Sponsorship Policy and How to Get One." *Front and Centre*, Vol. 3, nº 5 (September), p. 12–13. Distributed by the Canadian Centre for Philanthropy,

For Further Reference

Braun, M. 2000. "Courting the Media: How the 1998 Spoleto Festival USA Attracted Media Coverage." *International Journal of Arts Management*, Vol. 2, nº 2 (Winter), p. 50–58.

Chéron, E., and C. Bissonnette. 1992. "Les activités, les intervenants, les rôles et les critères dans le processus d'octroi des commandites par des organisations au Québec," in *Proceedings of the First International Conference on Arts Management*, F. Colbert and C. Mitchell eds. Montreal: Chaire de gestion des arts, École des HEC, August, p. 205–220.

Gardner, M.P., and D.J. Shuman. 1987. "Sponsorship: An Important Component of the Promotion Mix." *Journal of Advertising*, Vol. 16, nº 1, p. 11–17.

Larceneux, F. 2001. "Critical Opinion as a Tool in the Marketing of Cultural Products: The Experiential Label. *International Journal of Arts Management*, Vol. 3, nº 2 (Winter), p. 60–72.

Meenaghan, J.A. 1983. "Commercial Sponsorship." *European Journal of Marketing*, vol. 17, nº. 7, p. 5–73.

Pope, D.L, J. Apple and P. Keltyka. 2000. "Using an Integrated Ticket Donation Program to Increase Subscription Sales and Reach Underserved Markets: A Strategic Marketing Approach." *International Journal of Arts Management*, Vol. 3, nº 1 (Fall), p. 39–46.

Reiss, A.H. 2000. *CPR for Nonprofits: Creative Strategies for Successful Fundraising, Marketing, Communications, and Management.* San Francisco: Jossey-Bass.

Roschwalb, S.A. 1990. "Corporate Eyes on the Market: Funding the Arts for the 1990's." *Journal of Arts Management and Law*, Vol. 19, nº 4 (Winter), p. 73–83.

Schramm, W. 1960. "How Communication Works," in *The Process and Effects of Mass Communication.* Urbana, IL: University of Illinois Press.

Turgeon, N., and F. Colbert. 1992. "The Decision Process Involved in Corporate Sponsorship for the Arts." *Journal of Cultural Economics*, Vol. 16, (June), p. 41–52.

Vals Comes Home. 1987. "Information and Ideas for Arts Administrators." *ACUCAA Bulletin*, Vol. 30, nº 1 (January), p. 1–5.

Van Driessen, W., and M. Verlinden. 1993. "The Integration and Compatibility of Sponsorship Practice with Corporate and Marketing Communication Strategy: Five Case Studies," in *Proceedings of the Second International Conference on Arts and Cultural Management.* Jouy-en-Josas, France: Groupe HEC.

Plan

CHAPTER 9
Marketing Information Systems

OBJECTIVES

- Define internal sources of data
- Present and examine secondary sources of data
- Define and analyze the main primary sources of data
- Discuss the main methods of gathering data
- Outline the steps to follow in any research plan

INTRODUCTION

The marketing information system (MIS) is a fundamental part of the marketing process, since it provides the information needed to make enlightened decisions. The MIS represents an arsenal of tools useful in the decision-making process. Of course, no tool ever invented can replace good judgment!

An MIS uses three types of data: internal, secondary, and primary. Internal data represent all the information obtainable from within the company, such as sales and financial reports. Secondary data are published by public or private organizations in the form of reports made available to the public through the publishing organization or the library system. Primary data are obtained directly from the consumer. This information is usually collected through a market study, a poll, a survey, or business research. The company itself may do the work, or it may hire a specialized firm for the purpose. In this chapter, we will examine all aspects of the process, especially the sources and gathering techniques used for secondary and primary data.

9.1 INTERNAL DATA

The term "internal data" is used here to denote any information useful to the decision-making process found within the company. Internal data are usually derived from six sources (see table 9.1): the accounting system, sales reports, the client list, a website hits report, company staff, and previous studies. It should be pointed out that a survey or study performed by the company is

Table 9.1
Main Sources of Internal Data
Accounting system
Sales reports (ticket sales and billings)
Client, subscriber, supplier lists
Personnel
Previous surveys and studies

considered primary data gathering at the time of the study, but that the report retained as a file then becomes part of the internal data. These are all valuable tools for measuring the performance of cultural organizations.

The accounting system can furnish a great deal of interesting information – for example, the break-even point for the company as a whole or for each company product individually. It also enables the marketing manager to measure how profitable corporate marketing efforts have been. An analysis of the data supplied by the accounting system can orient the firm and the gathering of primary and secondary data.

Companies can also use data drawn from sales reports generated by the box office or customer billings. Box-office data enable the marketing manager to plot the sales curve of a particular event, compare it to previous years, and decide, if necessary, what measures to take. These measures may affect one or several variables in the marketing mix. For example, if there is always a drop in sales a few weeks after the start of an event, it might be worth increasing the promotion budget for this period in order to maintain or increase attendance figures.

Such data enable a company to correct a strategy, based on the results obtained. Over the years, company standards may develop as guidelines not only for analyzing or forecasting sales figures but also for enhancing the marketing planning process.

The client, subscriber, or donor list of an organization, be it commercial or non-profit, is a mine of interesting information. The geographic location of customers, for example, is actually a company's trading area. As seen in chapter 7, this is a simple method used to measure a company's penetration in a specific region or neighbourhood. This type of analysis points up spots where a company is well established and where it should focus its marketing efforts. Census data (section 9.2) can provide further details to flesh out the sociodemographic profile of consumers living in the sectors reached.

For other useful information, the marketing manager need look no farther than the staff members who actually come into contact with the customers. Employees in communications or sales can collect data that may prove highly relevant to those making the final decisions.

Of course, every analyst must be well acquainted with previous studies or surveys. Although the information may have become outdated, it can provide important clues on how to analyze the current situation. It might even be worthwhile repeating the experiment to compare the new data with the old.

Finally, thanks to the proliferation of Internet sites, it is relatively easy for a company to obtain information on a particular industry. For example, all professional associations in the arts and cultural sector have an Internet site, many of which provide direct links to the association's member organizations. In addition, a company can trace most of the visitors to its site by checking the statistics on the Hit Box, a service offered by most Internet providers.

9.2 SECONDARY DATA

9.2.1 General Considerations

Secondary data are those published by governmental organizations or by private groups. This kind of data is particularly useful to the marketing manager, since it provides the information needed to measure the size and evolution of product demand, the size and make-up of the product market, and even the structure of the industry itself.

The main advantage of using this type of data is the low cost, in terms of both time and money. Access to these documents involves few expenditures and the data can be gathered in a relatively short period, whereas several weeks or months may be needed to gather and collate similar information from a market study.

Secondary data also generate questions and hypotheses that actually orient primary-data research.

Secondary data include all information gathered for specific purposes from a perspective foreign to that suggested by the research problem set out by the company. Sometimes, the data actually provide a partial answer to the research problem or question. Sometimes, however, there is no pertinent information available on the specific issue or problem that the company has raised. Existing information may be out of date. In this case, the methodology used in the past to correlate data is an invaluable tool for the researcher who wants to repeat and update the study.

It should be pointed out that the more specific the set of problems is to the company and the more restricted the field of interest, the less information the secondary data will provide. In this case, primary data must be used.

9.2.2 Public- and Private-Sector Data

Secondary data may come from either the private or the public sector. Such data can be found in documentation published by various public organizations – for example, government departments, agencies, institutes, associations, and various government bureaus. Many polling firms and periodicals also publish study results.

These two different sources of secondary data have their strengths and weaknesses, as shown in table 9.2. In practice, the two sources complement each other.

In this section, we will use the example of Statistics Canada, which has an enviable international reputation in the field of data collection and processing. However, it should be noted that the characteristics discussed generally apply to other national statistical bureaus as well.

Scientific Method

Statistics Canada serves the needs of a broad range of people, such as politicians, students, analysts, and executives, who often base important decisions on Statistics Canada data. As a publicly funded government organization, Statistics Canada must

---

Table 9.2

The Strong and Weak Points of Public and Private Data

	Public data	Private data
Scientific methodology	+	−
Standardization of data	+	−
Possibility of studies conducted over time	+	−
Accessibility	+	±
Aggregation	−	+
Currency	−	+

take methodological precautions to ensure the validity of all the data it publishes. In fact, Stats Can, as it is popularly known, describes the research procedure for each study in a clear and detailed fashion. This is not always the case for private secondary data. Often, the authors of a privately published report do not specify the research method used; hence, the reader cannot detect their bias. Sometimes, such studies are in fact seriously biased. In short, it is easier to check the method employed in public studies than that applied in private studies.

Standardization of Data

Statistics Canada data are categorized in a standard fashion, which greatly facilitates searches and comparisons from one year to the next. This is not the norm, however, for private data, since the studies they are part of are usually carried out on behalf of a particular client seeking specific information. In most cases, it is impossible to compare data from two studies performed by a private-sector firm, since the objective of the study and type of information gathered may vary tremendously between any two studies. It may happen, however, that a study is repeated so that two sets of results can actually be compared.

Possibility of Time Series

The standardization in Statistics Canada data enables the researcher to create time series. Stats Can classifies information gathered in categories that remain the same from one year to the next. Periodically, minor adjustments are made to reflect changes in the social environment. For example, the videocassette recorder (VCR) did not exist in the pre-1980 category of "Leisure Equipment for Home Use," since the product was not yet available to the public at large. The VCR was recently added to reflect the new reality. By correlating data from one particular category over time, researchers can monitor the demand for a product. Information gathered by private firms does not allow for this type of tracking or follow-up.

Accessibility

Statistics Canada data can be found and consulted easily for little or no cost in large libraries. Private data are distributed but remain confidential and inaccessible. Moreover, the cost of buying private data can be rather high, or even prohibitive. All in all, accessibility to private data should be considered variable – somewhat like the weather!

Aggregation of Data

A research report published by a private firm usually summarizes a tremendous amount and vast variety of data. This is one of the main advantages of private data, since the synthesis of data makes the market analyst's task much simpler. For example, in a report produced by a research firm, the product market over fifteen years may appear in one graph or table, whereas the researcher would have to look through several Statistics Canada catalogues to construct the same demand curve. Hence the aggregative aspect of the information presented in a private report is a definite advantage.

Currency of Information

The complexity of Statistics Canada studies and the precautions it takes usually translate to a two- or three-year lag from research to publication stage. Research reports published by private firms, however, usually focus on recent events and the orders given by the client organization. Consequently, upon publication the data are still recent.

9.2.3 Public Data

National Statistical Agency

The main source of secondary data, as well as the most reliable and accessible, is unquestionably the National Statistical Bureau (NSG). As the federal statistics bureau, the NSB publishes a great deal of documentation on diverse topics. No matter what the framework or issue, the NSG has most probably published something pertinent.

NSGs publish, on a broad range of subjects, both general documents – for example, census data – and highly specific material – for example, studies on the performing arts. The marketing manager or researcher looking for documents on a particular country should first consult the general catalogue listing of the NSG publications to locate the most appropriate studies. (See, for example, in the United States, www.census.gov; in Canada, www.statcan.ca; in Australia, abs.gov.au; and in France, www.insee.fr.)

Of particular interest in Canada is the massive survey Statistics Canada conducts every two years on family expenditures in Canada (category 62-555). The results of this survey reveal, for example, average household spending and the percentage of families declaring expenditures on movies shown in theatres, on stage shows, and on admission fees to cultural establishments such as museums and galleries.

Other Governmental Agencies

Publications from various ministries and agencies are further sources of public secondary data.

In Canada, excellent sources of data are the Canada Council for the Arts Research Department, the Department of Canadian Heritage, and the Department of External Affairs, as well as the arts councils and cultural departments of the different provinces.

The National Endowment for the Arts in the United States, the Australia Council for the Arts, the Arts Council of England, and the Ministry of Culture in France also publish several studies each year. The Council of Europe represents another major source of data.

Other government organizations or departments in different countries also publish study results and documents of potential interest to those in the cultural milieu.

9.2.4 Private Data

Databases and Indexes

There are also various databases on the market that may be consulted free of charge. Until very recently, these databases provided only printed documentation. Now they are computerized and may provide a print-out, microfiche, or CD-ROM.

Computer-retrievable databases are usually located in one place and must be consulted via modem. Billing is calculated by minute or hour.

Databases on CD-ROM, like those on microfiche, may be consulted on-site, usually in a library, using the appropriate equipment. Indexes, which are generally printed on paper, provide key words that enable researchers to look up articles, books, theses, or any other material listed that is of potential interest. Some databanks and indexes include not only the code or call number of the document but also a short description of its contents, which facilitates the user's task considerably. These databases may be consulted in most public and university libraries.

Finally, one should not underestimate the wealth of information that can be gleaned from the Internet sites of companies in the arts and cultural sector; it is often possible to find an enormous amount of information on a particular company.

Publications by Private Organizations

The manager of a cultural or artistic enterprise can obtain useful information from private organizations, whether they focus on the arts or not. The Council for Business and the Arts in Canada and the Ford Foundation in United States are indirectly involved in culture or the arts and do publish reference material pertinent to arts management.

Professional associations are another source of useful information. Such associations may commission a special study or report in their own specific field and then publish the results.

Educational institutions that have an arts-management chair, department, or degree program are yet another fertile

source of interesting data. Such schools publish research results in monographs, bibliographies, or journals. The subjects covered represent a broad range of interests. These sources include: the arts-management chair at Montreal's École des Hautes Études Commerciales (HEC) (www.hec.ca/gestiondesarts), the Centre for Cultural Management at the University of Waterloo, Ontario (ccm.uwaterloo.ca), the Australian Key Centre for Cultural and Media Policy (CMP) at Griffith University (www.gu.edu.au/centre/cmp/home/html), and the Centre for Research of the Utrecht School of the Arts in the Netherlands.

The marketing manager may want to look at management journals such as the *Journal of Marketing*, or journals devoted to cultural affairs such as the *International Journal of Arts Management* (www.hec.ca/ijam), the *Journal of Cultural Economics*, the *International Journal of Cultural Policy*, or the *Journal of Arts Management, Law and Society*.

Table 9.3 lists the main sources of private data.

Table 9.3
Sources of Private Data

Indexes, databases, CD-ROMs
Specialized organizations
Professional associations
Private agencies
Educational institutions
International organizations
Magazines, academic journals
Websites

9.3 PRIMARY DATA

Primary data may be obtained by consulting the target market directly through data-collection techniques called "market study," "survey," or "poll." Data may be collated by the marketing manager, or a specialized firm may be hired to do the work. The procedure involves collecting data pertinent to a previously stated problem, analyzing the data, and then interpreting them with a view to making decisions.

The cost of collecting primary data should always reflect the value of the information sought. In other words, the manager in charge must calculate whether the study is worth the effort. It would be useless to spend $5,000 on a survey if the information obtained does not enable the company to save, or gain, at least $5,000. If the financial outcome of the decision were any lower, the entire project might not be worth the trouble.

There are three types of research for primary data: exploratory research, descriptive research, and causal research.

9.3.1 Exploratory Research

Exploratory research basically supplies qualitative data. It is not based on hypotheses or preconceived ideas and should be used only when little or no prior information is available. As a method, it is flexible, unstructured, and qualitative.

This type of research may serve several purposes. It may define a problem better, suggest hypotheses to be tested, generate ideas for new products, capture consumers' first reactions to a new concept, pretest a questionnaire, or determine which criteria play a role in selecting one show or film over another.

Exploratory research also reveals the consumer's vocabulary and centres of interest. All this makes the researcher and marketer more familiar with what may seem like a virtual terra incognita. Several techniques are available, including discussion groups, in-depth interviews, case studies, observation, and projection.

9.3.2 Descriptive Research

Descriptive research seeks specific information on a given topic. It usually starts from a hypothesis, which is tested and confirmed or disproved. This type of research is used only when the situation is fairly clear, with specific and well-defined information needs, frame of reference, and variables. Exploratory research often precedes descriptive research so that the research hypothesis and parameters involved can be defined more clearly.

While exploratory research is qualitative and uses a small number of respondents, descriptive research provides results that enable the researcher to proceed to a quantitative analysis from representative samplings of the population studied.

Descriptive research may, for instance, determine which factors intervene in the decision-making process for the purchase of a theatre ticket within a specific population. It may also provide a sociodemographic profile of museum visitors or outline the characteristics of popular music fans in a given area.

Data-Collection Techniques

There are three key data-gathering

techniques used in descriptive research: mail, telephone, and personal interviewing. The choice of one technique over another depends on the purpose or objective of the study and the resources available. The breadth and precision of the data collected, the time and effort required, the type of questions asked (open-ended versus closed), the cost associated with different techniques, and the administration required are all influential factors.

Mail-in Surveys

Mail-in surveys have two main advantages: they are inexpensive for the large number of people they can reach in comparison with either of the other two techniques, and they respect the respondent's wish to remain anonymous, which enables researchers to obtain more personal information while reducing any potential bias in the interviewer or in the respondent vis-à-vis the interviewer. The main disadvantages are as follows: the inability to control the identity of the respondent, who may consult a third party in replying; the lack of control over the order in which questions are answered; and the possible misunderstanding of terms.

With mass-consumption products, the rate of response for mail-in surveys ranges from 2% to 5%. A study carried out on a cultural matter may obtain a response rate of anywhere between 25% and 40%. The rate may rise significantly for a study carried out among a sampling of consumers related somehow to an establishment; for instance, "friends of the museum" will fill out a questionnaire more readily if it comes from the establishment they support or patronize.

The same pattern may be observed among the members of a professional association.

Telephone Surveys or Polls

The telephone survey is a quick way to reach a large number of people within a short period. By increasing the number of operators, a polling firm can reach several thousand people within a week.

The response rate is generally quite high, at approximately 80% to 90%. However, overuse of this technique in a region may lead to a higher rate of refusal.

The telephone survey allows the interviewer to clarify a question in the event that the respondent does not understand. This technique also proves more productive on a daily basis, since the interviewer does not have to travel anywhere to conduct interviews. Although more expensive than mail-in surveys, telephone surveys are cheaper than one-on-one interviews.

One disadvantage of the telephone interview is, obviously, the lack of visual support. It is also difficult, if not impossible, to use multiple-choice questions. In fact, the questions asked must be relatively simple. Further, they must be asked quickly, since the respondent will not stay more than fifteen minutes on the line unless the subject of the survey is of particular interest.

Personal Interviews

The personal interview is effective if the marketer wants to obtain fairly complex data. It enables the interviewer to use visual material and to clarify or repeat questions. This technique allows the respondent who has not understood a question to ask for additional information and lets the interviewer delve deeper into certain answers.

The personal interview costs much more in time and money than do the other two techniques. It is also more complicated and more open to potential bias caused by the presence of the interviewer.

Sources of Error

Regardless of the technique used, every researcher must try to minimize bias and sources of error that can creep into the data-collection process. There are four main sources of error: refusal to answer, sampling errors, vague or inaccurate answers, and human error caused by the interviewer. The researcher must always keep these possible sources of error in mind and try to minimize their influence.

If some members of the sample refuse to answer, a serious source of error develops. The higher the refusal rate, the greater the possibility of the statistics giving a biased view of reality. Since the researcher does not know what these people think, the results of a survey may not be accurate. Although the rate of refusal can never be eliminated, it must be kept to a minimum through the use of adequate evaluation tools.

Sampling errors can also yield results that are not representative of the over-all population being studied. These errors arise when the sampling method is inadequate or when the size of the sample is insufficient.

The third main source of error in descriptive research is obtaining vague or inexact answers. This error may be caused by sheer ignorance on the part of a respondent who wants to give any answer rather than appear stupid or who wants to answer

according to perceived consensus on a particular issue. It may be linked to forgetfulness if the data collection takes place too long after the facts to be analyzed took place. Attitude may also play a role, since respondents can voluntarily bias their answers for a variety of personal reasons. Common reasons are lack of time, general fatigue, a feeling that their privacy is being invaded, a natural tendency to furnish socially acceptable answers (e.g., inflating annual book purchases if the activity is perceived as valued), and even just the desire to please the interviewer. Some respondents may politely agree with the interviewer although they actually disagree completely.

The last source of error is the interviewer, who may unwittingly, through body language or speaking style, influence the respondent. Good interviewer training can reduce this potential bias to a minimum.

9.3.3 Causal Research

The third technique is causal in that it analyzes the effects of one variable on another. An example of this technique would be a study on the impact of distributing free tickets on the future consumption of a theatre troupe's product.

Relatively rigid and specialized, this type of research analyzes only one aspect of reality. Causal research is based on the principle that knowledge of a product is extensive and that several influential variables have already been defined and are relatively well known. This type of research seeks to find the cause-and-effect relationship that may exist between pairs of variables. It takes one or several hypotheses and then tests each one.

9.4 THE STEPS INVOLVED IN DESCRIPTIVE RESEARCH

Descriptive research attempts to meet objectives set out after the research problem has been defined. These objectives are to be met as inexpensively, accurately (low margin of error), and rapidly as possible. A marketing manager may decide to run a series of projects covering a part of the objectives rather than have a full study of all aspects of a problem.

Table 9.4 lists a series of fourteen steps which should be the basis of any research activity.

Table 9.4

The 14 Steps of Any Research Project

Step 1	Defining the problem
Step 2	Defining research objectives
Step 3	Deciding on the human and financial resources required
Step 4	Setting a schedule
Step 5	Choosing the appropriate tools and techniques
Step 6	Deciding on the sample
Step 7	Designing the questionnaire
Step 8	Testing the questionnaire
Step 9	Coding responses
Step 10	Gathering data
Step 11	Monitoring interviewers
Step 12	Compiling data
Step 13	Analyzing the results
Step 14	Writing the report

We can divide this fourteen-step series into two sections. The first four steps are common to all research. Only by answering the questions they pose can a manager or researcher select the appropriate technique or method to resolve the problem and choose the most appropriate form of data collection. The other ten steps, although given here within the framework of descriptive research, may be applied to both exploratory and causal research, depending on the situation. The content of some steps, however, may be different or not even applicable.

Step 1: Defining the Problem

Before beginning any form of data collection, the researcher or marketing manager must be sure that the problem to be studied has been properly defined. If the definition is specific, decisions throughout the subsequent steps are easier to make.

Since cultural enterprises usually have limited funds, market studies are not frequent. The risk, therefore, is that the company trying to squeeze every penny out of the study overloads its questionnaire and in the end respondents find it too long or complicated to answer.

A good definition of the problem being studied is one that lets the manager or researcher know just how helpful internal data or secondary data already available could be in solving all or part of the problem. In any event, it is wise to begin checking before the collection stage to ensure that the information does not already exist elsewhere.

The following situations may initiate the research process:

- The number of subscribers has dropped considerably over the previous year's figures.
- A corporate executive wonders about consumer reaction to a product price change.
- The company wants to enter an unknown market.

Step 2: Defining Research Objectives

An analyst can use the problem to be solved as a starting point to define research objectives. For instance, a theatre may want to find out why subscribers are not renewing their subscriptions, or know the percentage of consumers likely to react negatively to a price change, or define the consumption habits for residents of a specific area.

Step 3: Deciding on the Human and Financial Resources Required

The marketing manager must also calculate the staff and budget available for research purposes. Obviously, the subsequent decision will depend on study procedure and complexity, as well as on the way in which the research will be carried out – for example, by an outside firm or an in-house team. The budget allotted to the collection of primary data will be greater than that needed for gathering secondary data.

Analyzing the budget required for a market study provides an excellent opportunity to examine the value of the information sought in relation to the inherent cost of collecting it. The value of information provided by a market study is often difficult to estimate beforehand. Nonetheless, the marketing manager or researcher must try to answer this question so as not to waste time or money. According to Desormeaux,[1] every

marketing manager or researcher should ask the following eight questions before commissioning the collection of primary data.

1) Is the additional information really needed?

2) Does the project envisaged really correspond to the firm's information needs?

3) Is there too much uncertainty or inaccuracy?

4) Will the results influence future decisions?

5) Is there enough time to do the research?

6) What are the cost and probability of errors?

7) Is the expected level of certainty and accuracy appropriate?

8) Have secondary data already been used sufficiently?

Step 4: Setting a Schedule

Time is an important element in drawing up any study plan. The manager and company must know when the data will be available. A tight schedule in descriptive research might necessitate the use of telephone interviews, which may be carried out quickly but generate a limited amount of data.

Step 5: Choosing the Appropriate Tools and Techniques

Once the objectives have been set out, the marketing manager or researcher must choose, from among the three methods (exploratory, descriptive, causal), the one that will provide the necessary information at the lowest cost in terms of both time and money. The manager can then select the data-collection technique to be used; in descriptive research, for example, there are mail-in surveys, telephone surveys, and personal interviews. The choice of one technique over another depends on budget and schedule. There are other data-collection techniques, including observation and projections; however, the first three are the most commonly used by polling firms.

Step 6: Deciding on the Sample

Once the technique has been chosen – for example, descriptive – the researcher decides on the parameters of the sample. The sample must include a sufficient number of respondents chosen at random who represent the population studied in order to generate significant statistics. In some cases, such as if the population is fairly limited and heterogeneous, the marketing researcher will study the entire population.

Regardless of population size, the sample must include a minimum of thirty respondents. According to statistical laws, a sample is considered statistically significant once there are thirty respondents chosen at random. The accuracy and reliability of the results increase along with the size of the sample. The same rule applies when drawing conclusions about a subgroup of individuals within the main sample population: researchers must always have at least thirty respondents in any particular cell. Of course, it is possible to analyze seriously the results of a study or the subgroups of a sample with fewer than thirty respondents. In this case, non-parametric statistical methods are used, which do not allow a researcher to generalize the results as if they were the same for an entire population. (Readers

interested in these methods should consult *Non-Parametric Statistics* by Siegel.[2])

The size of the population studied does not determine the number of respondents needed to make up a representative sample. However, the size of the sample does determine the degree of accuracy. The more homogeneous the population, the more limited the sample will be. The laws of statistics prove that whether an opinion poll is conducted in a town of 5,000 or a city of 5 million, the same sample size provides the same degree of accuracy.

The size of a sample is calculated according to the number of people who respond to the questionnaire, not the number of people who receive it. For example, if a sample of 400 respondents is needed and the rate of response is usually 40% for this particular type of survey, 1,000 questionnaires should be sent out. A quick reminder: the larger the sample size, the higher the cost of the study and the longer the data-processing and analysis stages. The rate is also a function of the length of the questionnaire, the respondent's interest in the subject, and the motivation created by the questionnaire style. Various strategies can be used to increase motivation, such as a $1 included in each mailing or a postage-paid return envelope.

The size of the sample influences how much faith a manager should place in the information gathered (see table 9.5). The market researcher who selects 269 people has a 90% probability of not being wrong (maximum level of reliability sought) by more than 5% in any estimates (5% is, therefore, the maximum acceptable margin of error). If the sample includes 382 people, the manager's level of reliability rises to 95%

Table 9.5
Sampling Size According to Reliability Sought

Maximum Margin of Error	Reliability Sought	80%	90%	95%
	1%	4,100	6,715	9,594
More	3%	455	746	1,066
or	5%	164	269	382
Less	10%	41	67	96
	15%	18	30	43
	20%	10	17	24

with a maximum margin of error of 5%. For instance, if a survey based on a sample of 382 individuals shows that 30% of the respondents prefer a particular type of show, it actually proves that, with a probability of 95%, the percentage is between 28.5% and 32.5%.

Three methods are frequently used to develop a sample: the simple method, the systematic method, and the quota method.

Simple sampling consists of selecting at random, from the population studied, the individuals to be surveyed. In this method, each individual has the same probability of being chosen. If a company wants to send a questionnaire to a sampling of the residents of a town, the names and addresses of all those to be contacted are required. The strategy of asking passers-by at the intersection of two main downtown streets is not statistically significant, since each individual within the population studied does not have the same chance (or probability) of being at that corner at a specific time.

The simple method cannot be used in all circumstances; hence the utility of the systematic sampling method. This method consists of taking a slice of the population studied – for example, one person per x number of names. If the population studied were symphony subscribers, the marketing manager or researcher could simply draw one person's name per block of, say, ten names on the list until the sample had been completed. This method works particularly well when the total population comprises a known and finite number.

Lastly, the quota method seeks to represent the entire population studied by retaining certain common characteristics, which must be found in the same percentage within the sample. These characteristics could be age, gender, income, level of education, or any other variable of interest.

For example, in a telephone survey, if the company wants to reach a target of 51% female respondents, then interviewers could be instructed to interview no more women once that target has been met.

Step 7: Designing the Questionnaire

Designing a structured questionnaire is a delicate task. The questionnaire plays a key role not only in the quality of the information obtained, but also in the rate of response.

Questions must be worded so as not to bias the answers. The vocabulary must be readily understood by respondents.

The market researcher draws up a list of information to be gathered on the basis of the research objectives. This list is then transformed into a logically ordered series of questions, starting with the questions most likely to interest the respondent and ending with the most delicate or confidential, such as age and income.

Questions may be closed or open-ended. For closed questions, the respondent has a choice of answers and indicates this choice. Open-ended questions allow the respondent to answer freely. Closed questions are generally used in descriptive research in order to facilitate the analysis of results drawn from the long questionnaires used on a large sample.

For the highest possible response rate, the questionnaire writer must ensure that the final version is short and well laid out, with questions in a logical order. Closed questions are preferable. An introduction stressing the importance of the answers will encourage respondents to fill out the questionnaire.

Step 8: Testing the Questionnaire

The marketing manager or the head of the marketing-research team must have the questionnaire pretested before using it to collect data. This stage usually reveals any ambiguity in the questionnaire and allows for any necessary changes before the mailing begins. The pretest usually needs only a dozen respondents who fit as closely as possible the profile of the population studied.

One way of making a questionnaire even more efficient is to test it in a real situation. Researchers can survey a sample using a certain number of people, such as 100, who are asked to answer the questionnaire. The analysis of these data after compilation allows for any relevant changes to be made. Testing a questionnaire in a real situation is all the more necessary if there are many questions and the accuracy of the respondents' answers is essential.

This step is a crucial one that enables a company to improve a questionnaire and avoid costly errors.

Step 9: Coding Responses

Once the researcher is ready to gather data and the questionnaire is in its definitive version, the responses should be coded. This step facilitates the eventual processing of the data.

Step 10: Gathering Data

Once the questionnaire has been prepared and coded, the researcher can start collecting data. Interviewers are trained and respondents are contacted by mail, telephone, or in person.

Step 11: Monitoring Interviewers

Even if the interviewers are well-trained professionals, the company must monitor their work to ensure that the respondents are being reached and that the interviewers are following instructions. Usually, the contacts made by the interviewers are checked. This ensures that the respondent was both reached and asked questions properly.

Step 12: Compiling Data

Compiling data is a mechanical step that can be manual or computerized. If using a computer, the analyst can use specialized software that makes analysis easier. This step must be performed carefully, since errors in transcription can lead to false interpretations.

Step 13: Analyzing the Results

Caution should always be exercised in analyzing survey results. The popular expression "numbers say what we want them to say" is sad but true. The analyst must strive for rigour and not simply look for the answers that the company executive wants to hear.

It is at this point that the market study takes on its full meaning. Now, the researcher must transform disparate data into relevant analysis. Here it is important to understand the meaning of the responses and the links between them in order to interpret the data collected. The use of graphs and diagrams may make this task easier.

Step 14: Writing the Report

The results of a survey are usually presented as a written report. There are several excellent guide books on writing research reports available in bookstores and libraries. The first rule remains, however, that a well-written report is easy to consult. Since the report may be used later by the company or others to repeat the study so as to compare or update results, it is wise to detail the methodology used and attach a copy of the questionnaire itself in the appendix of the report.

SUMMARY

The MIS has three types of data: internal, secondary, and primary. Internal data are usually supplied by the company's accounting system. Others may contribute – for example, employees or even customers.

The two main sources of secondary data are public-sector and private-sector publications. The main source of public data is Statistics Canada. Other government departments and agencies also publish documents of potential interest to managers and executives. Private data can be accessed through databases. Public and private data have their respective strengths and weaknesses. In fact, they more or less complement each other. The main strengths of public data are standardization of data, precautionary methodological measures, comparative studies over time, and ease of access. The strength of private data lies in the aggregation and currency of the information.

Primary data are gathered through surveys or market studies. The research may be exploratory, descriptive, or causal. In the first case, variables are sought which might fit even though no hypothesis has been outlined. In the second case, the researcher starts with a hypothesis and sets out to prove or disprove it. In the last case, the causal relationship of one variable with another is examined.

Several techniques are used in exploratory research (group interviews, individual interviews, case studies, observation, forecasts, and projection). The group interview is often used to test a new product or formulation.

In descriptive and causal research, the research plan usually includes fourteen steps: defining the problem; defining the objectives; determining the financial and human resources; setting a schedule; choosing methods or tools; determining the size of the sample; writing the questionnaire; pretesting the questionnaire; coding; gathering data; monitoring interviewers; compiling data; analyzing results; and writing the report.

QUESTIONS

1. What are the three types of data used in an MIS?
2. What does "internal data" mean, and what are the main sources of internal data?
3. Why is it wise to consult different sources of secondary data before commencing a market study?
4. What are the strengths and weaknesses of public data and private data? Why do we often say that the strength of one is the weakness of the other?
5. What are the main sources of public data? Private data?
6. Define the following three types of research: exploratory, descriptive, causal.
7. Give an example of each of type of research.
8. Why is it important to define the research problem before starting a market study?
9. What is a random sample?
10. Does the size of a sample vary according to the population studied? If so, why?
11. What is quota sampling?
12. What are the basic rules to follow in writing a questionnaire?
13. Why do research firms monitor a certain percentage of the interviews conducted by the interviewing team?

Notes

1. Desormeaux, R. 1995. "La recherche marketing," in *Gestion du marketing, 2ᵉ édition*. F. Colbert and M. Filion, eds. Boucherville, Quebec: Gaëtan Morin Éditeur, chapter 5, p. 123–169.

2. Siegel, S. 1956. *Non-Parametric Statistics*. New York: McGraw-Hill, Series in Psychology.

For Further Reference

1. Gilhespy, I. 1999. "Measuring the Performance of Cultural Organizations: A Model." *International Journal of Arts Management*, Vol. 2, n° 1 (Fall), p. 38–53.

2. Kirchberg, V. 2000. "Mystery Visitors in Museums: An Underused and underestimated Tool for Testing Visitor Services." *International Journal of Arts Management*, Vol. 3, n° 1 (Fall), p. 32–39.

Plan

CHAPTER 10
Planning and Controlling the Marketing Process

10

OBJECTIVES

- Describe how marketing contributes to the corporate mission
- Set out the strategic marketing process
- Discuss key strategic approaches
- Study the contents of a marketing plan
- Consider the importance of controlling marketing within the firm

INTRODUCTION

Throughout this book, we have looked at the various components of the marketing model. Together, these components comprise a whole or a process that enables a company to reach certain objectives. This process is called the "planning and control cycle."

Planning and control are closely linked, complementary functions. In fact, control occurs only after some form of planning has taken place, planning that includes setting measurable objectives that enable the executive to judge the company's activities by comparing concrete results to original forecasts or target figures. Planning consists of defining the target to be reached, whereas control shows how successfully that target is being or has been reached. Control also assists the executive in future planning by indicating the effort required to obtain the expected results.

In this chapter, we examine the various components of the planning and control cycle in marketing. We start by defining the contribution of marketing to the overall mission of a company. We then look at the marketing planning process itself, which stems from the marketing plan and organizational structure. The marketing plan must be drawn up with a broader corporate strategy in mind, since any marketing strategy must contribute to the success of corporate strategies. Lastly, we focus on the key elements in controlling marketing activities.

10.1 HOW MARKETING CONTRIBUTES TO THE CORPORATE MISSION

A successful company usually assigns tasks and powers to its various departments or organizational units. Each unit contributes differently to the over-all mission of the company. For example, the marketing department contributes to the corporate objectives for growth, development, profitability, and general operations in a specific way. The responsibilities of this department are different from those of the finance and production departments, although they share the same general objectives. Once again, the synergy already applied to the marketing mix also applies to the different functions or departments of the company. The combined effort of all departments must produce an effect that is greater than the sum of the efforts made separately.

Marketing must be linked to the corporate mission before planning or monitoring are even considered. The company's mission leads to a series of over-all objectives. In any managerial planning process, the hierarchy of objectives corresponds to a hierarchy of strategies (see figure 10.1).

The marketing department must define its objectives within the framework of the over-all corporate objectives. The marketing objectives are then translated into a series of objectives related to each variable in the marketing mix. Each variable may then lead to a chain of specific objectives. Similarly, the company may use its over-all objectives to develop strategies, which support the marketing strategies which are in turn supported by the strategies for each

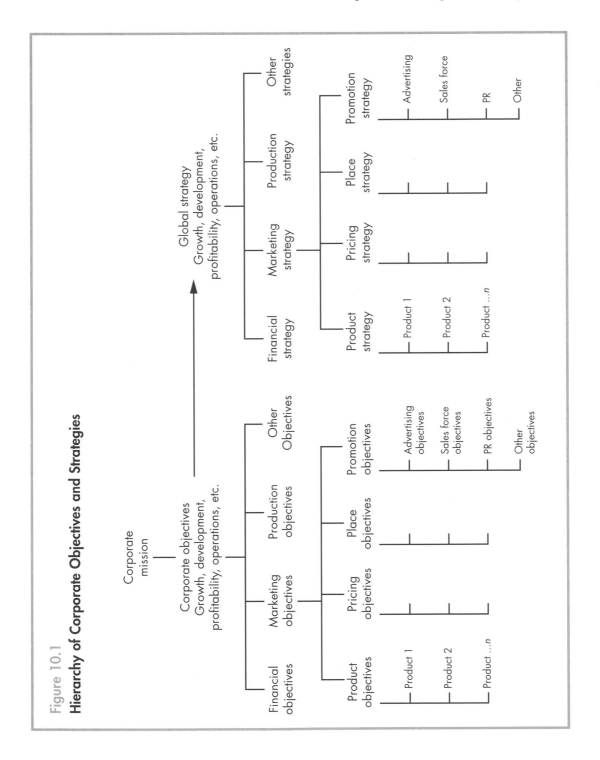

Figure 10.1
Hierarchy of Corporate Objectives and Strategies

variable in the marketing mix. Obviously, corporate planning includes the plans of each unit or department; consequently, marketing planning must fit into the overall corporate plan.

10.2 MARKETING PLANNING

10.2.1   The Process of Marketing Planning

Marketing planning (see figure 10.2) implies a series of questions related to the components of the marketing model. By answering these five key questions, the marketing manager can ensure that the marketing plan is well grounded:

1) Where are we as a company and where are we going? (situational analysis)

2) Where do we want to go? (setting strategic objectives)

3) What effort are we going to put into marketing? (assigning resources)

4) How do we want to get there? (marketing mix)

5) How can we do it? (implementation)

The procedure suggested in these five questions involves looking at the past, the present, and the future. The way in which a company behaves is largely due to its past actions. Similarly, the way in which a company will act in the future will reflect today's actions. These five questions encourage the marketing manager to draw up a plan with continuity in mind, be it a short-term or a long-term plan. In fact, a long-term plan usually comprises a series of short-term plans.

10.2.2   The Marketing Plan

The marketing plan is the result of a process. If it is broad and involves the company as a whole, the plan becomes a transposition of the company's strategic vision. The plan may also be limited to a particular sector and thus focus on one market, range, or product. The marketing plan (see table 10.1) is an analytical outline that may be applied to either situation.

Situational Analysis

The first part of a marketing plan requires that the manager analyze the situation. This analysis must answer two questions: Where are we now? Where are we going if we continue our current activities with no change in current objectives and strategies?

Markets

The various markets served by cultural enterprises evolve over time due to pressures from uncontrollable variables and the competition's actions. The marketing manager should check to see whether the consumer profile has changed, whether market segments have shifted, whether demand has evolved, and whether the intermediaries in the distribution network are still the same. The same checklist applies to the other two markets: sponsors and the state or various levels of government.

Competition and the Environment

Since competition and environmental variables affect the company and its markets, environmental trends – be they political, social, cultural, or technological – and changes in competitors' strategies should be studied.

Figure 10.2   The Marketing Planning Process

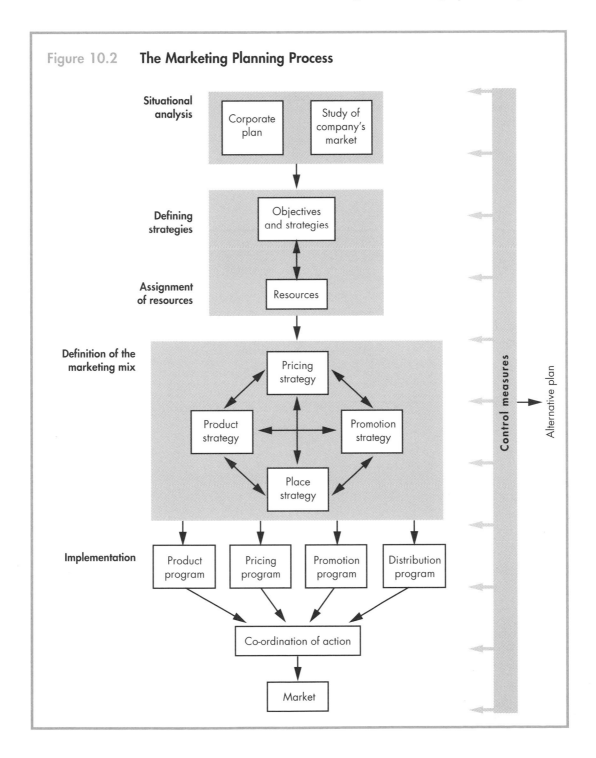

Table 10.1
The Marketing Plan

A. Situational analysis (Where are we and where are we going?)
Markets
  Consumers, demand, segments
Competition and the environment
Company
  Mission and objectives
  Strengths and weaknesses
  Distinct advantage

B. Setting objectives and defining strategies (Where do we want to go?)
Marketing objectives
  Sales, market share, contribution to profits
Marketing strategies
  Target segments, positioning desired

C. Assignment of resources (How much effort do we want to expend?)
Budget
Human resources

D. Definition of the marketing mix (How do we want to get there?)
Objectives and strategies

E. Implementation (How can we do it?)
Program of activities for each variable of the marketing mix
Definition of the responsibilities of each member of the marketing team
Co-ordination of operations
Schedule of activities
Alternative plan
Description of control measures

The Company

In a marketing plan, the big picture, or overall view of the company, is important, since the marketing department must strive for essentially the same objectives as the company. The marketing manager should look for consistency in the marketing objectives, the corporate mission, and the company objectives, and then weigh their strengths and weaknesses. Lastly, the situation ought to be seen in terms of a competitive advantage. The following questions should be asked: Is there such an advantage? Should it be redefined? How?

This quick, rather sweeping overview enables the senior manager to place the company within the internal and broader external environments and take stock of the situation. This is also an opportunity to ponder the future direction the company if no changes were made. The overarching question, given the evolution of the environment and the competition, becomes, "Are our current marketing strategies leading us where we want to go?"

Setting Objectives and Creating Development Strategies

Setting objectives means answering the following question: Where do we want to go?

The marketing department reviews its objectives, changes them as needed, sets sales targets, and determines market share or contribution to corporate profits to be achieved. Since these objectives are known, the manager can choose a marketing strategy that will assist the company in reaching them. This over-all strategy actually describes which segments are to be reached and the desired positioning.

Assigning Resources

Market objectives require both human and financial resources, both of which are normally limited. The answer to the question "How much effort can we put into it?" determines the means used to reach the objectives already set and also influences the viability of the strategies envisaged. In other words, objectives and strategies cannot be set or developed in a vacuum. Objectives, strategies, variables in the marketing mix, and available resources must all

be considered. The result may be the adjustment of certain objectives and strategies.

Determining the Marketing Mix

Once the marketing department has found its orientation, it must answer the question "How do we want to get there?" The time has come to make decisions for each one of the variables of the marketing mix.

While traditional marketing ponders which features a product should have, cultural marketing tries to identify product features, since they are predetermined. In both cases, pricing policy and distribution possibilities are decided and a balance of all four components of the promotion variable (advertising, PR/publicity, promotion, and personal selling) is struck.

Implementation

The last section of the marketing plan lists the operational aspects that will help the company reach its objectives.

The plan should be a detailed statement of the activities projected for each component of the marketing mix, including the responsibilities of each member of the marketing team, co-ordination of activities, and a schedule clearly indicating all deadlines.

A marketing plan should also include a fall-back or alternative plan. The marketing manager must go through a "future or anticipatory audit" and forecast all possible scenarios that might disrupt the schedule or objectives. Potential reaction by the competition is a key element of this exercise.

The answer to the last question, "How to proceed?", must include some description of the control system selected to measure the company's efforts in achieving its objectives.

In any company, the marketing plan is an essential tool that enables the marketing manager to plan, co-ordinate, implement, and monitor corporate marketing activities.

10.2.3   Organizational Structure

If a company adopts a marketing plan, the organizational structure of that company enables it to meet the objectives set out. Organizational structure may take many forms, depending on the size of the firm, the product range, and the variety of markets.

In small companies, the marketing team can be quite limited in size. In fact, it may comprise the promoter or entrepreneur working alone. In other cases, marketing activities are carried out by one manager with a small support staff. For instance, presenters who have a season that includes a few productions over eight to ten months may perform all managerial and marketing tasks. On the other hand, production companies in the performing arts and film, as well as record companies and publishing houses, normally have one employee in charge of PR/publicity or sales for the entire distribution market.

Large companies marketing many products and serving several very distinct markets require a more complex organizational structure, in which the major corporate functions are assigned to upper-level executives (e.g., marketing vice-president) who co-ordinate the activities of several managers from different specialized departments. Figure 10.3 provides an example of an organizational structure that large companies might use. This is, of course, only one of many possible structures.[1]

10.3 STRATEGIES

10.3.1   General Considerations

We have already underscored the fact that in any company there is a hierarchy of strategies ranging from the over-all corporate strategy and marketing strategy to strategies specific to each component of the marketing mix. Moreover, the over-all corporate strategy and the marketing strategy are easily confused. Often, the corporate strategy is defined in terms of the marketing mix. In the next section two corporate strategies are presented – competitive strategies and development strategies. Both are closely related to marketing strategy.

It should be mentioned that a strategy differs from a tactic. A strategy starts from a broad view of the means to be used in reaching a final objective – for example, obtaining a specific market share. A tactic is a timely adjustment of an element of a strategy – for example, inviting critics to the third night rather than the opening night of a production. The marketing manager can use various tactics to reach an objective without modifying the initial strategy.

10.3.2   Corporate Strategy

Every company must adopt an approach that takes into account the power ratio between that company and others within the same sector. This ratio is a function of the size of the company, its rivals, and the importance of its competitive advantage. That competitive advantage or edge may be linked to unique product features as these are perceived by the consumer. This power

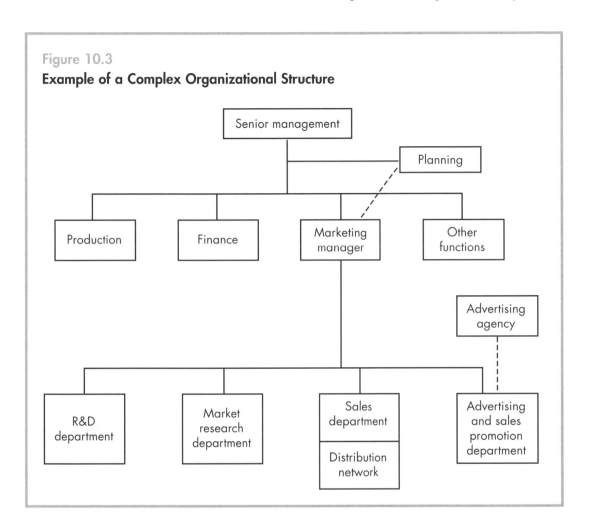

Figure 10.3

Example of a Complex Organizational Structure

ratio shapes both the competitive strategy and the development strategy of the company.

Competitive Strategy

There are four types of competitive strategy: leader, challenger, follower, and specialist.[2]

The Leader Strategy

The leader company dominates a market. This fact is recognized by the competition.

The leader is often a point of reference or a target to attack, a model to imitate, or an enemy to avoid. The leader sets the tone of the market and is constantly observed by the competition. The market leader has a host of strategies from which to choose, since it is in a strong position and dominates the market by size, market share, and economies of scale.

In the arts, however, a leader is not necessarily large, since artistic enterprises are usually modest in size. As a result, none can benefit from advantages of size. Actually, leadership in the arts is generally defined in terms of the product itself – that is, the capacity of the production to draw a large audience or to obtain peer recognition. Nevertheless, the leader in the arts does enjoy a choice of strategies.

The Challenger

The challenger is the company considered the main rival of the leader. Obviously, the challenger wants to be the leader. The challenger relies essentially on offensive strategies centred on one goal – taking the lead position in the marketplace. The challenger can confront the leader directly by using the same strategies as the leader. For example, the challenger can run an aggressive ad campaign, develop an impressive product, or offer highly competitive prices.

The challenger may work toward becoming top dog by taking advantage of the leader's weaknesses. It could try to infiltrate an underdeveloped network, offer the same product at a more advantageous price, give better service, or penetrate a region or segment that the leader has only partially covered. Obviously, the challenging company cannot simply throw caution to the wind in its choice of strategy. It must try to predict and judge the leader's reactions.

The Follower

The follower is a competitor with a fairly small market segment. It adapts all corporate action to the competition rather than trying for first place. The follower develops strategies to retain the company's market share without trying to increase it very

much. These strategies are found primarily in oligopolies, where there are few companies and no one really needs to upset the established pecking order.

This type of strategy is not, however, synonymous with laziness or laissez-faire. The follower does what the name says: it follows the competitors' actions very closely and adjusts its own conduct accordingly. These are active strategies based on the reality of the market and all firms active in that market.

The Specialist (or Nicher)

The specialist focusses on a fairly distinct market segment. Its strategies seek and carve out a niche that sets the company apart from the competition. The company then concentrates exclusively on that niche.

Specialization may stem from the originality of the product, the use of some unique technique, or a production capacity which in turn lowers retail prices. Any of these may prove a distinct advantage. This type of strategy is often adopted by a small company in the cultural sector that must compete against established giants.[3]

Development Strategies

Most companies want an increase in sales, profits, market share, or the actual size of the organization. All of the above are examples of development objectives. The manager seeking to reach these objectives can use different strategies based on the market-product pairing. Ansoff[4] outlines four strategies: market penetration, market development, product development, and diversification (see table 10.2).

Table 10.2 The Ansoff Model	Current market	New market
Current product	Market penetration	Market development
New product	Product development	Diversification

Through the first strategy, market penetration, a company attempts to increase product sales in existing markets by using different techniques. The company could, for example, create a more dynamic distribution network, launch a new promotional campaign, or set more advantageous prices. In any event, the company remains in the same niche with the same product.

Market development enables a company to increase sales by introducing its corporate products into new markets without changing the market segment already held. The company thus expands its clientele by offering the same product to new customers. A touring company that convinces presenters in other regions to buy its show and a promoter trying to break into the international market with a particular artist exemplify this strategy.

The product-development strategy enables a company to increase sales by offering completely new or modified products to currently held markets. The sale of spin-off products is part of this strategy.

The diversification strategy allows a company to improve its sales figures by offering a new product for new markets.

This strategy is riskier than the other three, since it involves two new unknowns: the product and the market. This is the strategy used by large corporate conglomerates that own companies in several cultural sectors – for example, film production, publishing, and electronic games.

Table 10.3 lists several examples of possible action for each of the strategies just discussed.[5]

Ansoff's grid enables a company to classify different scenarios according to the risk associated with a particular choice of strategy. The business risk rises with the newness of the product or market. Diversification as a strategy is therefore the riskiest, since new products are developed for new and unfamiliar markets. The penetration strategy is the least risky, since the company remains in terra cognita. The other two strategies represent interim situations.

This analytical tool may be used in various market contexts. For example, the agents in a specific region may use the grid to compare the strategic choices open to them in their bid to develop tourism.[6] Table 10.4 illustrates a hypothetical situation for a region that wants to lead a co-ordinated

---

Table 10.3
Possible Courses of Action for Ansoff's Four Strategies

1. Market penetration (increase current product use in existing markets)
Increase the customer's current rate of use
- Increase the purchase unit
- Increase the product's rate of obsolescence
- Advertise other product uses
- Offer bonuses for increased use

Attract the competition's clientele
- Improve brand differentiation
- Increase promotion

Attract non-customers
- Use samples, bonuses, and the like to encourage consumers to try the product
- Adjust prices up or down
- Advertise new product uses

---

2. Market development (sell current products in new markets)
Open up new geographic markets
- Regional expansion
- National expansion
- International expansion

Attract other market sectors
- Develop different versions of the product for other sectors
- Penetrate other distribution channels
- Advertise in other media

---

3. Product development (create new products for existing markets)
Develop new product features
- Adapt (to other ideas, other improvements)
- Modify (colour, movement, sound, scent, shape, line)
- Amplify (stronger, longer, thicker, greater value)
- Miniaturize (smaller, shorter, lighter)
- Substitute (different ingredients, new processes, other possibilities)
- Change the look (new design, new layout, new order, new component)
- Turn around completely (invert)
- Combine (mix, match, pair up elements, blend parts, objects, attributes and ideas)

Develop different degrees of quality
Create new models and formats (proliferation of products)

---

4. Diversification (create new products for new markets)
Any new product developed by the company is earmarked for a new market

---

Source: Adapted from Kotler P., and B. Dubois. 1973. *Marketing management, analyse, planification et contrôle*. 2nd ed. Paris: Publi-Union, p. 287.

Table 10.4
Use of Ansoff's Grid to Increase Regional Tourist Traffic

	Current market	New market
Current product	1 Penetration Intensive promotion	3 Market development Promotion abroad or packages
New product	2 Development of new products Opening of a nature- interpretation centre	4 Diversification Establishment of a summer theatre or other type of festival

offensive campaign to attract tourists. The possible choices are given in terms of the risk involved.

The strategy involving the least risk consists of trying to extend the tourist's visit and increase the tourist's expenditures through a co-ordinated promotion of the activities that already exist in the region (square 1). This objective can be reached by modifying the other three components of the marketing mix (price, distribution, and promotion), by organizing a promotional campaign that vaunts the various cultural products to the existing clientele, or by offering reduced prices to those who combine several activities.

A second strategy (square 2) that both extends the tourist's stay and increases the tourist's expenditures consists of offering a new activity (new product) to the current clientele. For example, a region that already attracts sports lovers for hunting and fishing might consider opening a nature-inter-

pretation centre that would reach the same specific clientele.

Marketers can also try to attract people not reached by current strategies, through a promotional campaign abroad or package deals offered to special categories of customers, such as seniors, who are not part of the current clientele (square 3).

Finally, there is the possibility of developing a new offering likely to interest another market segment, such as a summer theatre or festival (square 4).

10.3.3. Marketing Strategies

Strategic Choices

The main strategies available to a marketing department have been outlined in previous chapters (see also table 10.5).

These strategies can be combined to provide a firm with an array of strategic options. For example, the firm seeking positioning could opt for price skimming, selective distribution, and a push strategy.

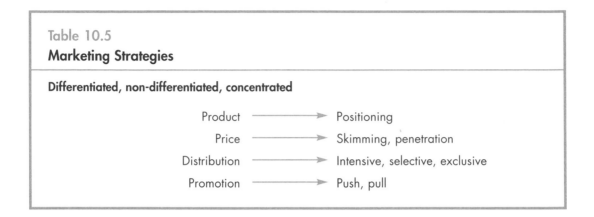

Table 10.5
Marketing Strategies

Differentiated, non-differentiated, concentrated

Product	$\longrightarrow$	Positioning
Price	$\longrightarrow$	Skimming, penetration
Distribution	$\longrightarrow$	Intensive, selective, exclusive
Promotion	$\longrightarrow$	Push, pull

Another firm might use penetration pricing, intensive distribution, and a pull strategy.

Analysis of Potential Marketing Strategies within a Market

Choosing from the arsenal of marketing strategies described requires some analysis of the strategic position of the company's product(s). The strategic position may be defined using the BCG model, developed by the Boston Consulting Group.[7] This model takes into consideration the position of the company or one of its products based on the market share relative to the market leader's share, and the rate of growth for that market. For instance, if one company has a market share of 20% while the leader holds 60% – a ratio of 1:3 – the situation is different from one in which the main competitor also holds 20%; – a ratio of 1:1. In the first case, there is a leader that can impose its will on the market, whereas in the second case, there are equal opponents competing for the consumer's patronage. Similarly, the strategic significance of these market shares would be different in a high-

growth market, where a firm can increase its sales by attracting new customers, and a stagnant market, where firms lock horns over market-share percentiles.

This analysis of a product market produces the BCG matrix, with four squares defining four probable situations. They are: (1) fairly large market share in a high-growth market; (2) fairly small share in a high-growth market; (3) fairly large share in a low-growth market; (4) fairly small share in a low-growth market (see table 10.6).

Stars

A company's star products are those that represent a large market share in a growth market. These products require a major injection of funds to finance growth. They are profitable when demand drops.

Problem Children

A company must withdraw the "problem child" products that it does not intend to improve in terms of market share. Simply maintaining these products in their market position drains away capital which cannot

Table 10.6
The BCG Model

Market growth		Relative market share	
		Large	Small
	High	Stars	Problem children
	Low	Cash cows	Dogs

be recovered. Other products in this category should be financed as necessary to improve their position vis-à-vis competing products.

Cash Cows

If the market is experiencing sluggish growth, a company may reap substantial profits from its products with a large market share. These profits should serve to fund star products and improve the competitive situation for "problem child" products.

Dogs

No company can afford to use its capital to increase its market share in a market with little potential for growth. The company has the choice of cutting its marketing costs to the bare bones for the dog product, knowing that this decision will lead to withdrawal of the product.

Product analysis based on the BCG matrix promotes the making of strategic decisions, such as supporting star products, investing selectively in problem children, maximizing profits from cash cows, and

cutting out dogs. The matrix also enables a company to gauge future financial needs, the potential profitability of products, and the balance required in its portfolio of products. This type of analysis applies particularly to large corporations whose objective is profitability – for example, in the cultural industries. The conceptual framework may also be used to analyze the market for small firms in the arts, since it allows for greater understanding of market dynamics and possible market changes or trends.

10.4 CONTROL

Control consists of examining all or part of the results of a marketing move in order to judge the impact of the tactic or strategy, and then making any necessary changes should there be a gap between projections and reality. The marketing manager using the marketing plan illustrated in figure 10.2 could monitor one, several, or all of the components. It is considered a marketing audit if all components are controlled.

10.4.1   Control by Cycle

Marketing activities should be monitored or evaluated in a continuous and regular fashion using specific tools. Control is part of this cycle, which includes planning and implementing corrective measures. Naturally, only if planning has occurred can there be any form of control.

The objectives of the marketing unit and of each variable or component of the marketing mix translate to a series of actions or programs. These objectives and courses of action must correspond to norms and criteria that measure the gap between projection and reality. Analysis of the causes of any differences should lead to the adoption of corrective measures affecting the objectives, the action taken, or both (see figure 10.4).

10.4.2   Control Tools and Measures

Tools used in marketing control vary according to what is actually analyzed and the light shed upon it through analysis, the objectives of the marketing department, the objectives of each variable in the marketing mix, the budget presented, and so on. Each one of these may be monitored and may require specific tools.

The objectives of the marketing department usually translate to sales figures, market share, or profit forecasts. The tools used are therefore tailored to these parameters. The marketing manager wants to know if the sales volume targetted was actually reached. This can be ascertained by comparing data obtained from sales reports, as detailed in the marketing plan, on an objec-

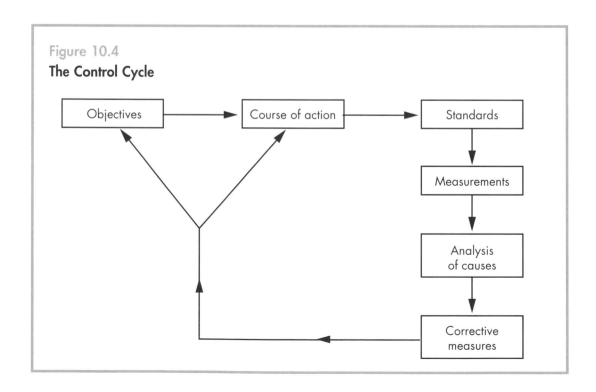

Figure 10.4
The Control Cycle

tive-by-objective basis. Similarly, the market share can be checked by comparing sales to demand according to the objective expressed in the marketing plan. Profitability can be reviewed by looking over the financial statement and comparing it to the objectives in the plan.

The next step is to check not only whether the objectives were reached, but also whether they were reached efficiently, for each component of the marketing mix (product, price, place, and promotion). The marketing manager or executive can check sales figures per product over time and scrutinize profitability per product or territory. The price levels of the company in comparison to those of the competition can be studied, as can the effectiveness of promotional tools currently or previously used.

The internal data and secondary data gathered from the company's MIS are vital to this exercise. Control may also involve the use of primary data, in which case the marketing manager can measure to see whether product positioning is what it should be, whether product awareness created through a promotional campaign corresponds to the objectives set, and whether members of the distribution network are satisfied.

The marketing manager or executive should develop specific criteria to monitor operations and periodically compare results, ensuring that the same criteria are being used. Dissimilar criteria are useless because they do not permit a real comparison of the results obtained.

A good example of using primary data for monitoring the effect of a strategy is "Metti una Sera a Teatro"; this is a particular form of season ticket which was first made available to Turin theatre-goers in 1995, in collaboration with the City of Turin and Agis (the General Italian Agency for the Performing Arts). Subscription holders can choose to attend one event in each of eight of the sixteen theatres participating, for a total of eight performances during the season. This arrangement is reasonably priced, at only $65, and allows audiences to become acquainted with the entire panorama of theatre in Turin. The number of subscribers has tripled in just three seasons: 543 season tickets were sold in the 1995-1996 season, while 1,499 were sold in 1997-1998.

The "Metti una Sera a Teatro"[8] initiative has been under constant monitoring since it was introduced. Five separate surveys were conducted over the course of three years, revealing some interesting trends concerning the consumer habits of subscription holders as well as their use of the subscription.

Positive approval ratings and the number of subscribers eager to renew their subscriptions offer ample evidence for the success of the initiative. Key factors in the positive feedback received at the end of each season were the freedom to choose from a variety of different events as well as the flexibility and savings offered by the subscription.

Results gathered from the surveys were used not only for *ex post* evaluation of the program, but also throughout the season in order to improve and fine-tune the subscription program.

Mail and telephone surveys of subscription holders at the end of each season indicated that subscribers wished for an increased number of performances from which to choose (one weak point indicated was that the subscription did not include the most important plays of the season) and greater cross-sectional representation, to reflect different types of performance (opera, dance, music, cinema).

As a result, the number of participating theatres has grown from twelve to sixteen in just three seasons, to include a number of small, specialized theatres offering puppet theatre, revues, and plays in dialect. Subscribers can now choose from over seventy performances (up from forty-three), including many of the most important events in each theatre's repertoire.

10.4.3   The Marketing Audit

The marketing audit is an in-depth, systematic, periodic critical study of a company's marketing orientation within its specific environment. This audit should enable a company to solve current problems, reinforce its competitive strengths, and raise the level of efficiency and profitability in its marketing activities.[9]

The marketing audit reviews the objectives, policy, organization, procedures, and staff of a company. The audit should be carried out regularly, and not only during a crisis. It should cover all corporate marketing activities, not only those experiencing difficulties. An independent firm or another department that the board of directors or company executive considers credible should perform the audit to ensure objectivity.

Table 10.7 is a checklist for a marketing audit. It includes all the questions that an organization should ask during an audit.

Table 10.7

Key Questions to Ask in a Marketing Audit

A. Situational analysis

Market and environment
- Which market(s) does the company already reach?
- Who are its customers?
- How are the market segments defined?
- What is the current and the potential demand?
- Who are the competitors? How big are they? What strategies do they use?
- Which environmental elements are likely to affect the company? How have they evolved and how might they evolve?

Company
- What is the company's mission?
- What are the company's corporate objectives?
- What are the company's over-all strategies?
- What are the company's strengths and weaknesses?
- Does the company have a distinct advantage? What is it?
- Does the company have a long-term plan? A short-term plan?

B. Analysis of the marketing plan

Objectives and strategies
- What are the marketing objectives?
- What results have been achieved through these objectives?
- What marketing strategies does the company use? Which market segments have been targetted? What is the company's positioning?
- Do these strategies correspond to the over-all corporate strategy?
- Which control measures has the company put in place to evaluate the marketing objectives and efficiency of corporate strategies?

Marketing mix
- Which objectives have been defined for the variables of the marketing mix?
- What is the product strategy?
- What is the positioning sought for each product?
- Is the product mix consistent?
- Is the service offered adequate?
- How does the product itself help the company reach its marketing objectives?
- What is the pricing strategy?
- Which factors have been considered in setting the product price?
- How does the price compare to that of the competition?

(continued)

Table 10.7 (continued)
Key Questions to Ask in a Marketing Audit

- How does the pricing strategy work toward achieving the corporate marketing objectives?
- Which distribution strategy has been adopted?
- Are the distribution networks adequate? Effective?
- Are relations positive among the members of the distribution channel?
- How does the distribution strategy work toward achieving the corporate marketing objectives?
- What is the promotional strategy?
- What is the role of each component of the promotional mix?
- Has the promotional mix been tested? How, and with what result?
- How does the promotional strategy work toward achieving the corporate marketing objectives?
- Do the strategies of each variable in the marketing mix correspond to the over-all marketing strategy?

C. Analysis of the marketing program
- Is there a written plan of the activities (programs) for each variable of the marketing mix?
- What role does each member of the marketing department play in the success of the marketing plan? Have the tasks been assigned clearly?
- Is there a schedule? Is it followed?
- How are the various functions co-ordinated?
- Is there an alternative marketing plan? Is it realistic?

D. Forecasts
- How are the environment and competition developing?
- What effect have they had on the organization?
- Is the company ready to handle changes foreseen in the environment?
- What interesting business opportunities are available to the company?
- What are the keys to success for the company? How can the company acquire the new skills or knowledge it needs?

E. Suggestions
- What changes should the company make in its objectives and strategies?
- How can the company effect these changes?
- What will the cost be?
- What additional information is needed to make relevant decisions?

SUMMARY

Marketing planning and control are two complementary parts of the same process. Planning – the setting of operational objectives and drafting of specific policies – must necessarily precede any monitoring of marketing activities. Only with reference to objectives and policies can the marketing manager assess the results of marketing activities.

Marketing planning depends on two things: the creation of a marketing strategy and the drafting of a marketing plan. Planning relies on the answers to the following five questions:

- Where are we and where are we going?
- Where do we want to go?
- What effort are we going to expend?
- How do we want to get there?
- How can we do it?

Before choosing a marketing strategy, the marketing manager may want to define the company's strategic position in the marketplace. The BCG model may prove useful, as it positions competitors' products according to the market share of each competitor or according to market growth. The company can choose between two types of strategies: competitive and development.

Competitive strategies take into account the power ratio that already exists among firms active in the sector. The strategies based on the respective position of each firm are called the leader, the challenger, the follower, and the specialist.

The development strategies categorized in Ansoff's grid set out parameters based on the product and the market. Depending on degree of novelty, or newness, a company may decide to concentrate on its current market with an existing product, launch its product in a new market, or introduce a new product into a new market.

A marketing plan consists of five steps: situational analysis; definition of marketing strategy (marketing objectives, target markets, positioning, and other strategies); assigning of financial and human resources (budget); decision on the marketing mix; and implementation (alternative plan, control mechanisms).

Marketing control consists of tracking and evaluating how well objectives are being met based on qualitative and quantitative standards. It should be seen as a cycle. Beyond the results provided by sales figures and market share, the marketing manager usually controls the results for each variable of the marketing mix. The manager may also want to fully and systematically review all marketing operations – in other words, proceed with a marketing audit.

QUESTIONS

1. What is the planning and monitoring cycle?

2. How does the strategic planning process in a cultural enterprise differ from that of a traditional business?

3. Where does the "distinct advantage" fit into a marketing strategy?

4. Why is the diversification strategy riskier than the penetration strategy, according to Ansoff's grid?

5. Describe the four competitive strategies.

6. What are the main elements of a marketing plan?

7. Provide examples of the elements that a manager can control for each variable of the marketing mix.

8. What is a marketing audit?

Notes

1. Colbert, F. 1995. "La planification et le contrôle marketing," in *Gestion du marketing, 2nd ed.* F. Colbert and M. Filion, eds. Boucherville, Quebec: Gaëtan Morin Éditeur, chapter 11, p. 461–485.

2. Lambin, J.-J. 1989. *Le marketing stratégique, 2nd ed.* Paris: McGraw-Hill.

3. Valentin, M. 1993. "Le marché du disque : un oligopole avec frange concurrentielle," in *Proceedings of the Second International Conference on Arts and Cultural Management*, Jouy-en-Josas, France: Groupe HEC.

4. Ansoff, I. 1957. "Strategies for Diversification." *Harvard Business Review* (September–October).

5. Kotler, P., and B. Dubois. 1973. *Marketing Management, Analyse, planification et contrôle, 2nd ed.* Paris: Publi-Union.

6. Colbert, F., and J.-M. Boisvert. 1988. "Le consommateur culturel comme segment de marché de l'offre touristique." *Téoros, revue québécoise de recherche en tourisme*, Vol. 7, n° 1 (March), p. 17–20.

7. Lambin, J.-J. 1989. *Le marketing stratégique, 2nd ed.* Paris: McGraw-Hill.

8. Reproduced with the permission of Allessandro Bollo, Fondazione Fitzcarraldo, Turin, Italy.

9. Maria, M., in M. Filion et al. 1990. *Gestion du marketing*. Boucherville, Quebec: Gaëtan Morin Éditeur.

For Further Reference

Einola, K., and N. Turgeon. 2000. "International Marketing of Canadian Television Programs: Industry Players, Export Successes and Strategic Challenges." *International Journal of Arts Management*, Vol. 3, n° 1 (Fall), p. 46–62.

Conclusion

The marketing model presented in this book provides the manager of a cultural or artistic enterprise with a framework and an analytical outline. It ties together the different aspects involved in any marketing process. Of course, readers have realized by now that marketing is not an exact science but rather a blend of science and art. It is a science in that problems can be rigorously analyzed using recognized models, and an art in that marketing concepts and strategies are rarely applied under textbook or clear-cut circumstances. The marketing manager must therefore make decisions without all the necessary information, in a situation that is in perpetual flux, and must therefore know how to trust his or her intuition.

Our knowledge of the cultural consumer remains quite limited. The models developed to explain consumer behaviour in other purchasing situations are useful only in the sense that they enable us to understand phenomena related to all purchasing situations, including those involving cultural products. Research on the special behaviour of cultural consumers must continue, since this information will help the marketing manager support the artistic mission of the company. Naturally, further research in cultural marketing is needed, and just as traditional marketing evolved from other sciences by developing its own models, cultural marketing must borrow relevant traditional concepts while still acquiring its own specific body of knowledge.

Anyone considering a marketing career in an artistic or cultural enterprise should have the same qualities as any other good marketer – intuition, imagination, empathy, analytical skills, and the ability to summarize material and deal with uncertainty. The ideal marketing manager will be able to understand and explain a cultural product and, above all, enjoy taking risks and making miracles happen on a shoestring budget. Lastly, like an artist, the marketing manager needs talent to succeed – tools may be acquired, but not talent.

The following, final, figure summarizes the marketing model for culture and the arts, including the main concepts touched upon in this book. We ask readers to consider the model as a starting point for their own marketing career in the cultural milieu.

The Marketing Model for Culture and the Arts

Enterprise

Company	Product
Mission	All profits
Objectives	Dimension
Resources	• referential
• human	• technical
• financial	• circumstantial
• technical	Complexity
Image	Life cycle
Competitive advantage	Marketing plan
Marketing plan	New-product development
Organization	• R&D
Strategies	• risk
• corporate (competitive/development)	Line and range
• marketing	Brand
Control	
• cycle	
• marketing audit	

Time

Specificity of the company

Market information system

Internal data

Secondary data	• public
	• private
Primary data	• exploratory, descriptive, and causal research
	• 14 steps

Residual marketing mix

Price	Promotion
$ – Effort expended	Tools
– Associated costs	• advertising
Skimming – Penetration	• personal selling
	• PR
	• sales promotion
Place	Respective role of each tool
Channels – Physical distribution – Location	Communications plan
Intensive distribution – Selective distribution – Exclusive distribution	Push – pull

Competition

Leisure industry

Fragmentation

Globalization

Markets

Consumers	Distribution
Demand	Intermediaries
Behaviours	
Segmentation – Positioning	
Differentiation – Non-differentiation – Concentration	
State	Sponsors
Federal	Donations
Provincial	Sponsorships
Municipal	Decision-making process

Macro-environment
- economic
- political-legal
- demographic
- cultural

Selected Bibliography

The following bibliography offers readers a broad range of documents published in the field of culture and arts marketing. Many different countries are represented. The bibliography has been divided into three parts: books, articles and monographs, and studies and surveys.

BOOKS

Argano, L. 1997. *La Gestione Dei Progetti Di Spettacolo*. Milano, Italy: Franco Angeli s.r.l.

Baskerville, D. 1985. *Music Business Handbook & Career Guide*, 4th ed. Los Angeles: The Sherwood Company.

Boulet, Y. 1989. *La commandite d'événement: un nouvel outil marketing*. Montreal: Agence d'Arc.

Chalendar, J., and G. de Brebisson. 1987. *Mécénat en Europe*. Paris: La Documentation française.

Charron, J.-M.1991. *L'État des médias*. Montreal: Boréal; Paris: La découverte/ Média pouvoir/CFPJ.

Creton, L. 1994. *Économie du cinéma : perspectives stratégiques*. Paris: Nathan Université.

Creton, L. 1997. *Cinéma et marché*. Paris: Armand Colin/Mason.

Cummings, M.C., and J.M.D. Schuster. 1989. *Who's to Pay for the Arts? The International Search for Models of Arts Support*. New York: ACA Books.

Diggles, K. 1986. *Guide to Arts Marketing: The Principles and Practice of Marketing as They Apply to the Arts*. London: Rhinegold Publishing Limited.

Dupuis, X., and F. Rouet. 1987. *Industries culturelles, Vol. 3*. Paris: La Documentation française.

Durand, J.-P. 1991. *Le marketing des activités et des entreprises culturelles*. Paris: Les éditions Juris Service.

Féral, J. 1990. *La culture contre l'art: essai d'économie politique du théâtre*. Sillery: Presses de l'Université du Québec.

Fink, M. 1989. *Inside the Music Business: Music in Contemporary Life*. New York: Schirmer Books.

Fisher, V., and R. Brouillet.1990. *Les commandites: la pub de demain*. Montreal: Éditions St-Martin.

Fitzgibbon, M., and A. Kelley. 1997. *From Maestro to Manager: Critical Issues in Arts & Culture Management*. Dublin: Oak Tree Press.

Ford, N.M., and B.J. Queram. 1984. *Pricing Strategies for the Performing Arts*. Madison, WI: Association of College, University and Community Arts Administrators Inc.

Ghalinger-Beane, R. 1988. *The Canadian Artist's Survival Manual*. Kapuskasing, ON: Penumbra Press.

Globerman, S., and A. Vining. 1987. *Foreign Ownership and Canada's Feature Film Distribution Sector: An Economic Analysis*. Vancouver: The Fraser Institute.

Green, J. 1981. *The Small Theatre Handbook: A Guide to Management and Production*. Boston: The Harvard Common Press.

Greffe, X. 1990. *La valeur économique du patrimoine : la demande et l'offre de monuments*. Paris: Anthroppos Economica.

Hehner, B. 1989. *Making It: The Business of Film and Television Production in Canada*. Toronto: The Academy of Canadian Cinema and Television.

Hendon, W.S. 1979. *Analysing an Art Museum*. New York: Praeger Publishers.

Hendon, W.S., J.L. Shanchan and A.J. MacDonald. 1980. *Economic Policy for the Arts*. Cambridge, MA: ABT Books.

Jefferson, B.T. 1985. *Profitable Crafts Marketing*. Portland, OR: Timber Press.

Jeffri, J. 1983. *Arts Money: Raising It, Saving It and Earning It.* New York: Neal-Shuman.

Johnson-McAllister, W., and F.K. Smith. 1991. *Art Gallery Handbook.* Toronto, ON: Association of Art.

Kotler, N., and P. Kotler. 1998. *Museum Strategy and Marketing,* San Francisco: Jossey-Bass Publishers.

Kotler, P., and J. Scheff. 1997. *Standing Room Only-Strategies for Marketing the Performing Arts.* Boston: Harvard Business School Press in association with Americans and the Arts.

Langely, S. 1990. *Theatre Management and Production in America: Principle and Practice.* New York: Drama Book Specialists Publishers.

Leroy, D. 1980. *Économie des arts du spectacle vivant.* Paris: Economica.

Levasseur, R. 1982. *Loisir et culture au Québec.* Montreal: Boréal Express.

Lord, B., and G.D. Lord. 1997. *The Manual of Museum Management.* London: The Stationary Office.

Lord, J.G. 1981. *Philanthropy and Marketing: New strategies for fund raising.* Cleveland: Third Sector Press.

McIntyre, C. 1985. *Road Signs: A Guide to Foreign Touring.* Ottawa: External Affairs. Art Promotion Division, Government of Canada.

Melillo, J.V. 1995. *Market the Arts.* Revised Edition, Brooklyn, NY: Patricia Lavender, Arts Action Issues.

Mokwa, M.P., W.M. Dawson and E.A. Prieve. 1980. *Marketing the Arts.* New York: Praeger Publishers.

Monaco, B., and J. Riordan. 1988. *The Platinum Rainbow: How to Succeed in the Music Business without Selling Your Soul.* Chicago: Contemporary Books.

Morison, G.B., and J.G. Dalglersh. 1987. *Waiting in the Wings: A Larger Audience for the Arts and How to Develop It.* New York: American Council for the Arts.

Morison, G.B., and K. Fliehr. 1968. *In Search of an Audience.* New York: Pitman Publishing Corp.

Newman, D. 1977. *Subscibe Now! Building Arts Audiences Through Dynamic Subscription Promotion.* New York: Theatre Communication Group.

Papolos, J. 1988. *The Performing Artist Handbook.* Cincinnati: Writer's Digest Book.

Pick, J. 1980. *Arts Administration.* London: E. & F. N. Spon Ltd.

Pilon, R. 1991. *L'état des médias: groupes et stratégies.* Edited by J.-M. Charron. Paris: Éditions Boréal.

Reiss, A.H. 1979. *The Arts Management Reader,* 3rd ed. New York: Marcel Dekker Inc.

Riordan, J. 1988. *Making It In The New Music Business.* Cincinnati, OH: Writer's Digest Book.

Stolper, C.L., and K.B. Hopkins. 1989. *successful Fundraising for Arts and Cultural Organizations.* Phoenix: Oryx Press.

Throsby, G.D., and G.A. Withers. 1979. *The Economics of the Performing Arts.* New York: St. Martin's Press.

Tool, R.C. 1982. *The Entertainment Machine: American Showbusiness in the Twentieth Century.* Toronto: Oxford University Press.

Tremblay, G. 1990. *Les industries de la culture et de la communication au Québec et au Canada.* Sillery: Presses de l'Université du Québec.

Wolf, T. 1993. *Presenting Performances: A Handbook for Sponsors*, 5th ed. New York: American Council for the Arts.

ARTICLES AND MONOGRAPHS

Ames, P. 1992. *Effective Education for Everyone: Accommodating Assorted Abilities, Providing for Particular Preferences, and Telling the Targeted*. Montreal: Chaire de gestion des arts, École des HEC, in collaboration with le Musée de la civilisation.

Andreasen, A.R., and R.W. Belk. 1980. "Predictors of Attendance at the Performing Arts." *Journal of Consumer Research*, Vol. 7, n° 2 (September), p. 112–120.

Baumol, W.J. 1967. "Performing Arts: The Permanent Crisis." *Business Horizons*, Autumn, p. 47–50.

Bayon-Eder, T., and A. Herrman. 1995. "On the Necessity of Anchoring Marketing in the Management of German Government-Supported Theatres." *Journal of International Marketing and Marketing Research*, Vol. 20, n° 1 (February), p. 15–30.

Beaulac, M., F. Colbert and C.P. Duhaime. 1991. *Le marketing en milieu muséal: une recherche exploratoire*. Montreal: Chaire de gestion des arts, École des HEC.

Benghozi, P.-J. 1992. *Musées et activités commerciales*. Montreal: Chaire de gestion des arts, École des HEC.

Bergadaà, M., and S. Nieck. 1995. "Quel marketing pour les activités artistiques : une analyse comparée des motivations des consommateurs et producteurs de théâtre." *Recherche et applications en marketing*, Vol. 10, n° 4, p. 28–45.

Bhattacharya, C.B., and M.A. Glynn. 1995. "Understanding the Bond Identification: An Investigation of Its Correlates Among Art Museum Members. " Journal of Marketing, Vol. 59, no 4 (October), p. 46–57.

Biles, G. E., and V.B. Morris. 1982. "Charitable Giving to the Arts: Quo Vadis." *Journal of Arts Management and Law*, Spring, p. 57–62.

Blamires, C. 1992. "What Price Entertainment? " *Journal of the Market Research Society*, Vol. 34, n° 4 (October), p. 375–388.

Bouder-Pailler, D. 1999. "A Model for Measuring the Goals of Theatre Attendance." *International Journal of Arts Management*, Vol. 1, n° 2 (Winter), p. 4–16.

Browning, E.L.A. 1993. "Personality Museum as a Tourist Attraction." *Economic Development Review*, Vol. 11, n° 4 (Fall), p 78–80.

Burke, A.E. 1996. "The Dynamics of Product Differentiation in the British Record Industry." *Journal of Cultural Economics*, Vol. 20, p. 145–164

Chamberlain, O. 1986. "Pricing the Performing Arts." *Journal of Arts Management and Law*, Vol. 16, n° 3 (Autumn), p. 49–60.

Colbert, F., and J.M. Boisvert. 1988. "Le consommateur culturel comme segment de marché de l'offre touristique." *Téoros*, Vol. 7, n° 1 (March), p. 17–20.

Colbert, F. 1989. *La recherche et l'enseignement en gestion des arts à l'aube des années 1990*. Montreal: Chaire de gestion des arts, École des HEC.

Colbert, F. 1989. "Les arts: un marché pour les commandites." *Gestion, revue internationale de gestion*, Vol. 14, n° 2 (May), p. 58–65.

Colbert, F., C.P. Duhaime and M. Lanctôt. 1990. *Le processus d'achat de la clientèle des galeries d'art contemporain*. Montreal: Chaire de gestion des arts, École HEC.

Colbert, F. 1997. "Changes in Marketing Environment and Their Impact On Cultural Policy." *Journal of Arts Management, Law and Society*, Vol. 27, n° 3 (Fall), p. 177–187.

Colbert, F., C. Beauregard and L. Vallée. 1998. "The Importance of Ticket Prices for Theatre Patrons." *International Journal of Arts Management*, Vol. 1, n° 1 (Fall), p. 8–16.

Comer, L.B., and J.A.F. Nicholls. 1994. "Hispanics at the High Arts: In Search of a Culturally Relevant Attendance Experience, " in *Developments in Marketing Science*. Proceedings of the Academy of Marketing Science. Vol. 17, p. 272–

Cooke, M., and R. Morris. 1996. "Music Making in Great Britain." *Journal of the Market Research Society*. Vol. 38, n° 2 (April), p. 123–134.

Cooper-Martin, E. 1992. "Consumers and Movies: Information Sources for Experiential Products," in *Advances in Consumer Research*. Proceedings of the Association for Consumer Research, Vol. 19, p.756–761.

Cooper, P., and R. Tower. 1992. "Inside the Consumer Mind: Consumer Attitudes on the Arts." *Journal of the Market Research Society*. Vol. 34, n° 4 (October), p. 299–311.

Cornwell, T.B. 1994. "Advertising, Ethnicity and Attendance at the Performance Arts." *Journal of Professional Services Marketing*, Vol. 10, n° 2, p. 145–146.

Crompton, J.L., and L. Love. 1994. "Using Inferential Evidence to Determine Likely Reaction to a Price Increase at a Festival." *Journal of Travel Research*, Vol. 32, n° 4 (Spring), p. 32–36.

Crowley, M.G. 1991. "Prioritising the Sponsorship Audience." *European Journal of Marketing*, Vol. 25, n° 11, p. 11–21.

Currie, G., and C. Hobart. 1994. "Can Opera be Brought to the Masses? A Case Study of Carmen Opera." *Marketing Intelligence and Planning*. Vol. 12, n° 2, p. 13–18.

Currim, I.S., C.B. Weinberg and D.R. Wittink. 1981. "Design of Subscription Programs for a Performing Arts Series." *Journal of Consumer Research*, Vol. 8, n° 1 (June), p. 67–75.

Curry, D.J. 1982. "Marketing Research and Management Decision." *Journal of Arts Management and Law*, Vol. 12, n° 1 (Spring), p. 42–58.

Duckworth, E. 1990. "Museum Visitors and the Development of Understanding." *Journal of Museum Education*, Vol. 15, n° 1 (Winter), p. 4–6.

Duhaime, C.P., A. Joy and C.R. Ross. 1989. *A Picture Speaks a Thousand Words: The Consumption of Contemporary Art*. Montreal: Chaire de gestion des arts, École des HEC.

Dunn, S. 1992. "Predictive Dialing: The Next Step for the Performing Arts." *Fund Raising Management*, Vol. 23, n° 1 (March), p. 39–43.

Eliashberg, J., and S.M. Shugan. 1997. "Film Critics: Influencers or Predictors? " *Journal of Marketing*, Vol. 61 (April), p. 68–78.

Elliot, R., and E. Hamilton. 1991. "Consumer Choice Tactics and Leisure Activities." *International Journal of Advertising*, Vol. 10, p. 325–332.

Evrard, Y., and P. Aurier. 1996. "Identification and Validation of the Person-Object Relationship." *Journal of Business Research*, Vol. 37, n° 2 (October), p. 127–134.

Felton, M.V. 1989. "Major Influences on the Demand for Opera Tickets." *Journal of Cultural Economics*, Vol. 13, n° 1 (June), p. 53–64.

Fronville, C.L. 1989. "Marketing for Museums: For-Profit Techniques in the Non-Profit World." *Curator*, Vol. 28, n° 3 (September), p. 169–182.

Gainer, B. 1989. "The Business of High Culture: Marketing the Performing Arts in Canada." *Service Industries Journal*, Vol. 9, n° 4 (October), p. 143–161.

Gainer, B. 1993. "An Empirical Investigation of the Role of Involvement with a Gendered Product." *Psychology and Marketing*, Vol. 10, n° 4, p. 265–283.

Gainer, B. 1993. "The Importance of Gender to Arts Marketing." *Journal of Arts Management, Law and Society*, Vol. 23, n° 3, p. 240–251.

Gainer, B. 1995. "Ritual and Relationships: Interpersonal Influences on Shared Consumption." *Journal of Business Research*, Vol. 32, p. 253–263.

Gallanis, B. 1983. "Entertainment Marketing: The New Business of Show Business." *Advertising Age*, n° 54 (December), p. m9–m11, m20–m24.

Gardiner, C., and M. Collins. 1992. "Practical Guide to Better Audience Surveys." *Journal of the Market Research Society*, Vol. 34, n° 4 (October), p. 289–297.

Gardner, M.P., and D.J. Shuman. 1987. "Sponsorship: An Important Component of the Promotion Mix." *Journal of Advertising*, Vol. 16, n° 1, p. 11–17.

Gary, C.M. 1998. "Hope for the Future? Early Exposure to the Arts and Adult Visits to Art Museum." *Journal of Cultural Economics*, Vol. 22, n° 2-3, p. 87–98.

Godbout, A., N. Turgeon and F. Colbert. 1991. *Pratique de la commandite commerciale au Québec: une étude empirique*. Montreal: Chaire de gestion des arts, École des HEC.

Gross, A.C., M.B. Traylor and P.J. Schuman. 1987. "Corporate Sponsorship of Arts and Sports Events in North America." *European Research (Netherlands)*, Vol. 15 (November), p. S9–S13.

Hardy, L.W. 1981. "Theatre Objectives and Marketing Planning." *European Journal of Marketing*, Vol. 15, n° 4, p. 3–16.

Hendon, C.R. 1992. "Arts Participation: Comparing the Elderly and Non-Elderly." *Journal of Cultural Economics*, Vol. 16, n° 1 (June), p.83–92.

Hendon, W.S. 1990. "The General Public's Participation in Art Museums: Visitors Differ from Non-Visitors, but Not as Markedly as Case Studies." *American Journal of Economics and Sociology*, Vol. 49, n° 4 (October), p. 439–457.

Hermann, A., F. Franken, F. Huber, M. Ohlwein and R. Schellhase. 1999. "The Conjoint Analysis as an Instrument for Marketing Controlling, Taking a Public Theatre as an Example." *International Journal of Arts Management*, Vol. 1, n° 3, p. 59–70.

Hinds, N., and T. Waters. 1992. "A Small Arts Organization's Approach to Market Research." *Journal of the Market Research Society*. Vol. 34, n° 4 (October), p. 345–360.

Hirschman, E.C. 1983. "Aesthetics, Ideologies and the Limits of the Marketing Concept." *Journal of Marketing*, Vol. 47 (Summer), p. 40–55.

Hirschman, E.C., and B.M. Holbrook. 1982. "Hedonic Consumption: Emerging Concepts, Methods and Propositions." *Journal of Marketing*, Vol. 46, n° 3 (Summer), p. 92–101.

Holbrook, M., and R.M. Schindler. 1989. "Some Exploratory Findings on the Development of Musical Tastes." *Journal of Consumer Research*, Vol. 16, p. 119–124.

Holbrook, M., and R.M. Schindler. 1994. "Age, Sex and Attitude Toward the Past as Predictors of Consumers' Aesthetic Tasted for Cultural Products." *Journal of Marketing Research*, Vol. 31 (August), p. 412–422.

Holbrook, M., and R.M Schindler. 1996. "Market Segmentation based on Age and Attitude Toward the Past: Concepts, Methods and Findings Concerning Nostalgic Influences." *Journal of Business Research*, Vol. 37, n° 1 (September), p. 27–39.

Kangun, N., G. Otto and D.C. Randall. 1992. "Marketing Strategies for Increasing Symphony Season Ticket Purchases Among College Students." *Journal of Cultural Economics*, Vol. 16, n° 1 (June), p. 25–39.

Kelly, R.F. 1993. "Vesting Objects and Experiences with Symbolic Meaning: Summary of a Special Session," in *Advances in Consumer Research*. Proceedings of the Association for Consumer Research. Vol. 20, p.232–234.

Lacher, K.T., and R. Mizerski. 1994. "An Exploratory Study of the Responses and Relationships involved in the Evaluation to Purchase New Rock Music." *Journal of Consumer Research*, Vol. 21, n° 1 (September), p. 366–380.

Laczniak, G.R, and P.E. Murphy. 1977. "Marketing the Performing Arts." *Atlanta Economic Review*, Vol. 27, n° 6 (November-December), p. 4–9.

Legum, L.T., and W.R. George. 1981. "Analysis of Marketing Management Practices of Dance Companies." *Journal of the Academy of Marketing Science*, Vol. 9, n° 1 (Winter), p. 15–26.

Mayfield, T.L, and J.L. Crompton. 1995. "The Status of the Marketing Concept Among Festival Organizers." *Journal of Travel Research*, Vol. 33, n° 4 (Spring), p. 14–22.

McLean, F. 1994. "Services Marketing: The Case of Museums." *Service Industries Journal*, Vol. 14, n° 2 (April), p. 190–203.

Meenaghan, J.A. 1983. "Commercial Sponsorship." *European Journal of Marketing*, Vol. 17, n° 7, p. 5–73.

Morisson, W.G., and E.G West. 1986. "Child Exposure to the Performing Arts: The Implications for Adult Demand." *Journal of Cultural Economics*, Vol. 10, n° 1, p. 17–25.

Nantel, J., and F. Colbert. 1992. "Positioning Cultural Arts Products in the Market." *Journal of Cultural Economics*, Vol. 16, n° 2, p. 63–73.

Papadopoulos, N., L.A. Heslop and J.J. Marshall. 1990. "Domestic and International Marketing of Canadian Cultural Products: Some Questions and Some Directions for Research," in *ASAC Conference*, Whistler, BC. p. 232–240.

Petroski, R.A. 1991. "Extending Innovation Characteristic Perception to Diffusion

Channel Intermediaries and Aesthetic Products," in *Advances in Consumer Research. Proceedings of the Association for Consumer Research*, Vol. 18, p. 627–634.

Prince, D.R. 1990. "Factors Influencing Museum Visits: An Empirical Evaluation of Audience Selection." *Museum Management and Curatorship*, Vol. 9, n° 2, p. 149–168.

Pronovost, G. 1997. "Shifting Cultural Practices: An Intergenerational Perspective," in *Colloquium Proceedings, Cultural Organisations of the Future*, F. Colbert, ed. Montreal: École des HEC, November, p. 89–113.

Robbins, J.E., and S.S. Robbins. 1981. "Museum Marketing: Identification of High, Moderate and Low Attendee Segments." *Journal of the Academy of Marketing Science*, Vol. 9, n° 1 (Winter), p. 66–76.

Scheff, J. 1999. "Factors Influencing Subscription and Single-Ticket Purchases at Performing Arts Organisations." *International Journal of Arts Management*, Vol. 1, n° 2 (Winter), p. 16–28.

Scheff, J., and P. Kotler. 1996. "Crisis in the Arts: The Marketing Response." *California Management Review*, Vol. 39 (Fall), p. 28–52.

Scheff, J., R. Dodge and H. Welch. 1999. "Turning on the Next Generation to Classical Music," in *Proceedings of the 5th International Conference on Arts and Cultural Management*, L. Uusitalo and J. Moisander, eds. Helsinki: Helsinki School of Economics and Business Administration, p. 307–314.

Semenick, R.J., and C.E. Young. 1979. "Market Segmentation in Arts Organization," in *1979 Educators Conference Proceedings*, Chicago: American Marketing Association, p. 474–478.

Sexton, D.E., and K. Britney. 1979. "A Behavioral Segmentation of the Arts Market," in *Proceedings of the 10th Annual Conference, Advances in Consumer Research, Volume VII*, San Francisco: Association for Consumer Research, p. 119–120.

Steinberg, M., G. Miaoulis and D. Lloyd. 1982. "Benefit Segmentation Strategies for the Performing Arts," in *1982 American Marketing Association Educators Conference*, Chicago: AMA, p. 289–294.

Thomas, E.G, B.D. Cutler. "Marketing the Fine and Performing Arts: What Has Marketing Done for the Arts Lately?" *Journal of Professional Services Marketing*, Vol. 10, n° 1, p. 181–199.

Tian, S., J.L. Crompton and P.A. Witt. 1996. "Integrating Constraints and Benefits to Identify Responsive Target Markets for Museum Attraction." *Journal of Travel Research*, Vol. 35, n° 2 (Fall), p. 34–45.

Turgeon, N., and F. Colbert. 1992. "The Decision Process Involved in Corporate Sponsorship for the Arts." *Journal of Cultural Economics*, Vol. 16, n° 1 (June), p. 41–53.

Yavas, U. 1996. "Regional Symphony Orchestras: A Marketing Challenge." *Journal of Professional Services Marketing*, Vol. 13, n° 2, p. 123–136.

Yorke, D.A., and R.R. Jones. 1984. "Marketing Museums." *European Journal of Marketing Planning*, Vol. 18, n° 2, p. 91–99.

STUDIES AND SURVEYS

ACCUCA. 1984. *The Professional Performing Arts: Attendance Patterns, Preferences and Motives*, Vols. 1 and 2. Madison, WI: Association of College, University & Community Arts Administrators Inc.

Brokensha, P., and A. Tonks. 1986. *Culture and Community: Economics and Expectations of the Arts in South Australia.* Wentworth Falls. Australia: Social Science Press.

Busson, A., and Y. Evrard. 1987. *Portraits économiques de la culture.* Paris: La Documentation française.

Canada Council. 1986. *A Survey of Arts Audience Studies: A Canadian Perspective 1967–1984.* Ottawa: Research and Evaluation.

Colbert, F. 1990. *Un marché en turbulence: huit ans plus tard.* Montreal: Groupe de recherche et de formation en gestion des arts, École des HEC.

Colbert, F., and J.M. Boisvert. 1985. Étude sur les dimensions économiques des activités à caractère culturel: le *cas de l'orchestre symphonique de Montréal, du Musée des beaux-arts de Montréal et du Festival international de jazz de Montréal.* Montreal: CIDEM and Ministère des Affaires culturelles du Québec.

Cooper, J. 1983. *A Study of the Effects of Pre-performance Materials on the Child's Ability to Respond to Theatrical Performance.* Athens, GA: University of Georgia.

Couture, F., N. Gauthier and Y. Robillard. 1986. *Le marché de l'art et l'artiste au Québec.* Quebec City: Ministère des Affaires culturelles du Québec.

Donnat, O. 1996. Les *amateurs – Enquêtes sur les activités artistiques des Français.* Paris: Ministère de la Culture, Département des études et de la prospective.

Donnat, O., and D. Cogneau. 1990. *Les pratiques culturelles des Français 1973-1989.* Paris: Ministère de la Culture et de la Communication, La Documentation française.

Fitzhugh, L.D. 1983. *Introducing the Audience: A Review and Analysis of Audience Studies for the Performing Arts in America.* Washington: The American University.

Ford Foundation. 1974. *The Finances of the Performing Arts.* Vol. 2. New York: Ford Foundation.

Les Consultants Cultur'inc., and Decima Research. 1992. *Profil des Canadiens consommateurs d'art 1990-1991– Constats.*

McCaughey, C. 1984. *A Survey of Arts Audience Studies: A Canadian Perspective 1967–1984.* Ottawa: Research and Evaluation Canada Council.

Myerscough, J. 1986. *Facts about the Arts 2, 1986 Edition.* London: Policy Studies Institute.

National Endowment for the Arts. 1993. *Arts Participation in America: 1982–1992.* Washington: Research Division Report n° 27.

National Endowment for the Arts. 1996. *Age and Arts Participation: With a Focus on the Baby Boom Cohort.* Washington: Research Division Report n° 34.

Schuster, J.M. 1985. *Supporting the Arts: An International Comparative Study.* Cambridge: Department of Urban

Studies and Planning, Massachusetts Institute of Technology.

Young, V.L.F. 1988. *Segmenting the Audience for the Performing Arts: An Empirical Study*. Saint-John: University of New Brunswick.

Index

AGMV Marquis

MEMBRE DU GROUPE SCABRINI

Québec, Canada
2001